Rocky Mountain
Memories

Rocky Mountain
Memories

Frances Melrose

Denver Publishing Company

International Standard Book Number: 0-914807-05-6
Library of Congress Card Catalog Number: 86-72343
Copyright (c) 1986 by Denver Publishing Company
All rights reserved.
Printed in the United States of America

Cover photograph by David L. Cornwell
Cover design by Ed Stein
Book design by Richard Kohen

First printing October 1986

Foreword

IT seems somehow appropriate that Frances Melrose's Colorado roots reach as deeply into the state's history as those of the *Rocky Mountain News*.

Hugh Hudson Melrose, one of her grandfathers, came to the state during the Gold Rush of 1859. It was in the spring of 1859 that the *Rocky Mountain News* was brought to life in the attic of Uncle Dick Wootton's saloon near the banks of Cherry Creek. The same gold rush brought both Melrose and the redoubtable founder of the *News* to what was then a brawling boom camp.

Frances' other grandfather, dentist George Milton, arrived in Creede after the Civil War.

It should be noted that both men sought gold in Colorado, but never found it. It's probably just as well for us that they didn't. Who knows, if they had found wealth, Frances might never have pursued a journalistic career.

But pursue it she did, for 43 years. And the *Rocky Mountain News* and Colorado have been the richer for it.

She started at the *News* on June 28, 1943, as an assistant to advice columnist Molly Mayfield at $15 a week and so impressed her employers that she was made a reporter a month later. Her career was on its way.

In her career Frances Melrose worked at various times as a feature writer, entertainment editor, movie and drama critic and travel editor.

In 1946, she started the Sunday magazine, then called *Everybody's Section*.

She also started the Golden Wedding Party, a public service event the *News* still holds annually after 32 years.

In addition, Frances started Showagon, another public service event, the Show Plane project and she revived the Spelling Bee after World War II.

Frances always has had a tremendous interest and curiosity concerning Colorado history and this led her, 5 years ago, to begin a weekly column on the subject. The result was *Rocky Mountain Memories*.

When Frances retired in March 1986, I asked her to continue to write the column on a freelance basis. The column continues to run in the *News* every week.

We decided to produce this collection of some of the *Memories* columns after many requests from the public. This is the fifth such collection the *News* has published since columnist Gene Amole's *Morning* in 1983. Others were cartoonist Ed Stein's *Stein's Way (1983), Amole Again* (1985) and *John Coit (1986).*

The Melrose columns provide stories of some fascinating events from Colorado history, many of them the kind of offbeat happenings that many history books miss. I'm sure you will find them as enjoyable as I did.

Ralph Looney
Editor, *Rocky Mountain News*
October 1986

Introduction

THE West — wide, wild and wonderful — is the star of this volume.

We all know that the scenery in this part of the world is magnificent. And there are men and women to match the mountains. No wonder there are so many tales to tell in a Rocky Mountain setting.

But this book never would have come about without the help of many people, many of them not westerners.

Ben Blackburn, managing editor of the *Rocky Mountain News,* several years ago conceived the idea of the *Rocky Mountain Memories* column to celebrate the West, and asked me to write it. Ralph Looney, editor of the *News,* saw the column's potential as a book and set the production machinery in motion.

In between, thanks are owed to many people who helped make both columns and book a reality.

The toughest job was handled by Zoe Lappin, a many-times prize winner from the *News* copy desk, who is the book's editor. She is a perfectionist who worked endless hours trying to see that everything is just right, down to the last comma.

The dedicated librarians in the Western History Department of the Denver Public Library and the library of the Colorado Historical Society searched diligently and long seeking answers to difficult questions from readers. The *Rocky Mountain News* library staff also cheerfully added their efforts to many a search.

I am grateful also to the *News* photo staff, especially Dick Davis, who copied many of the photos for reproduction, and David Cornwell, who made the cover photograph.

Ed Stein, *News* editorial cartoonist, gave the book its handsome cover design. Richard Kohen designed the book.

Chris Power, *News* special projects editor, did a great deal to publicize and sell the volume.

Acknowledgment also should go to many other *News* staffers who took an interest in the column, made suggestions and helped in the production.

Finally, I thank my mother, the late Allene Milton Melrose. She came to Colorado from Dodge City, Kan., in 1890, looked, listened and absorbed many happenings, and when I was a child, shared her observations with me. Many of the things she told me inspired some of these columns.

I am proud and happy to be a product of the West, and I hope these little stories will entertain both easterners and westerners, old-timers and newcomers.

Frances Melrose

Table of Contents

Chapter 1

Rocky Mountain News

Judge Ben Lindsey, his wife Henrietta and daughter Benetta were a compassionate family as they left Denver to live in California. He had been disbarred, but the disbarment later was rescinded.

Lindsey led the way with juvenile courts

THE Colorado legislature scored a bull's eye in the circle of jurisprudence when it established Denver Juvenile Court in 1903.

Judge Ben B. Lindsey, one of the most controversial figures ever to sit on the bench in Denver, outlined the law that established the court and, for many years, was the presiding judge.

Lindsey was controversial for several reasons — partly because he was a flamboyant showman who courted publicity for his causes, but also because some of his causes were "far out" for their day.

"The little judge," as he often was called, was a native of Jackson, Tenn. He came to Denver as a child. He was 5-foot-5 and weighed 100 pounds. He had a feisty disposition — a David ready to

take on any Goliath.

He was loved and admired by hundreds and hated by other hundreds. His admirers ranged from the struggling poor to President Theodore Roosevelt, who referred to him as "the bull mouse." A national poll in 1914 rated Lindsey as one of the 10 greatest living Americans.

It is hard to believe that a man of Lindsey's professional stature would be disbarred, but that happened, and the judge left Colorado in 1929. He later became a Los Angeles Superior Court judge and died in office there at the age of 73.

Lindsey was admitted to the Colorado Bar in 1894, and was elected county judge on the Democratic reform platform in 1900.

He was concerned with the law's failure to

distinguish between adult and juvenile prisoners, and one of his first works as judge was to organize the Association for the Protection and Betterment of Children. The law establishing the Denver Juvenile Court followed.

Lindsey's methods of dealing with those who appeared before the court were unusual and unorthodox. He would give young offenders carfare to the State Training School 15 miles away. Out of several hundred, only five betrayed his trust and didn't show up.

Young unwed mothers who feared the stigma of returning home with their babies were given a helping hand by Lindsey. The judge would perform a marriage ceremony between the girl and a fictitious man, then provide her with annulment papers. The girl would return home with a marriage certificate, annulment papers and a baby.

The late Judge Philip B. Gilliam, who presided over the Juvenile Court from 1940 to 1973, admired Lindsey and wrote about him at length. Gilliam recalled that Lindsey, upon his disbarment, gathered from his files the personal histories of those who had appeared in his court, heaped them on the courthouse lawn and set fire to them in front of assembled reporters.

As the flames shot upward, Lindsey took a folder off the heap, opened it, read briefly and remarked, tossing the folder back into the blaze:

"Mary, your secret dies with me."

The judge became a spokesman for the sexual freedom of the 1920s. Writing in the *Ladies Home Journal,* he said his courtroom observation was that sexual ignorance was a major cause of "broken homes, desertions, sorrow and the great mass of social ills. . . ." He advocated the dissemination of birth control information.

Lindsey's idea of companionate marriage — trial marriage without children, so common to-day — became a scandal of the 1920s, arousing the ire of both public and pulpit. Thousands of letters of protest were delivered to him. The fire-eating preacher, Billy Sunday, called Lindsey's proposal "barnyard marriage — nothing but free love." Lindsey responded by saying Sunday "would be burning witches . . . if he had his way."

Through it all, however, Lindsey made it plain that he expected the participants to go through a legitimate marriage ceremony. He did not favor premarital living arrangements.

Disapproval of Lindsey's espousal of companionate marriage is believed to have played a role in his disbarment, although the disbarment involved another issue.

Lindsey was disbarred by the Colorado Supreme Court in December 1928 on charges that he had accepted a $37,500 "gift" from Helen Elwood Stokes while he was a juvenile court judge for services he performed in helping her obtain custody of her children after a divorce and for helping her gain a $1.4 million settlement from the estate of her ex-husband.

In 1936, the Colorado Supreme Court reinstated Lindsey and ordered his name restored to the state's list of attorneys. By then, however, he was living and working in California.

When Lindsey died, his widow brought his ashes to Denver and, following his request, scattered them near the site of the courthouse where he had presided. The courthouse, which stood at 16th Street and Court Place, had been torn down and the site had been turned into a park, where the ashes were scattered.

The juvenile court Lindsey founded in Denver lives on, as do many modeled after it around the world.

July 12, 1981

Bring back the melons of days gone by

GROWING up in Denver, I regularly went grocery shopping with my mother. She was a canny woman who believed every girl should be taught such things as how to recognize a bargain, the way to select bananas and that a housewife's best friend is her butcher.

About this time of year, it seems to me, we were always prodding and sniffing melons and bringing in sacksful of Golden Bantam or Country Gentleman corn.

The cantaloupes we looked for were called either Greeley Wonder or Rocky Ford — the latter characterized by its green flesh, not the pink-orange we know now. It occurred to me recently that I haven't seen either of them in the market for years. And while I've occasionally spotted some Golden Bantam corn, it must be at least 25 years since I've seen any Country Gentleman.

The Greeley Wonder was a big elliptical cantaloupe with deep ridges running lengthwise. It sometimes was as big as a small watermelon, and by following the ridges, it was easily sliced into neat wedges. Or, if you sliced it across the rings, the rings had a pretty scalloped look because of the ridges.

The Rocky Ford cantaloupe was nationally famous for its sweet flavor and small core. They were shipped all over the country and were a prize of the market.

Country Gentleman corn was a pearly white variety that grew on very large ears with small close-set kernels. It was tender and had a delicate sweet flavor when fresh. Golden Bantam was equally good, and some even liked it better. It was a smaller ear filled with sweet yellow kernels. Once started, a kid could eat a dozen of them.

What became of these gustatory delights? John Cretti, Colorado State University Extension horticulturist in charge of the Denver Cooperative Extension Office, said we no longer have them because large seed companies which wholesale the seed to farmers phased them out

Piles of famous Rocky Ford melons were exhibited at the Arkansas Valley Fair in 1904.

P.E. Kennedy

On the last day of the fair, the huge crowd of fairgoers rushed for the free melons.

when demand declined. Fickle farmers turned to other varieties they liked better.

Cretti made some educated guesses on why the demand for these particular varieties faded. The Greeley Wonder melon probably lost its popularity because of its size, less desirable as families grew smaller. The famous old Rocky Ford cantaloupe, a nice, small round melon, fell out of favor when a melon of similar size and shape was developed with orange meat, which the public found more eye-appealing.

"The melon with orange flesh still is called a 'Rocky Ford,' Cretti said, "but it doesn't seem to get the merchandising and advertising of its predecessor. Old-timers around Pueblo, Rocky Ford and La Junta still grow a few of the original melons, which they maintain have a better flavor. The newer Rocky Ford is a good melon, but different."

Country Gentleman corn went out when a new variety, Silver Queen, came in, Cretti said.

"Country Gentleman was delicious if it could be eaten the day it was picked," he said, "but the longer it lay around in a market, the more of its sweetness it lost. Silver Queen, on the other hand, is a white corn with better keeping quality. It holds its sugar content longer after picking."

But all is not lost, Cretti said. We still may bring back Greeley Wonder melons, the original Rocky Ford cantaloupes and Country Gentleman corn if we really want to.

"The National Seed Storage Laboratory, which is located in Fort Collins and is a part of Colorado State University, has saved seeds from many rare and outmoded crops," Cretti said, "Any recognized seed producer or plant breeder may borrow some of these seeds and grow a crop, with the understanding that he will return a certain number of seeds from the new crop. The office isn't open to ordinary farmers or gardeners."

Let's hope someone will get busy and popularize these delicious foods again. I can taste them now.

July 26, 1981

The readers said . . .

FREDA Chenburgh of Arvada sent us some wonderful old pictures of Watermelon Day that were taken in Rocky Ford in 1904.

"My foster grandfather was Sen. John Crowley, for whom Crowley County was named," she said, "and I know he always played a prominent part in this Rocky Ford celebration. It was such a festive occasion that many people who were working away from Rocky Ford would try to return for it, just as they did for Christmas."

Watermelon Day, which still is celebrated in Rocky Ford, began in 1877 as part of the Arkansas Valley Fair, according to Ellenor Brenneman, Rocky Ford city clerk.

"Big piles of watermelons were placed on the fairgrounds at the beginning of the fair," she said. "Then on the final Saturday, the starting signal was given, and the crowd rushed to the pile of melons to grab what they could. In the very beginning, I understand the melons were given as dessert to a big potluck supper staged as the finale of the fair."

Half-a-dozen years ago, however, policing the pile of melons became such a chore that now they are held in a warehouse until the parade on Friday, when they are paraded through town on National Guard trucks. Then they are distributed free to all comers by the Rocky Ford Rotary Club on Saturday.

"Donations are collected during the year," said Brenneman, "and the melons are purchased from local produce dealers through these donations for Watermelon Day."

September 6, 1981

The Liberty Bell
had its day in Denver

WE always think of America's famous Liberty Bell ensconced in its well-guarded surroundings in Philadelphia, but Freda Chenburg of Arvada writes that she remembers when the Liberty Bell visited Denver.

"I was a small child," she wrote, "and it has to be at least 60 years ago when the bell came to Denver. It was parked on a flatbed railroad car at Union Station, and my parents took me down to see it. A big crowd had turned out at the station to see the bell.

"That's about all I remember about it. Can you give me any other details of the time and the event?"

Dear Mrs. Chenburg:

The front page of the *Rocky Mountain News* reported May 6, 1915, that "the Liberty Bell, which clanged forth in joy when the Declaration of Independence was signed, July 4, 1776, is coming to Denver." The visit was announced for late July, but the paper said it was hoped the date could be changed to August 1, Colorado Day, the anniversary of Colorado statehood.

The date was not changed, however, and the July 11, 1915, edition of the *News* reported that 150,000 people had "paid homage to the bell in Denver yesterday, as it stood on the tracks."

"From early morning till noon, when the brass-mouthed flat car pulled out, people walked by, rapt with thoughts of history in a seeming daze," the paper reported. Many visitors held out a key, a coin, a card — anything they could touch to the bell and keep as a souvenir.

Guards from the Navy and the Philadelphia Police Department accompanied the 2,800-pound bell on the trip, and it was reported that mothers would pass small children over to one of the guards so they could be held up to kiss the bell. During the Liberty Bell's stopover in Denver, music was provided by a band, plus three drums and a fife.

The bell had left Philadelphia on July 3, 1915, headed for a West Coast exposition. The day after its Denver visit, it stopped in Salt Lake City, and it was reported that "the largest crowd ever gathered in Utah saw the bell at Salt Lake City." While it was parked in a corner of Pioneer Square between 11 a.m. and 3 p.m., more than 400,000 people visited it.

"A great rivet was holding the crack together," the paper reported, and the clapper had been stilled.

The Liberty Bell was cast and molded by hand in England at the Whitechapel Bell Foundry in 1752. It is 77% copper and 23% tin. The bell's inscription, "Proclaim Liberty Throughout the Land, to All the Inhabitants Thereof," had nothing to do with the American Revolution. Isaac Norris, an assemblyman in Pennsylvania, asked the colony's London agent to buy the bell for Philadelphia's new statehouse at a time when Pennsylvania still was loyal to England. The verse Norris chose comes from Leviticus 25:10.

The *News* was wrong when it said the Liberty Bell was rung July 4, 1776, when the Declaration of Independence was signed. The bell was not sounded until July 8, when the first public reading of the declaration took place outside the statehouse in Philadelphia.

The bell got a tiny crack early in its career, but the major crack that made it dangerous to ring developed when the death of Chief Justice John Marshall was being tolled in 1835.

Personnel at the English bell factory, refusing to admit that the crack came from imperfect workmanship, said that poor handling at the hands of "ignorant Colonials" caused the crack.

Colorado has a replica of the Liberty Bell standing on the grounds of the former state Historical Society Building at East 14th Avenue and Sherman Street. (In July 1986, the bell was moved to a spot west of the capitol between Lincoln and Broadway, the eventual site of a veterans' memorial.)

It and 52 other replicas of the famous bell were cast in France in 1950. They were donated to the U.S. government by "American industry and free enterprise." One bell went to each state and the district of Columbia, and two are missing.

September 6, 1981

Rocky Mountain News

The Liberty Bell was in Denver in 1915 as it toured the nation so the citizens could pay homage to it. About 150,000 people went to Union Station to see the famous bell, crack and all.

Two famous broncs busted their riders

CHEYENNE Frontier Days, with its sun-fishing broncs and high-flying bronc bust-ers, brought to mind two of the greatest bucking horses that ever lived — Midnight and his bud-dy, Five Minutes to Midnight. These examples of equine dynamite made rodeoing particularly lively during the 1920s, '30s and early '40s.

Midnight, a coal-black 1,600-pound stallion, had a reputation as the meanest thing ever tied up in horsehide when he had a man on his back. But as soon as the rider had been bucked off, he mildly trotted away. He never tried to stomp a rider and never kicked one.

Midnight became a shining star of the rodeo circuit, from Madison Square Garden to Pendle-ton, Ore., and especially at Denver's National Western Stock Show and Cheyenne Frontier Days. People bought tickets to rodeos just to see Midnight do his worst.

The late Verne Elliott, longtime rodeo produc-er who bought Midnight in 1926 when the horse was 10 years old, said the beast had made a study of pitching cowboys into the dust. There was no doubt he was a master at it. He threw some of the best bronc riders in the world — Earl Thode, Pete Knight, Eddie Woods, Paddy Ryan and Doff Aber among them.

Midnight was part thoroughbred and part Morgan, with a dash of Percheron

He had worked out a bucking technique that began with a few stiff jumps, which most wad-dies could withstand, then went on to lower his head with a jerk, throw his hind legs straight in the air and make a fast sideways twist. It was the sideways twist maneuver that threw riders.

Elliott maintained that Midnight was success-fully ridden only when he was sick. It happened at Fort Worth, Texas, in 1933, when an unknown cowboy managed to stay on the bronc's pitching back until after the whistle blew. Elliott said then that the horse had a cold. He also was 17 years old.

After that, Elliott retired Midnight to his ranch outside Platteville, stating that the horse had thrown every great bronc rider in his time, and he wouldn't now let a lot of unknown cow-boys ride him when he was old and sick.

Midnight died Nov. 7, 1936, having spent his last days in green pastures. He was buried on Elliott's ranch with a gravestone that said;

"Under this sod lies a great bucking hoss,
"There was nary a cowboy he couldn't toss.
"His name was Midnight — his coat black as coal.
"If there is a horse heaven, please, God, rest his soul."

Midnight was a hard act to follow, and Five Minutes to Midnight, or Old Five, as the cow-hands called him, never was quite as famous. Five Minutes to Midnight was smaller, a gelding weighing only 900 pounds. He also was black, wiry and shaggy, and he bucked like a coiled spring coming loose.

A news item on the National Western Stock Show in 1940, when Old Five was 22, reported that he had been ridden only 17 times out of 2,000 tries.

Elliott, who also owned Old Five, had bought him for $5 at a horse pound in Calgary, Alberta. It was the best bargain he ever made.

Like Midnight, Five Minutes to Midnight was retired to spend his declining years on Elliott's ranch. He and Midnight were pals, and he was said to be one of the only two horses Midnight would allow near his herd of mares.

Five Minutes to Midnight died on the ranch in 1947. He was 29. He, too, was buried on the pre-mises.

In 1966, 30 years after Midnight's death, the remains of both horses were exhumed, to be re-buried at the National Cowboy Hall of Fame and Western Heritage Center in Oklahoma City.

August 2, 1981

'Silv'ry Colorado Wends Its Way'

OLD-TIME songs of the West are the subject of a letter from Ora Lee Ritterspach of Denver.

"Recently, I enjoyed a beautiful concert of Victorian music given by Dana Krueger, who sang the role of Augusta Tabor in *The Ballad of Baby Doe* at Central City," she writes. "One of the songs was *Where the Silv'ry Colorado Wends Its Way*, and it made me wonder whether it was inspired by the river in the state of Colorado or Arizona."

Dear Mrs. Ritterspach:

Your inquiry opened a treasure box of information on songs about the West, in addition to the cowboy type. Fortunately, the Western History Department of the Denver Public Library has a large file of sheet music devoted to songs of the West or written by western composers.

Where the Silv'ry Colorado Wends Its Way, with music by Charles Avril and words by C.H. Scoggins, was published in 1901 by the Tolbert R. Ingram Music Co. of Denver.

The cover contains a number of advertising plugs for the song, such as "Introduced with great success by Lottie Gilson, 'The Little Magnet,'" "Played by Helen May Butler's Ladies Military Brass Band of 50 Members," and "The Ballad Which John D. Rockefeller Sings and Whistles." Apparently John D. Rockefeller Jr. had provided the composers with financial backing on this project.

Avril and Scoggins, writers of many successful songs, surprisingly were a pair of Denver letter carriers who wrote songs as a hobby. Most of their output was published by the Home Music Co. of Denver, and included *Dreaming on the Silv'ry Rio Grande, Baby's Laughing in His Sleep, In the Shadow of the Everlasting Hills,* and *The Girl I Loved Out in the Golden West.*

Nothing has been published about the locale of *Where the Silv'ry Colorado Wends Its Way,*

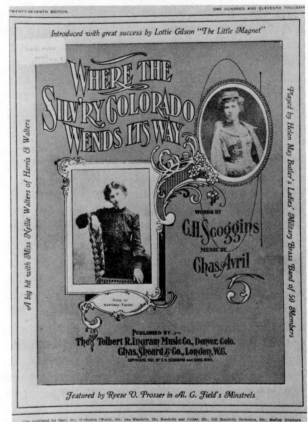

Western History Department, Denver Public Library

Where the Silv'ry Colorado Wends its Way, by two Denver mailmen, was published in 1901.

which was one of those sad, four-handkerchief songs, but the writers lived in Colorado, and the words sound as if the setting is Colorado. The end, for instance says:

"Now she sleeps beneath the lilacs,
"And she'll ne'er come back again
"Where the silv'ry Colorado wends its way.

The sheet music cover of *Dreaming on the Silv'ry Rio Grande* amused us with the artistic license it took with geography. A picture of a stream, presumably the Rio Grande, is shown tumbling down from the Mount of the Holy

Cross.

Another prolific turn-of-the-century song writer was Estelle Philleo whose output included the music for one of the most famous of all, *Out Where the West Begins.* Words to this classic were by Arthur Chapman. Philleo also wrote *Farther West,* with words by Roscoe Stockton; *Roundup Lullaby,* with words by Badger Clark; and the more famous *Way Out West in Wyoming.* Lettering under a drawing on the sheet music cover of *Out Where the West Begins,* states that the "skyline sketch is by Harold Bell Wright from *When a Man's a Man.*" Chapman's verses for *Out Where the West Begins* have been quoted often. Here they are in part:

"Out where the handclasp's a little stronger
"Out where the smile dwells a little longer,
"That's where the West begins!
"Out where the sun shines a little brighter,
"Where the snows that fall are a trifle whiter,
"Where the bonds of home are a wee bit tighter —
"That's where the West begins . . . "

There are dozens of other songs about the West. It's amazing how mountains and streams and the ways of the West have inspired the creation of music. There are romantic songs, serious songs and a few funny ones. One of the classics, of course, is *When It's Springtime in the Rockies,* by Mary Hale Woolsey and Robert Sauer, which was published in 1923, and still is virtually the anthem of the mountain states.

Another of the most famous, which schoolchildren were taught to sing a few years ago, is *C-Oh! Hello! Hooray D-Oh! C-O-L-O-R-A-D-O,* written in 1926, with both words and music by Roscoe K. Stockton. Stockton was a widely known Denver radio producer-writer and for several years taught a course in radio writing and production at the University of Denver. Many remember him as "Old Waggin' Tongue," narrator of a series of western radio dramas.

Stockton's Colorado song is bouncy and rollicking, with a clever play on words. The chorus goes:

"C-Oh! Hello! Hooray D-Oh!
"I'm a mile high feelin' fine,
" 'Cause I just got back to my mile-high shack
"In this healthy, wealthy, wonderful state o' mine.
"As I Stop! Look! Listen! not a hilltop's missin',
"And the sun just loves to shine.
"Co-Lo-Hip Hip Hip Ra-Do
"Tell the world I'm feelin' fine."

And we shouldn't overlook our state song, *Where the Columbines Grow,* adopted as Colorado's official song by the legislature in 1915. Words and music were by A.J. Fynn, and the song, a waltz, was published by the Daughters of Colorado, with a dedication to the Colorado pioneers. It never caught on like some of the others.

Silver Dollar Echo Tabor, daughter of the silver king, H.A.W. Tabor, and his second wife, Baby Doe, also contributed a Colorado song. Her composition, the words to a march composed by Professor Anthony S. Lohmann, was entitled, *Our President Roosevelt's Colorado Hunt.* The cover of the sheet music carried a dedication "To my beloved father, H.A.W. Tabor." The music also gives her name only as Silver Echo Tabor.

Denver, too, has had its share of songs. Among them are *Good Old Denver Town,* with words and music by J.R. Shannon, written in 1913, for the 32nd triennial conclave of Knights of Templar of the USA; *Seeing Denver, the City of Lights,* song and words by Gus Brohm, a widely known comedian and entertainer, in 1908; and *City of Lights,* a march-two step, written in 1907, by Enrico Gargiulo.

In more recent times, there has been *The Beautiful People of Denver,* from the musical, *The Unsinkable Molly Brown,* by Meredith Willson and Richard Morris.

August 23, 1981

City Park trotters

DENVER socialites, who included many of the city's leading businessmen had an obsession with harness horse racing at the turn of the century.

The hub of the activity was an organization called the Gentlemen's Driving and Riding Club, organized in 1898. Members informally had been indulging their interest for many years before that.

We got launched on this subject when a Denver resident of only 26 years, Joe Mills, wrote that some years ago, he ran into an old-timer who mentioned the "old race track at City Park." Mills asked what we could tell him about the City Park track.

An article in *Denver Municipal Facts* for May 7, 1910, said the Gentleman's Driving and Riding Club was organized solely "for the pleasure its members would derive from horse competitions and exhibitions."

Charter members included W.W. Porter, George M. Black, J.A. Osner, J. Fred Roberts, William McGath, John D. Ross, J.J. Joslin, R.G. Webster, M.J. Lawrence and Alfred Butters.

In the early 1880s, this group had a clubhouse in a large frame building with first and second

The grandstand at City Park race track was built in 1898 by public subscription. Members of the Gentlemen's Driving and Riding Club raced their trotters on the half-mile track.

floor verandas, at what now is East 4th Avenue and Downing Street. They maintained a stable there for horses that raced on nearby Arlington Park track.

Maj. Jacob Downing came into possession of the building during the 1880s, and maintained it as a clubhouse. When he died in 1907, his wife turned it into the Downing Home for Old People. By then, the Gentlemen's Driving and Riding Club had moved from Arlington Park to City Park.

It seems the gentlemen drivers had a penchant for running their sulkies on East 17th Avenue, and the mayor ordered them off the street because of the traffic hazard. As a conciliation, he offered them the northeast corner of City Park, which then was largely undeveloped, where they could race.

In 1898, the city built a half-mile track at a cost of $10,000, and the grandstand costing $15,000 was built by popular subscription. The wooden bleachers and dirt track occupied the area north of the Museum of Natural History that's now used for football, softball and soccer.

It was considered to be one of the best half-mile riding and driving tracks in the United States, and the Gentlemen's Driving and Riding Club was said to be the largest amateur driving club in the world. It also had a polo team.

In the starter's tower on 26 alternating Saturday afternoons, the bell rang for racing. In summer the Denver Muncipal Band played.

Seven racing events were held at each matinee. An average of 36 horses started during the afternoon.

There was no admission charge. Denver's elite turned out in all their finery. Often the matinees began with a parade of horses and sulkies around the track.

One account said that it cost each member of the Gentlemen's Driving and Riding Club about $800 for horse and equipment, and another $45 per month to keep the horse in training. These were considerable sums for the times.

By 1910, three world records had been established at the City Park track, and all state records over a half-mile track had been broken. In 1904, a horse named Jim Perry, owned by Albert Wright, trotted a half-mile to a road wagon in 1:02¾ minutes, which stood as a world record in 1910.

At the end of the season, horses were raced to road wagons, with silver loving cups and gold medals as prizes.

September 20, 1981

Silver Dollar Tabor lived in chaos

BOOKS, plays and countless articles have been written about H.A.W. Tabor, Colorado's renowned "silver king," and his beautiful and controversial second wife, Baby Doe. But what of the Tabor children, Lilly and Silver Dollar? The children are hardly mentioned in the books and plays. The story of Silver Dollar, however, is nearly as tragic and dramatic as that of her mother.

An inquiry from Patricia Patty of Lakewood sent us on a search for information on Silver

Colorado Historical Society

In 1914, Silver Dollar Tabor worked briefly as a bit actress with a Colorado Springs company.

Dollar's fate. Much of the information for our answer was supplied by the late Caroline Bancroft, author of *Silver Queen,* and a nationally recognized authority on the Tabor history. (Miss Bancroft died in October 1985.)

Rosemary Echo Silver Dollar Tabor came into the world in 1889, in the Tabor Mansion at 1260 Sherman St., a little princess of silver, born to luxury. Her father, the silver king, spared no expense to show her off. Her layette was fashioned of the finest fabrics, and gold clasps on her tiny dresses were set with diamonds.

Wherever they went, Silver and her sister, Elizabeth Bonduel Lilly, who was 4 years older, were the center of attention, as daughters of the silver king. Blond Lilly resembled her mother, but Silver Dollar had the dark looks of her father.

The Tabor fame and fortune came tumbling down around them when Silver Dollar was only 4. The Panic of 1893 sent the price of silver skidding. By 1896, the mansion was gone and all but a few jewels had been sold. A short time before his death in 1899, Tabor got a political appointment as Denver postmaster, but died before he could benefit from it.

Tabor died April 10, 1899, in the Windsor Hotel. His funeral, a tribute to a man who had helped "put Colorado on the map," was one of the most elaborate the town had seen. Flags were flown at half-staff, and an elaborate funeral cortege wound up to the capitol, where Tabor's body lay in state to be viewed by thousands.

Leadville, the town where Tabor struck it rich, sent a cornucopia of roses 6 feet high. His funeral was in a different class from the modest ceremonies after the later deaths of Baby Doe and Silver Dollar.

Following Tabor's death, Baby Doe and her daughters moved to Leadville to live in a little mining cabin, faithful to Tabor's deathbed dictum: "Hang on to the Matchless." The Matchless was the mine which once had brought fortune to the family.

Baby Doe's frozen body was found in the mine shack on a March morning in 1935. She was alone, because by then, both daughters had gone.

Lilly, scornful of her mother's belief in the mine, and hating the life she lived in the mining camp, obtained money from her mother's brother, Peter McCourt, and took a train to Oshkosh, Wis., to live with relatives. She later married a cousin, John Last, in Wisconsin.

Silver Dollar, who dreamed of seeing the Tabor name restored to fame and grandeur, had died 10 years before Baby Doe, as Bancroft says, "under tragic and mysterious circumstances."

As a child, she stayed on at the Matchless with her mother, occasionally attending school in Leadville, but mainly trying to help Baby Doe work the mine. Although she had little formal education, she was interested in writing, and dreamed it might be a way to attain new fame for the Tabors.

When President Theodore Roosevelt visited Leadville in 1908, Silver Dollar rode into town to see him and later wrote a poem, *Our President Roosevelt's Colorado Hunt,* which was set to marching music by A.S. Lohmann of Denver.

Two years later, Silver Dollar, by then working on the *Denver Times,* pressed close to the platform when Roosevelt made an appearance in Denver and handed him a copy of the song. They were photographed together, and Denver newspapers carried the picture.

Her days on the *Times* were limited and not particularly successful, and for a very short time she edited a little newspaper, *Silver Dollar Weekly,* which failed. She also wrote a novel, *Star of Blood,* which found no success. By 1914, she was working, again only briefly, as a bit performer with a film company in Colorado Springs.

Silver Dollar is reported to have become involved in romantic escapades in Leadville and Denver. One story has it that Baby Doe managed to drive away the man Silver Dollar loved.

From film company work, she joined a variety show troupe playing the Midwest and even-

tually arrived in Chicago. She was reported to have become an alcoholic there.

From Chicago, Silver Dollar wrote her mother that she was entering a convent and would not be heard from again. In another letter, she wrote Baby Doe that she was married and happy.

On Sept. 18, 1925, a woman who had given the name Rose Norman, but who proved to be Silver Dollar Tabor, was found dead in a sleazy Chicago rooming house. She was 36 years old.

A coroner's jury reported the death was caused by her "being scalded, either accidentally or otherwise." One account is that she died in a bathtub of scalding water. The other is that she was drying her hair in front of a radiator on which sat a pan of scalding water that she accidentally pulled over on herself.

A copy of her book, *Star of Blood,* was found in the room, and in it, she had underlined a phrase — "only the grave brings peace."

During the investigation, two men, both reputed to be her lovers, were questioned, but they were released.

Baby Doe clung to the belief that Silver Dollar was in a convent and would not admit that the woman who died in Chicago was her daughter, according to Bancroft. An aunt, however, identified the body.

Lilly also denied her relationship to the dead woman, claiming instead to be a daughter of John Tabor, H.A.W. Tabor's brother. She later also denied that she was Baby Doe's daughter.

Funeral expenses — $200 — were provided by Peter McCourt, the uncle who always had come up with a little money when his nieces needed it. He didn't, however, provide enough for a gravestone.

On Sept. 18, 1957, on the 32nd anniversary of Silver Dollar's death, a simple marker was placed on her unmarked grave in Holy Sepulcher Cemetery in Chicago.

The headstone was a gift of Bancroft, Bert Baker, an engineer from St. Paul who had become interested in the Tabor story, and Tom Peavy of United Press, who had been a personal friend of Baby Doe.

Smoky Hill Trail lives in loving legend

CROSSING the Great Plains in a covered wagon, heading into an uncertain future was one of the most daring and romantic adventures ever undertaken in the history of our country.

Lela McQueary of Denver, whose husband, Ralph G. McQueary, is a member of a pioneer Colorado family, wrote to *Rocky Mountain Memories* conerning one of those historic wagon treks.

"My husband's father came by wagon train from Missouri to Denver in June 1873. The following paragraphs are taken from his memoirs of the trip:

"We left the railroad at Fort Wallace and cut southwest to the Big Sandy River, then cut south and west again through what was called the Bison Basin country and the Divide country, somewhere near the head of Cherry Creek. From there we went to the old 100-Mile House, stopping place for travelers, 100 miles from Denver.

"From there we went to the 50-Mile House, 50 miles from Denver, and then drifted back to the Big Sandy and followed it until we were about east of Denver. We then turned west and came into Denver about where East Colfax Avenue is now.

"We have been unable to find anything about the 100-Mile House and the 50-Mile House. Can you give us any information?"

Dear Mrs. McQueary: It sounds to me as though your father-in-law was traveling on the Smoky Hill Trail which stretched between Atchison, Kan., and Denver, and wound up at what is now the intersection of East Colfax Avenue and Broadway. The spot is marked by the Pioneer Monument, which was dedicated to the brave and hardy pioneers who opened this frontier.

Not quite 50 years ago, Margaret Long wrote a book about this trek called *The Smoky Hill*

Rocky Mountain News

People packed Colfax and Broadway intersection in 1911 to dedicate Pioneer Monument.

Trail, which details many of the markers along this pioneer route.

The Smoky Hill trail began at Atchison, followed the Smoky Hill River across Kansas and entered Colorado near Cheyenne Wells, Long wrote.

"From the indefinite headwaters of the Smoky Hill, it crossed the Big Sandy and snaked westward across Kiowa and Bijou creeks, until it reached the headwaters of Cherry Creek, then followed this into Denver," Long said.

The Overland Trail followed the South Platte River to Julesburg, then took the Fort Morgan cutoff to Watkins and on into Denver.

In connection with the Smoky Hill Trail, I found mention of six stage houses located in the Cherry Creek Valley between Parker and Denver — the 20-Mile House, 17, 12, 9, 7 and 4-mile houses. These served travelers on the two branches of Smoky Hill as well as the Cherokee Trail and Santa Fe Stage Road.

I could not find mention of a 100-Mile House or a 50-Mile House. The old Kiowa Creek Express station was about 64 miles from Denver, fitting neither description.

Mention of the Pioneer Monument, which is one of Denver's best known landmarks, brings to mind another story.

The monument, dedicated in 1911, was a gift to the city of Denver from several groups and individuals who wanted to honor the pioneers. Its total cost was $75,000, for which the city appropriated $7,500 and the state $10,000. The rest was met by contributions from citizens. Donations included $3,000 from Thomas F. Walsh of Camp Bird Mine fame.

The sculptor selected was Frederick MacMonnies, an American artist living in Paris. He was given no specific instructions on what kind of monument was wanted, and so, in his preliminary sketch, he created a handsome model of an Indian on a rearing horse for the main figure. The base of the monument depicted figures of the Hunter, the Prospector, the Pioneer Mother and Child and the Cowboy, along with overflowing cornucopias.

Pioneers who saw the sketches were incensed at the idea of using an Indian at the top of the Pioneer Monument. Indians, some of them contended vociferously, had caused the pioneers nothing but trouble. It was ridiculous and insulting to put one atop the monument.

The uproar was enough to bring about an order for a redesign of the sculpture. It was decided that the scout and pathfinder, Kit Carson, should be used for the main figure.

MacMonnies visited Denver to straighten out the problem. Unconvincingly — to that audience — he explained that the crowning figure of a monument is not necessarily the hero of the occasion.

Undaunted, the Denver Real Estate Exchange, which headed the group commissioning the monument, stood firmly by the idea of Kit Carson. They even sent a picture of Carson, along with the scout's jacket and powder horn, to MacMonnies in Paris and told him to get busy. He complied. The contract for the work was signed in 1907, and the dedication was in 1911.

October. 11, 1981

The readers said . . .

A Denver fireman, Bob Isett, who works out of Station No. 4 at 19th and Lawrence streets, was interested in a *Rocky Mountain News* article on the Pioneer Monument at West Colfax Avenue and Broadway.

"When I was a young fireman, I used to talk a lot with an old assistant chief, Bill Bryan," Isett said. "He told me that in the early days there was a firehouse where the Pioneer Monument now stands. They had horse-drawn hose wagons then, and he described the feeling of excitement as the horses would come tearing out of the station and go galloping down Broadway.

"After it was decided to erect the Pioneer Monument at West Colfax and Broadway, because that was the 'end of the trail' as the pioneers came to Denver, they had to move the firehouse. The old building was torn down, and a new firehouse was built. The 'new' building is the Firehouse Museum at 1326 Tremont Place."

February 6, 1983

Ivy Baldwin reveled in challenging death

WHEN Colorado aviation pioneers get together, the talk sooner or later swings around to Ivy Baldwin. He was one of the great ones, one of the first to be honored with nomination to the Colorado Aviation Hall of Fame.

Baldwin, who weighed a scant 100 pounds, had more courage and derring-do encased in his 5-foot frame than 100 bigger men. He flirted with danger all his life and loved every minute of it.

He made his last big splash at the age of 82 when he walked a high wire stretched 125 feet above South Boulder Canyon at Eldorado Springs, to celebrate his birthday, July 31, 1948. News wire services carrried the story around the world.

That, however, was only one of 86 crossings Baldwin made across the canyon, most of them 582 feet above the canyon floor. It once was described by Robert Ripley as "the highest tightrope walk in the world." The lowered height on Baldwin's 82nd birthday was a concession to age and the fact that he hadn't performed the stunt for 20 years. Just to prove that his successful feat at 82 was no accident, Baldwin did it again the next day, walking backward across the chasm while a crowd of hundreds screamed.

Wire walking was only one of the ways in which Baldwin challenged death. He also did stunts out of balloons, developed, flew and manufactured an early airplane, and crashed in

Colorado Historical Society

Ivy Baldwin walked a high wire over South Boulder Canyon at Eldorado Springs on his 82nd birthday in 1948. Just to prove it was no fluke, he did it again the next day — backward.

planes 19 times, proving that he never got up very high and also had more lives than a cat.

Baldwin, whose real name was Will Ivy, was born in Houston in 1866. As a boy, he shined shoes and sold papers to earn enough to see every circus and carnival that came to town. One of his heroes was Charles Blondine, world-famous tightwire walker who several times walked a wire across Niagara Falls.

At 13, Will Ivy ran away from home to join a small circus, having trained himself into considerable skill as a wire walker. His first job at the circus, however, was doing tricks in a balloon when the regular balloonist showed up drunk at performance time. Ivy performed successfully, doing aerial stunts on the balloon's ascent and descent, dangling from a trapeze attached to the balloon which rose to nearly 5,000 feet. For this, the boy earned a permanent job with the circus.

A few years later, he changed his name to Ivy Baldwin, taking his last name in admiration of Thomas Baldwin, a famous acrobat and wire walker, with whom he was working.

In 1890, John Elitch brought Ivy Baldwin to Denver where he became a star attraction doing balloon ascensions and parachute drops at Elitch Gardens. He made a number of high-wire walks at Elitch's in following years, and also at the old Manhattan Beach, on Sloans Lake.

With the outbreak of the Spanish-American War, Baldwin enlisted as an expert on balloons. He was sent up as an observer to get information on the Spanish fleet at the battle of Santiago, Cuba. He spotted the fleet, but his balloon was punctured by small-arms fire and it made an unscheduled drop. The only thing that saved Ivy Baldwin that time was landing in a creek. He returned as the only aeronaut to serve under fire with the Army in that war.

After the war, the Wright Brothers started their flying experiments, and Baldwin became involved with several associates in the manufacture of planes in Sacramento, Calif. He described the planes as "pusher type, with the engine in back of the pilot." Test flying those planes accounted for some of his 19 crashes.

The crashes also interested Baldwin in parachute jumping. He became the second man in the United States to make a parachute jump. Tom Baldwin was the first.

Willing to try anything, Ivy Baldwin also made the first plane takeoff from water in Colorado. He took off from Sloans Lake in one of his pusher-type planes, which fluttered only a few feet over the lake for about 200 feet, then came down in a spectacular splash landing. He wasn't hurt.

When he was 41, in 1907, Ivy Baldwin made the first of his 86 crossings over Boulder Canyon at Eldorado Springs. He once was lashed by wind and hail and forced to hang on the wire by his hands and knees for 30 minutes before he could get up and continue the walk.

But Baldwin maintained that the most dangerous walk of his life took place in 1885 in San Francisco. He was 19, then, and skittered over a wire perilously stretched over the Pacific Ocean, from San Francisco's Cliff House to Seal Rocks. He said the pounding surf made him dizzy as he teetered on the wire, but he performed that stunt periodically for a couple of years.

Baldwin's stunts took him around the world, and he once performed for the emperor of Japan. The emperor was so impressed that he had a crew of women sit up all night sewing Baldwin a dressing gown embroidered with balloons and parachutes. The robe became one of his good-luck pieces.

Although Ivy Baldwin did most of the crazy things he could think of in his lifetime, he failed to realize one ambition. He wanted to walk the wire across South Boulder Canyon an even 100 times. But the next time he wanted to go up, in his mid-80s, his family cracked down on the idea and prevented his doing it.

At the age of 87, in 1953, Baldwin died in bed in the Arvada home of his son, Harry Baldwin, where he spent the last years of his life.

November 1, 1981

Early Denver's whistle wet by artesian wells

THE new buildings going up in downtown Denver started us thinking about the artesian wells that once supplied many of the city's office buildings. Are they still used, or what became of them?

An article in the *Denver Times* on Sept. 30, 1900, reported there were about 150 artesian wells in the city. A number of the larger buildings had put in their own artesian wells, the *Times* said, because it was cheaper than obtaining water from the city system.

Artesian wells get their name from the province of Artois, France, where they have been used for hundreds of years. A well at Pas de Calais had been flowing steadily since 1126 A.D., according to the *Times*.

Three conditions are necessary to produce an artesian well, the *Times* article said. They are: The fountain head must be higher than the area where the boring is done; there must be a moderate downward dip of the strata toward the site of the well; and alternate layers of porous and impervious strata must lie under the surface soil.

Depth has nothing to do with creating an artesian well, according to Jeris Danielson, state engineer in the Division of Water Resources. It depends on the water's confinement, which creates pressure, and this can occur at any level, but generally is very deep, he said.

The Windsor Hotel, which stood at 18th and Larimer streets, had an artesian well 1,100 feet deep, but the deepest well in the city was said to be the one bored for Gov. John Evans in the rear of the Lawrence Street Methodist Church. (We can't find any Methodist church by that name in 1900, but there was the Paul Quinn Methodist Church at 23rd and Lawrence streets.)

Boring on the church well was stopped at 1,140 feet, but the well later was plugged at 710 feet. During the digging, the well had produced some petroleum, and Evans was afraid natural gas would follow, causing an explosion.

The deepest well still in use in the city, according to the *Times*, belonged to Henry C. Brown "on Capitol Hill." Brown, who had built the Brown Palace Hotel, at the time had his residence at 1311 Sherman St. No depth is given for the well except that "it is over 1,000 feet."

Brown put in three artesian wells for the hotel that he built in 1892, one going down 740 feet, according to Corinne Hunt, historian for the Brown. That well is still used at the hotel, and another was added 3 years ago.

One of the city's oldest artesian wells, as well as the most popular one, was that supplying a fountain in front of the old Courthouse Building, which occupied the square block between 15th and 16th streets and Court and Tremont places, where May D&F now stands.

This well, bored in 1882, went down 900 feet. At 620 feet, small particles of silver were brought up, and it was believed that a rich vein of silver was in the vicinity. However, as in the case of the church well, water was considered more important than oil or silver, and the water drilling went on.

When the well was completed, it was an instant hit.

"People would sample the waters all day and would bring jugs and jars to fill and take home, believing the iron it contained was beneficial to their health," the *Times* article said. "At first, it was necessary to pump the water with an old-fashioned pump handle, but about 1899, the old pump was taken out and the well was put down another 100 feet to increase the flow of water. A hydrant was inserted, and then it was only necessary to turn a spigot."

People came for miles to get this "germ-free" water, a later article said. Water from the Windsor Hotel was compared to the Courthouse water and was found to be "of entirely different nature . . . with no taste of iron . . . as clear and tasteless as any that can be found."

Because of the importance attached to the Courthouse well, imagine the public dismay when the *Times* on Aug. 10, 1903, reported that lazy city employees, finding it too much trouble to keep the pump running, were filling the tank from a faucet supplying water from the South Platte River.

Not all attempts to bore an artesian well were successful. At one point, an effort was made to put one in on the capitol grounds. After going down 200 feet, the contractor lost his drill. Another bore was started, and at the same depth, the drill slipped again, so the project was abandoned.

An attempt was made also to drill a well in the alley between the Tabor Opera House at 16th and Curtis streets and the old Post Office Building, later the Customs House, at 16th and Arapahoe streets. Here the contractor lost the drill in quicksand several times before giving up.

Among the many successful wells, we found mention of one in 1886, at "12th Street and Colfax." Twelfth Street later became Elati Street. This well, probably on property now owned by the *Rocky Mountain News,* went down 720 feet and was fed from four streams. It supplied 52 families in the area and possibly accounts for some of the water problems encountered by contractors building an addition to the *News* building about 14 years ago.

Several artesian wells were bored in the area of the railroad yards. The Kansas Pacific shops and the Union Pacific hospital each had one. An artesian well at Denver Union Station reportedly was supplying 223,000 gallons of water daily.

Dorathy Cohn, real estate agent who handled the sale of the Beatrice Creamery Building at 1801 Wynkoop St. in 1980, said the 1890's build-ing was supplied by an artesian well. The artesian water was used in the firm's manufacture of 5 million pounds of butter annually. This well was rebuilt in 1977 and still is used.

In addition to the Brown Palace and the Windsor Hotels, the Albany Hotel at 17th and Stout streets had an artesian well.

In the course of this research, we turned up still another interesting tidbit. In the early years of the Equitable Building at 730 17th St., the building's elevators were run by the pressure from an artesian well.

During the intervening years, so much pumping has taken place in the whole Denver basin that there no longer is sufficient pressure for the natural flow of artesian wells, Danielson said. However, they still can be pumped, and the Brown Palace, for instance, pumps its artesian water.

No registration of wells was required in the state until 1957, according to Danielson, so he doesn't know how many artesian wells may be in operation in Denver. He thinks there aren't many left, however.

"Since the wells at most of these locations no longer are flowing, the usual procedure is simply to cap them and not use them," he said.

William H. Miller of the Denver Water Department said the department has no artesian wells — no wells at all except some shallow ones on the Platte river. When artesian wells are in use, they are not connected to the Denver water system, and most buildings using artesian water also have a backup system from the city.

Wouldn't it be nice if Denver someday could uncap its old artesian wells and started pumping that wonderful water again?

November 8, 1981

The Dead Brother was the caption on a drawing of the Blue brothers in an 1867 book, *Beyond the Mississippi,* by Albert D. Richardson. The Blues' story was told by Daniel Blue in his journal.

Blue brothers ate a place in infamy

ALFERD Packer was the only man ever tried in the United States on a charge of cannibalism. The story began when he left Bingham Canyon, Utah, in November 1873, as a guide for a group of men seeking gold in Colorado territory.

The trip was plagued with snow and extreme cold, and the only one to survive was Packer, who emerged well-fed and healthy after weeks in the wilderness. He admitted living off the flesh of his companions, and after a trial in Lake City, he was convicted of killing five fellow travelers.

So much has been written about the celebrated Colorado cannibal that we don't plan to go into detail about him. Instead, we will concentrate on some other local cannibals, the Blue brothers, whose activities have been almost overlooked. The difference, possibly, is that the Blue brothers waited until their victims died natural deaths, while Packer was said to have killed his victims.

The Blues' story is told in an original account by Daniel Blue. The original journal, *Thrilling*

Narrative of the Adventures, Sufferings and Starvation of Pike's Peak Gold Seekers on the Plains of the West in the Winter and Spring of 1859, was republished by Ye Galleon Press, Fairfield, Wash., in 1968.

Daniel Blue, middle of the three Blue brothers, with his older brother, Alexander, younger brother, Charles, a cousin, John Campbell, and Thomas Stevenson, all of Whiteside County, Ill., set out for Pikes Peak in a quest for gold Feb. 22, 1859. Alexander left a wife and four young children. The other men were bachelors.

In Lawrence, Kan., they purchased a pack horse and after getting supplies, they continued their journey. In Topeka, they joined a party of nine others being guided by John "Captain" Gibbs. Two others also joined the group there.

At Fort Riley, Kan., Gibbs decided to lead the group over the Smoky Hill route rather than the more northerly Republican route, because he said he was familiar with it. Before the day's end, they were overtaken by a terrible storm, and Daniel and Charles Blue tried to persuade the party to take the other route. They would not. The others also insisted that Daniel leave behind a tent he had purchased, leaving them with no protection at night except the blankets they wrapped themselves in.

After about 9 days, Gibbs halted the party to renew provisions while they still were in buffalo country. The original Blue party of five, plus George Soley, decided to go on.

It was an ill-fated trip from the beginning. The group was traveling without a guide, without a compass but with plenty of misinformation. Two days later they were lost, and that night their packhorse wandered off or was stolen. By then, Alexander Blue, the first to falter, had become so ill they had to stop and let him rest a few hours.

Somewhere along the way, they had been rejoined by two of the Gibbs' group and a third person who had become lost from another expedition.

They reached the head of the Smoky Hill trail March 17, and then believed themselves to be only 55 miles from Denver. Actually, the distance was 170 miles. By then, they had consumed the last of their provisions, had been through several storms and were suffering from severe cold.

"Because of the distance, we thought we would go on without stopping to hunt for game," Daniel Blue wrote. "Oh! It was a fatal and terrible mistake, this information as to the real distance."

Lacking a compass, they had been charting their course by the sun, but a blizzard struck, obscuring the sun, and they "traveled in uncertainty for 5 days." At storm's end, they found they had been traveling in a circle.

Alexander Blue's condition worsened, and Charles also became ill. By then, the men were living on snow, an occasional rabbit and a dog that followed them. One night when they were exhausted by hunger, the talk turned to eating one another.

"Horrible thought!" wrote Daniel. But the group decided that whoever died first should be eaten by the rest.

The next day they saw a mountain peak in the distance, but it was too late for Alexander, who could no longer walk without help. Several of the party left, ostensibly to get help, leaving the three Blue brothers and Soley behind. By then they had been without food, with the exception of boiled roots and grass, for 8 days.

The next morning, Soley who had been uncomplaining but had grown steadily weaker, died. That left only the three Blue brothers. With his last words, according to Daniel's account, Soley asked the others to preserve their lives by eating his flesh.

"The dead body lay there for 3 days, we lying helpless on the ground near it, our craving for food increasing continually, until driven to desperation, wild with hunger and feeling, in its full force, the truth of the sentiment that 'self preservation is the first law of nature,' we took our knives and commenced cutting the flesh from the legs and arms of our dead companion and ate it! This was the hardest of our trials. . . ."

Although they all rallied somewhat, it was too late for Alexander, and he died several days later, after first writing a short farewell note to his wife and children. Alexander also urged the others to eat his body for their own preservation.

"After he had been dead two days, the uncontrollable and maddening cravings of hunger impelled Charles and I to devour a part of our own brother's corpse! It was a terrible thing to do, but we were not in a condition of mind or heart to do as we or other men would have done amid ordinary circumstances," Daniel wrote.

Daniel and Charles then traveled on, until Charles died. Broken in spirit, Daniel said he had made up his mind to die. He lay there for 3 days, occasionally eating some of Charles' body, but eventually he lost his sight and fell asleep.

He didn't know if it was hours or days later that he was awakened by three Arapaho Indians. The Indians put him across a pony and carried him to the Arapaho camp, where they fed him antelope meat and raw antelope liver and blood.

"I relished them well," Daniel said. "They strengthened and revived me. I was soon able to raise my head. In a day or two I could sit up, and my eyesight was restored." Daniel thanked the Indians for taking care of him.

The Indians then took him to a westward-bound encampment of the Pikes Peak Overland Express Co. After first stopping to bury Charles' body, the express party took Daniel to the nearest station and left him to be put on the next coach for Denver.

He arrived in Denver nearly 3 months after he had left Illinois. Soon after his arrival, he ran into Gibbs and another of his party. Only five made it to Denver of the 17 who started from Illinois.

In Denver, Daniel Blue found that the tales of gold had been greatly exaggerated, and he couldn't find work. Three weeks later, he arranged to travel east as far as the Missouri River with an Iowan who had a mule team. At Omaha, he caught a steamer to St. Louis, and then went by train to his home in Whiteside County, Ill.

He got there with 50¢ in his pocket and a burning desire to stay home.

November 15, 1981

The flood of 1933

A devastating flood — one of the worst ever to strike Denver — roared down Cherry Creek in the early morning of Aug. 3, 1933.

"Much of the information may be obtained from Ingrid Mosher, who was one of the telephone operators on the old Sullivan Exchange," said Malvina Sprague Robbins of Denver, writing to suggest a column on the flood. "She and others were at the switchboard nearly all night, telephoning warnings to people in the flood path."

That was a good suggestion, Mrs. Robbins, and we have been able to find a great deal of information about the flood, including what some

Rocky Mountain News

After Cherry Creek flooded in 1933, downtown businesses were left with tons of mud and water to get rid of. It was a 40-mile path of destruction, and damage was about $1 million.

Denver socialites wore on the occasion.

A headline in the *Rocky Mountain News* for Aug. 4, 1933, said "Breaking of Castlewood Dam — Menace Hanging Over City for 40 Years — Leaves 40-Mile Path of Destruction."

Two people died in the flood, and damage was estimated at more than $1 million, which would be equivalent to $4 million or $5 million today. Bridges at Colorado Boulevard, Stout and Champa streets were torn out by the flood and the debris it swept along. Basements were flooded from the Denver Country Club area to the warehouse district where Cherry Creek joins the South Platte River.

Castlewood Dam was built in 1899 for the Denver Land and Water Co., mainly for farm irrigation. The structure was situated in Wildcat Canyon and was 60 feet high, 8 feet wide and 600 feet long.

A blowout occurred beneath the dam in 1899, while the reservoir was full of water, and resulted in instability of the foundation, the news account indicated. The dam did not rest on bedrock, said the paper, but its foundation was on boulders forming the floor and walls of the canyon. The dam had been inspected only a few months before the flood and appeared safe, according to the state engineer, M.C. Hinderlider.

One of the heroes of the flood was Hugh Paine, who had been caretaker of the dam for 20 years. Heavy rains had been falling several days before the break, and Paine in an interview said he and his wife late at night heard "a low rumbling" and knew something was wrong. Paine dressed and ran to the dam.

"I saw it was going," he said. "It seemed to be breaking up in the middle where a well runs down through the dam to the bottom."

Paine's telephone was out of order, so after picking up a neighbor, Ed Hall, he traveled to Castle Rock, 12 miles away, over roads made slippery and dangerous by the rain.

At Castle Rock, he telephoned Denver police and informed them about the impending flood. He also notified August Deepe, telephone operator at Parker. Deepe, too, had notified Denver police he thought a flood was on the way, and had contacted Mrs. E.R. Henderson, operator at Sullivan.

With the help of other operators — Ingrid Mosher, Nettie Driskell and Fay Davis — Mr. and Mrs. Henderson, Mr. and Mrs. Paine and Deepe got busy trying to spread the warning to residents along the footpath.

"Castlewood Dam has gone out," came the message, nearly shouted. "Get to the high ground." Men on horseback rode out to warn those who had no phones.

The dam began breaking up around midnight, but the first thrust of the flood wasn't felt in Denver until 5:40 a.m. when the rising waters rushed under the bridge at Colorado Boulevard. The river crested in waves 25 feet high as the water entered the walled section of Cherry Creek.

Within 30 minutes, the broken dam had emptied 5,000 acre feet of water into Wildcat Canyon. Spreading out from the canyon, the flood path sometimes was a mile wide on each side of the creek. Fields were ruined, cattle drowned, homes and barns were crumpled and thousands of dollars worth of feed supplies were damaged. "Huge trees were carried along like jackstraws," said one account.

While telephone operators were busy notifying rural residents, and lights were flashing on in farm homes all over the Cherry Creek valley, Denver police cars raced along Cherry Creek, sirens screaming to inform both Country Club dwellers and denizens of the Platte River bottoms of the danger. At South Madison Street, near Cherry Creek, the 4-story mortar plant owned by the Brannan Sand & Gravel Co. was uprooted and whisked away.

The flood spread out for several blocks among the fine homes of the Country Club area, and Anne New, *Rocky Mountain News* society editor, plunged out into the flood with notebook in hand, gathering news of the rich and famous. Later she wrote:

"There was weeping and wailing in Country Club place . . . and there were dry throats, for many cellars were flooded . . .

"For the first time in many a moon, society awakened with the dawn as warning of the flood was relayed by telephone or sounded by police sirens.

"The galaxy of nondescript clothing that adorned our elect was beyond description. Evening trousers accompanied pajama coats, and negligees made their appearance on the street in company with the very latest in fall millinery. ... Mrs. Arthur Roeder disregarded her many works of art, lovely silver and chinaware and costly bric-a-brac and took out into the water-laden streets only a pair of stirrups. Mrs. Edgar Wilson Mumford rushed to her wardrobe, decked herself in a new fall Hattie Carnegie gown which she was saving for a gala affair, thrust her jewels in her handbag, grasped her small son, Arthur, and was prepared for the worst. ... Many rushed to the higher ground at the George Cranmer home. ...

"And," finished New, "it is difficult for even a lowly flivver to make its way along Speer Boulevard because of the streams of costly motor cars bearing Denver's wealthy and socially elevated who are curious to see what the raging waters did."

The Castlewood Dam never was rebuilt, but its remains are there for sightseers.

Jack Unitt, park manager of the Tri-Lakes Project at Chatfield Dam, in the U.S. Army Corps of Engineers, said that after the Castlewood Dam went out, the city of Denver built the Kenwood Dam, which was completed in 1936, just below the present Cherry Creek Dam.

"After a flood on the Republican River (in eastern Colorado), which could have been disastrous to Denver if it had taken a slightly different direction, it was decided to call for federal help," Unitt said. "A federal study was made of the entire basin, and the Cherry Creek Dam was authorized under the Flood Control Act of 1940. The dam, fed by the same waters as those of Castlewood, was delayed because of World War II. It became one of the first postwar projects and was completed in 1950."

In 1975, Chatfield Dam, at the confluence of Plum Creek and the South Platte River, was completed. That dam was prompted by the South Platte flood of 1965.

"Chatfield has overcome all the problems of Denver flooding," Unitt said. "Bear Creek, Cherry Creek, Plum Creek and the Platte River, all of which presented dangerous flood problems, are under control now."

November 22, 1981

Anna Bassett — a queenly enigma

QUEEN Ann of Brown's Park — what a woman she must have been! This fiery little woman with gray eyes and auburn hair piled high was something of a mystery, even in her own day.

Anna Bassett, who became known as Queen Ann, was born in 1878, and grew up in wild, lonely, primitive country under frontier conditions. She refused to learn to ride sidesaddle as her ladylike mother did, but by the age of 8 was wearing a divided skirt and riding astride.

She was an expert horsewoman and a crack shot. She rolled her own cigarettes in a day when "nice" women didn't smoke, and she liked liquor. She could salt her conversation with classical references or be as profane as most men.

Paradoxically, she had received one of the finest of finishing school educations, and had a lifetime love of music and books and a passion for pretty clothes. She was one of the most widely known frontier women in Colorado, with a reputation as one of the toughest in the West.

Western History Department, Denver Public Library

Anna Bassett was mysterious and romantic. Was she a cattle rustler, a lady, or both?

Anna Bassett's cabin stood in Brown's Park, a 35-mile canyon along the Green River.

There were many stories about her, but she denied two of the most colorful: that she headed the Bassett Gang of outlaws and that she was a cattle rustler.

The subject of Queen Ann came up this week in a letter from Jeanne Winder of Denver:

"For many years my husband's family owned a sheep ranch in Moffat County, the Two Bar Ranch near Craig," she wrote. "Queen Ann was reputed to be the leader of a group of men who were cattle rustlers. Her cabin was on the land before S. Norman Winder and Leo Winder bought it around the start of World War I. Can you give me any information about this woman?"

Dear Mrs. Winder:
Much of this woman's unusual story was written by Queen Ann herself in her later years. She entitled it *Queen Ann of Brown's Park.*

Her parents, Herbert and Mary Elizabeth Bassett, she recorded, came west from Springfield, Ill., in 1871, headed for California in a covered-wagon train that included 11 other couples. Her father, she said, had been a teacher in Illinois, and played several musical instruments.

En route, they stopped to visit Bassett's brother, Samuel Clark Bassett, who had settled near Rock Springs, Wyo. From there, they discovered Brown's Hole, a canyon 35 miles long by 6 miles wide, running along the Green River in an area where the states of Colorado, Wyoming and Utah meet. Winters were mild in the canyon, the grass was green, flowers were beautiful and game was abundant.

The Bassetts and the other families traveling with them decided to forget California and settle in Brown's Hole.

Access to the canyon was difficult, and it received its name from its reputation as "a good place to hole up." Because of its inaccessibility, Brown's Hole became a rendezvous for outlaws, mainly Butch Cassidy and his Wild Bunch, who appreciated the fact that even if lawmen managed to track them into the canyon, they could escape quickly into another state.

Impressed with the beauty of her surroundings, Bassett later changed the name of Brown's Hole to Brown's Park.

The Bassetts built a 10-room log cabin, and their furnishings included many classical books, feather beds and an organ shipped from the Virginia plantation of Ann Bassett's maternal grandfather. Ann, or Anna as she was christened, was born in the cabin in 1878. She records that her mother's milk was insufficient to feed her. A band of Utes was camped about 200 yards away, so arrangements were made for the baby Bas-

sett to be wet-nursed by an Indian with an infant son. This arrangement lasted about 6 months until the Bassetts acquired a cow.

Bassett grew up in this wild and beautiful country with four brothers and sisters. She recalled that in addition to riding, she learned to "flank a calf and stick a wild cow's head through a loop."

Bassett's mother died when the girl was 14. In an effort to correct her tomboyish ways, her father sent her first to convent school in Utah, and later to Miss Porter's School in Boston. Although she loved the gentle nuns in Utah, Bassett detested the training in Boston and the kind of women it produced.

At Miss Porter's, excellent rider that she was, she prodded her horse into bucking and rearing, to the delight of the other girls in the class. The "riding mawster," as she called him, was livid. She answered him with:

"Go to hell, you repulsive little monkey-faced skunk." She left the school a short time later.

Queen Ann's cattle rustling days, if such they were, began when she was 8. She started innocently with a "dogie," cow-country name for an orphaned or stray calf.

When Bassett was 6, she found one of these bovine orphans belonging to the big Middlesex Cattle Co. operating in the area. Her tender care saved the calf's life, and the Middlesex company manager gave it to her, although it carried the Middlesex brand.

Roving cowboys from other companies sometimes checked out cattle on the ranches they passed through, looking for strays from their own herds, Bassett recorded in her memoirs. One day a cowpoke spotted Bassett's dogie with the Middlesex brand, roped it and took it with him.

At the age of 8, a determined little girl confronted the manager of the big Middlesex company and demanded the return of the calf that had been given to her. She won her case, and when she got the calf home, she persuaded one of her father's wranglers to help her change the brand on it. It was her first experience at altering a cattle brand.

While it was a center of thriving ranches,

Brown's Hole also became known as a rendez-vous spot for outlaws.

"The question has frequently been asked," Bassett wrote, " 'How could a people permit themselves to harbor committers of crime without becoming involved in the deals?' The answer is simple. We were in a constant struggle to protect our own interests on the range where our living was at stake. Bank robbers were not a menace to personal interests, and we had no reason to carry the ball for banks and trains. . . . Law officers were elected and paid by the taxpayers to assume jurisdiction over legal matters of the country. . . ."

One of the outlaws with whom Bassett was familiar was Elza Lay, whom she describes as a "likable young Englishman who came to the Bassett ranch on a hay crew." Lay later joined Butch Cassidy's gang, and Bassett commented, "but we did not pry into his affairs. . . . We had accepted Elza Lay as our friend, and friendship among those youthful pioneers was no light bond. . . . But if the law wished to come into our country and make an arrest not one hand would have been raised to protect an outlaw."

It was customary on the frontier to feed strangers who dropped in at mealtime. Bassett comments:

"I knew several badmen. They were not welcome in our neighborhood, yet they were treated with courtesy and fed."

December 13, 1981

Cattlemen made Anna fight back

WHAT is the truth about Anna Bassett Willis? Was this woman, who came to be known as "Queen Ann of Brown's Park," a cattle rustler and leader of a gang of bandits? Or was she merely a tough-talking, hard-driving frontier woman whose determination to protect her property earned her a reputation she didn't deserve?

Last week's *Rocky Mountain Memories* column told of Queen Ann's early years in the wild, lonely, primitive country of Brown's Park, where she was born in 1878. This fiery little auburn-haired woman grew up riding and cursing like a man. She smoked cigarettes and drank whiskey. She also had an expensive Eastern finishing-school education, loved music and books and beautiful clothes.

Brown's Hole, in the wild country where the states of Colorado, Wyoming and Utah meet, became known as a hideout for outlaws, including Butch Cassidy and the Wild Bunch. It was rumored that Queen Ann gave aid and comfort to outlaws. She denied that she did any more than treat the outlaws with the same courtesy accorded anyone living in the area. When they came to her ranch at mealtime, they were fed just as any other traveling stranger.

Throughout her life, Queen Ann, a name which grew out of her imperious ways, contended that the troubles that beset the Bassett ranch, as well as her own reputation as a cattle rustler, were fomented by the cattle companies trying to drive out small ranchers and settlers. It was the old story of big ranches against small ones, and at times, sheepmen against cattlemen.

Queen Ann contended one company in particular aimed to drive her out. This offender, owned by Ora Haley, was the mammoth Haley Livestock and Trading Co., which operated the Two Bar Ranch. Queen Ann insisted that the hired killer, Tom Horn, had been assigned by Haley to do away with her. When she was 19, Matt Rash,

Western History Department, Denver Public Library

In her later years "Queen Ann" Bassett was a well-known Colorado ranching character.

her fiance, who was believed to have been a cattle rustler, was shot as he walked out of his cabin.

She believed Horn shot Rash. Queen Ann expressed her opinion loudly and widely, and one night as she was playing solitaire, two bullets smashed through her cabin door and into the wall behind her. Once again, she blamed Horn.

Queen Ann was imaginative in her campaign against the big companies and their intruding cattle herds trying to drive her off the range. She and a companion spent some of their time "jerking" Two-Bar cattle — throwing a lariat over their rumps and flipping them in the air. Sometimes the animals broke their necks in the fall. This fighting woman also drove trespassing cattle over cliffs, and is said to have rustled some.

In one stroke of genius, she devised a plan of encircling Brown's Park with sheep to prevent cattle from drifting in off other ranges, although Brown's Park legally was open to all. Under this scheme, many cattle could not find food, but would not cross the path of the sheep. Queen Ann thus established a reputation as the ruler of the Bassett gang.

"We were in a constant struggle to protect our own interests on the range, where our living was at stake," she wrote in her memoirs many years later.

Although she lived in primitive country and often did men's work, Queen Ann was not immune to romance. In April 1904, she married Hi Bernard, who, surprisingly, was a foreman for the Haley company. They met when Bernard, a good-looking fair-haired man, attempted to bring cattle into Brown's Park on land Queen Ann said belonged to her. He was greeted by the militant woman who leveled a shotgun at him and ordered him off.

But while Bernard may have dismissed Queen Ann from his mind, she didn't forget him. Three years later, she sent him a note, inviting him to dinner, stating that she had a business deal to discuss.

When Bernard arrived on the appointed night, Queen Ann, wearing a stylish blue gown and with auburn hair piled high and shining, greeted him cordially.

Before the evening was over, Bernard, who was 46, had proposed to Ann, who was 26. The marriage lasted 6 years, and when it ended in divorce, Bernard left the area.

In 1911, Queen Ann was brought to trial on charges of cattle rustling. The head, hide and hooves of a Two-Bar calf had been found buried near her house. She was arrested and charged with cattle rustling, but insisted that the calf's remains were a "plant" to incriminate her.

Queen Ann and her ranch manager, Thomas Yarberry, in March 1911, had the first case tried in the new county of Moffat. For days, the trial was the main topic of conversation in Craig, and it was widely regarded as a battle of small ranchers against big cattlemen.

Newspaper accounts said the cattlemen of Routt and Moffat counties were helping the prosecution, and had spent thousands of dollars on the case. Private detectives had been hired for months of investigation.

Testimony for the prosecution said that Yarberry and Eb Bassett, one of Ann's brothers, had killed the calf in question, in her presence.

For the defense, Chick Cowen, a cowpuncher, testified that W.M. Patton, foreman of the Two-Bar, had told him a year before that Queen Ann was in the way, and the cattlemen needed the water on her ranch.

The trial ended in a hung jury, and Ora Haley insisted on a second trial. Two years later, Queen Ann was retried on the same charges and she was found not guilty. The verdict resulted in a gala celebration by the residents of Brown's Park.

As the open range began to disappear, she sensed the change and took a course in forestry at the University of Arizona. Queen Ann applied for the position of ranger on the national reserve adjoining Brown's Park, but was turned down. Of this she wrote:

"For the slapdash reason that I happened to be a female, I was forced to withdraw my application."

In 1923, Queen Ann married Frank Willis, also a former Haley company foreman. They operated cattle ranches until she became interested in mining. For many years, she spent the summers at her old place in Brown's Park, and she spent winters in Leeds, Utah.

In 1953, she suffered a heart attack in Leeds and died 3 days later. With her death, the book was closed on one of the most colorful passages of the Old West. Not long before her death, she said:

"I've done everything they said I did and a helluva lot more."

December 20, 1981

Tales of Christmas past

THE spirit of Christmas past lingers in Colorado in even greater variety than the spirit that haunted the dreams of Ebenezer Scrooge.

The earliest recorded Christmas celebration in Colorado was observed by Lt. Zebulon Pike and his party who had been sent to explore the

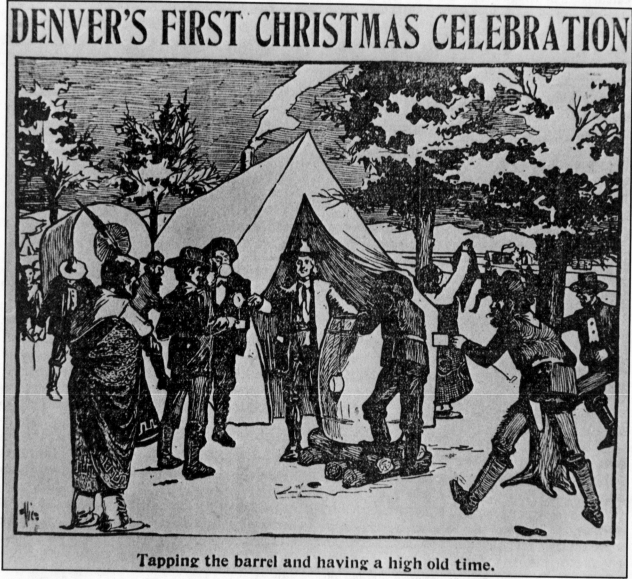

DENVER'S FIRST CHRISTMAS CELEBRATION

Tapping the barrel and having a high old time.

The Denver Times in 1900 published this sketch of Denver's first Christmas in 1858. It wasn't much different from other days in the settlement, although Santa, played by a frontiersman, showed up.

Red and Arkansas rivers.

The story of that Christmas, which hardly could be called "merry" is told in *Zebulon Pike's Arkansas Journal*. At the time, Dec. 25, 1806, Pike and his men were camped on the north bank of the Arkansas, below the mouth of Squaw Creek. After they broke camp the next day and marched on, they passed the present site of Salida.

"We appeared generally to be content, although all the refreshment we had to celebrate that day with was buffalo meat without salt or any other thing whatever. . . . " Pike wrote in his journal. "It being stormy weather and having meat to dry (we had eight beeves in our camp) I concluded to lie by this day. Here I must take the liberty of observing that in this situation, the hardships and privations we underwent were on this day, brought more fully to our minds, having been accustomed to some degree of relaxation and extra enjoyments..."

After civilization of sorts had reached the confluence of Cherry Creek and the South Platte River in camps set up by gold seekers waiting out the winter there, another Christmas celebration was observed in December 1858.

Two versions of that Christmas, which have come down from men who were there, vary rather widely. It seems agreed, however, that the weather that Christmas Day, 1858, was "as soft and genial as a May Day."

O.A. McGrew, one of the pioneer arrivals at Cherry Creek, wrote a letter on Dec. 29, 1858, which was printed in the *Omaha Times* on Feb. 17, 1859.

McGrew explained that the gold seekers were living in several settlements, including Denver, which had been selected as the county seat; Arapahoe City, about 5 miles above it; and Plum Creek Settlement, 7 miles above Denver. Auraria was across the creek. The Curtis Ranch was 3 miles below Denver City, and on the opposite side of the river was Spooner's Ranch.

In his account, McGrew commented on the "spring weather."

A meeting was held at Camp Spooner, Dec. 21, he said, to plan the celebration of Christmas Day. When the day came, he said:

"The boys, with their invited guests, lolled lazily around on the logs, smoking pipes or spinning innumerable yarns about their gold prospecting and hunting expeditions.

"The cooks, or rather, 'culinary professors,' were steaming over their different departments, now turning a choice saddle of venison, then looking to the pastry to see that it was done to a nicety," McGrew said. "One was molding fresh rolls of butter into all sorts of fantastic shapes, another cracking the nuts. Anon, a head would appear from a cabin door with a cry of " more wine for the pudding sauce.' "

The menu he recorded includes "salmon trout with oyster sauce, venison and grizzly bear a la mode, buffalo, smothered elk, mountain sheep, mountain pig, mountain pheasant, mountain rabbits, turkeys, ducks, sage hens, prairie chicken, black mountain squirrel, prairie dogs, mountain rats and hill cranes, quails and white swans. Potatoes baked and boiled, rice, beans baked and boiled, and beets, squashes and pumpkins stewed."

Dessert was mince pie, currant pie, apple pie, rice pie, peach pie, mountain cranberry pie, bread pudding and rice pudding. A considerable wine list went along with the meal. Do you get the feeling that this may have been a tongue-in-cheek account of some of the things they would have liked to have had on that Christman Day?

After dinner, McGrew said, there were toasts and songs including *The Star Spangled Banner, The Girl I Left Behind Me, Rosalie, the Prairie Flower* and *The Home of My Boyhood*. Gen. William Larimer then spoke about the future of the territory.

At day's end, the celebrators went to Auraria where they "found the town alive with an influx of miners, some of whom were dressed in the most fantastic and grotesque manner that an active imagination and the application of skins of wild beasts could devise."

"In a short time an immense fire was blazing in the public square. . . . Light hearts, merry countenances and active feet were soon in motion, and the dance continued until midnight. Groups of Indians with their squaws and papooses filled up the background."

Henry Edward Warner, the other chronicler of Denver's first Christmas, described an entirely different celebration. Warner told his story in the *Denver Times* of Dec. 23, 1900 from his memories.

Denver and Auraria, great rivals, were comprised of 200 men and "only five white women, four of them married" on that first Christmas, according to Warner. There also were "two squaws, half-blood Sioux, wives of John L. Smith and William McGaa, two frontiersmen."

Denver and Auraria, together known as "Cherry Creek settlement," had been is existence 60 days, Warner wrote. "There were a few log cabins scattered about and more wigwams and rough, homemade tents."

Frontiersmen were not used to celebrating holidays, Warner said, so there was no advance cleaning of cabins, no hanging of stockings. The first Christmas tree in Colorado was put up by Countess Katrina Marat, wife of the camp barber, Count Henri Marat, who decorated it with gingerbread figures of children, animals and stars and hand-dipped candles.

Christmas Day in Cherry Creek settlement began like any other day, Warner said. "There was a breakfast of buffalo steak or some wild meat in each cabin, and the men went about their work as usual."

But the sun hardly had risen, said Warner, "when Santa Claus made his appearance." This Santa, he said, was "an ordinary frontiersman who had fought Indians and scouted and hunted across the vast and fertile Plains. He carried a rifle and was smooth shaven. He had a couple of wagons laden with frontier merchandise, chiefly in barrels."

The newcomer gave his name as Richens L. Wootton, from Fort Union, N.M.

" ... Wootton put up a tent beside his wagon. rolled his stock inside, then rolled a barrel onto a log platform, smashed in the top with an ax and invited the onlookers to 'Pitch in and he'p y'r selves!' in honor of Christmas," Warner wrote.

Reindeer were stabled in Civic Center in downtown Denver during the 1920s for Christmas.

"The liquid was what was in those days termed 'Taos Lightning'. It came from Taos, N.M., and was warranted to kill at 40 yards. . . . None felt obliged to resist temptation. Convenient wagon wheels were soon being used as crutches by those who had allowed themselves to gather in the influence. . . . Men lying flat on their backs because of physical inability to stand held out their hands for more.

"One by one the pioneers went down and out, and when the sun crept into bed that night, there were forms stretched out in deep slumber over the prairie.

"Nobody ever has forgotten that Christmas . . . the first Christmas in Denver. Before night, the generous distributor of whiskey was known as 'Uncle Dick,' and the name has stayed with him. . . . He opened up a place of business the next day and before the New Year of 1859 started, he was the leading merchant of the Rocky Mountain region."

We'll cast a vote for Warner's account as a more logical Christmas on the frontier. The real story probably is a composite of both yarns.

December 27, 1981

Chapter 2

Rocky Mountain News

Legendary catacombs wind away to mystery

DENVER "underground" is the subject of a question from Barbara Raichle of Denver who writes:

"I wonder if you can tell us about some of the tunnels under Denver streets, leading to or from some of the hotels in early days. Some of them, I've heard, also led to shady doings."

Dear Mrs. Raichle:

In digging around, should I say, through Denver tunnels, I've found that many were mentioned, but apparently few actually existed. They were romantic figments of the imagination of some of the writers and some of the good storytellers of the time, and have been repeated so often they are regarded as fact.

For instance, I can find absolutely nothing to substantiate the story that a tunnel ran under Tremont Place from the Brown Palace Hotel to the gambling house and brothel in the old Navarre Restaurant Building. It was an amusing tale that probably was inspired by the tunnel leading under 18th Street from the long-gone Windsor Hotel at 18th and Larimer streets to the Windsor Baths in the Barclay Block at 1751 Larimer St.

The Windsor-Barclay tunnel evidently was one of the few that actually existed, although it had been walled up many years before the Windsor was razed in 1960. Accounts of Windsor guests who used the tunnel are some of the main evidence of its existence.

The Windsor Hotel, built in 1880, was Denver's finest, catering to newly made millionaires who were seeking a luxury they never before had known. When the Barclay Block was built in 1884 by Denver Mansion Co., the same English firm which built the Windsor, the Windsor Baths were installed as one more touch of luxury. There the travel-stained or the hungover could soak out the miseries.

The baths were of polished white marble, with trim of fine woods and decorations of stained glass. There were Turkish baths, Russian baths, Roman baths and "electric" baths, all fed by the two artesian wells in the Windsor. White-robed attendants catered to the guests, and the baths were advertised as "preventing poisonous ferments in the body."

These baths were closed many years ago — no one knows quite how long ago — but the Windsor continued in operation for years after the baths ceased to be a feature.

Intrigued with the stories of the baths and the tunnels, *Rocky Mountain News* photographer Bill Peery (now retired) and I went to see them about 30 years ago. It was an adventurous trip.

In the basement of the Windsor we were shown a large pile of stones which presumably sealed off the tunnel to Union Station. It was such a mess we couldn't be sure. Any sign of a tunnel to the Barclay Block had disappeared.

A street urchin who had tagged along, fascinated by the big Speed Graphic Peery carried, told us he had seen the baths and would show us how to get to them.

We crossed the street and went down into the bowels of the Barclay Block on the heels of our 10-year-old guide. After leading us past a battery of ancient furnaces and through a maze of heating pipes, the boy pointed to a door in the wall, about 8 feet up. The baths, he said, were up there, and he supplied a rickety ladder which we ascended to the door.

We pried open the rusty old door and were struck by an icy blast of air. A dark space lay ahead. The only light was the flashlight we carried. The dust we kicked up was thick and fine, possibly undisturbed for 30 years.

A few feet farther on, we could pick our way by the slanted gray light coming through a half-covered, dust-covered window. High old-footed bathtubs still were there, in separate cubicles, some standing properly in place, some cracked,

Rocky Mountain News

In 1949, *News* photographer Bill Peery took this photograph of the dusty remains of the swimming pool that was part of the Windsor Hotel Baths, across 18th Street from the hotel on Larimer Street.

and some overturned.

Once-elaborate gilt lettering, chipped and faded, designated the "Sudatorium," "Frigidatorium," "Lavatorium" and "Shampoo Room."

In another room, we came to a darkened area that the boy said had been a swimming pool. Peery held up his camera and took a flash picture.

We didn't actually know what we had seen until later, when he developed the picture that is printed with this story. We felt a sense of awe when we considered that such long-ago celebrities as Buffalo Bill Cody, Oscar Wilde, John L. Sullivan, Lillian Russell, Emma Abbott, Edwin Booth and Frederic Remington had bathed here.

The baths were destroyed when the Barclay Block was torn down in 1970, part of an Urban Renewal project.

The late Edmund W. Carr, a former city engineer who was thoroughly familiar with the city's plat books, was interviewed on the subject of Denver's understreet tunnels in 1968. He said real estate maps dating back to 1887 showed no tunnels. Carr said he believed the Windsor-Barclay tunnel existed, however, along with a shorter underground passageway across the alley from the hotel to the servants' quarters in the Little Windsor.

Other tunnels were said to have run west from the elegant Windsor to Union Station, and east, to the streetcar barn, at 18th and Arapahoe streets.

Carr said he believed a tunnel once existed from the Windsor Hotel to Union Station. He based his opinion on the fact that in the early 1960s, a sidewalk along 18th Street near Blake

Street began to collapse. Investigation revealed a tunnel leading in the direction of the Windsor. Carr did not explore the tunnel, because he found it was filled with rats. He ordered it filled and covered over.

Some years ago, Howard Parker who lived at 1414 Tremont Place, told me he had made a study of Denver tunnels. He had heard, but had not been able to authenticate, that a tunnel ran from the Windsor to the old Union Pacific Depot at 22nd and Wazee streets for use in inclement weather.

Parker said he had talked with a Denver plumber, name unknown, who described making a trip through the tunnel, carrying an acetylene torch to keep rats away. Similar stories are told about the tunnel to the streetcar barns at 18th and Arapahoe streets.

The stories exist, but did the tunnels? We think there is more romance than truth in these legends.

January 3, 1982

The readers said . . .

THE tunnels beneath Denver streets, described in a column, Jan. 3, 1982, prompted several letters, most of them begging to differ with us. (We said these tunnels are legends, some true, some only fanciful stories.)

We wrote that one tunnel, for which we could find no substance, is said to have led across Tremont Place between the Brown Palace Hotel and the old Navarre Restaurant.

One letter writer, Rep. Patricia Schroeder, D-Colo., said of the column:

"This was like the news there is no Santa! What — no tunnel from the Brown!"

Dear Ms. Schroeder:

Or should I say: "Yes, Patricia, there is a Santa Claus." At least there was, indeed, a tunnel under Tremont Place, between the Navarre and the Brown, according to several correspondents.

One, a former waiter at the Navarre, who asks that his name not be used, wrote: "I worked at

the Navarre Restaurant from November 1951 to May 1957. Our menu had a picture of the original building on the front cover. The backside gave the Navarre's history, from boarding school, on through the bawdy period, up to its then-current operation under the late John Ott and his wife, Esther.

"How I wish I had a copy of that menu now. The prices would make one sick — a full lunch at $1 and a complete prime rib dinner at $3.50.

"During my period of employment, I made it a point to go through the building from the top, right down to the basement.

"The basement was where the liquor supply was stored, and in that room the famous rumor became a reality. There was a narrow-gauge railroad track leading right to a wall facing Tremont Place and the Brown Palace. The wall, as I recall, was of cinderblock, and at some period it had been put up to seal off the entrance to the Navarre basement.

"On the track was a small flat-bed car that was said to have been pulled through the tunnel during its heyday. During my time, we used the car to pull the liquor back and forth. I used to try to visualize the famous gents of the period arriving on that little car for an evening of forbidden pleasure.

"Regarding the tunnel between the Windsor Hotel at 18th and Larimer streets and the Union Station — that, too, did exist.

"During the summer of 1962, I paid a visit to a friend who had a small business on the northwest side of 17th and Larimer. His shop stood next to the alley between Larimer and Market streets.

"We stood in his shop doorway watching a city worker operate a machine cutting away a portion of the curb. When the worker had cut through, he removed the curb, got down on his hands and knees and started talking to the curb. I thought he must be nuts. The conversation over, he got up and walked away.

"I had to find out what was going on. I went over to the curb, and on hands and knees, peered into a hole he'd left there. As I looked down, I saw a lightbulb and a tunnel that had white tile walls. I feel sure it was the famous tunnel I had heard about.

"Several years later when buildings on this corner were being torn down, a friend of mine was in the area when they dug down and exposed the tunnel. He went into the tunnel, which showed not only the white tile, but also brick. He said the tunnel ran north in the direction of the former Windsor Hotel, and west toward the Union Station."

Agnes Conley of Denver, also wrote confirming that a tunnel led from the Navarre to the Brown.

"I was the cashier in the Navarre Restaurant during the late 1950s and early '60s," she wrote. "One day, accompanied by the kind caretaker, I visited the basement and saw the rickety little car parked on two rails leading under Tremont Place. . . . Since the building has been designated as a historic landmark, the tunnel must still be intact."

A similar letter came from members of a group signing themselves "The Werewolves of Denver."

"As members of this city's only known group with expertise in the exploration of abandoned historic buildings, we feel some additional information is necessary on Denver's catacombs," they wrote.

"Some evidence does exist that a tunnel ran under Tremont Place from the Brown Palace to the Navarre. . . . Twice, in April 1979 and September 1981, members of our group explored the Navarre and on both occasions found evidence.

"On the basement wall of the structure, facing Tremont Street and the Brown Palace, there still exist the remains of a tunnel which juts about 25 feet away from the building and under the sidewalk and street. The tunnel ends abruptly at a solid brick wall.

"Inside the tunnel are small rails, which according to some version of the story, were used to transport customers through the tunnel in small cars. Why did these rails end so abruptly and why does this passageway cross the original foundation of the Navarre? We were forced to

conclude that it is indeed the remains of the famous passageway of history."

Paul W. Rader, a Denver architect, wrote:
"I have read and heard of these tunnels, but there is one which never is mentioned.

"When I was working for an architectural firm around 1950, we were commissioned to remodel the Cosmopolitan Hotel at East 18th Avenue and Broadway. During the work, we found in the basement evidence of an old tunnel which had been walled shut. We were informed that this tunnel originally connected the Brown Palace Hotel to the old Metropole Hotel. And, as I understand, the southern portion of the Cosmo was the old Metropole. (The Metropole opened May 25, 1891, slightly ahead of the Brown Palace.)

"We were told that the gentry used the tunnel from the Metropole, over to the Brown, and then from the Brown, across Tremont Place, to visit ladies of the night housed in the old Navarre . ."

Dale Scott, of Vancouver, British Columbia, who became manager of the Cosmopolitan in January 1981 when the hotel was purchased by Bramalea Ltd. of Toronto, also was intrigued by the tunnel stories.

He invited Rader and me to tour the Cosmo-Metropole basement. Virgil Kidwell, assistant manager who had been with the hotel many years, accompanied us. (The Cosmopolitan was torn down in May 1984, 2 years after this column was published.)

Kidwell pointed out a passageway, at one time a tunnel, which led from the Cosmopolitan into the Metropole and eventually went through a trap door in the old Broadway Theater, which was housed in the Metropole building.

"Some of the hotel employees used to sneak through that tunnel and up into the theater to see the show," Kidwell recalled. We saw another area of the basement which possibly led across Broadway to the Brown, but it was not conclusive proof.

January 17, 1982

Sensational murder on Castle Rock

GOLDEN'S Castle Rock prompts several questions from M.J. Christenson of Arvada. She writes:

"Recently I visited a museum in Golden and found a post card with a cog-wheel (conveyor) going up the 'Castle Rock.' You can still see where the cog once was.

"Someone told me there was a dance hall on top of the rock. Then someone fell off, and they closed it down. Now there is nothing.

"I have never heard of any of this before. I've even asked some of Denver's older citizens who have lived here all their lives, and they know nothing about it. Can you give me some information?"

Dear Mrs. Christenson:

There were two funicular railways in the Golden vicinity about 70 years ago. One was the Castle Rock Scenic Mountain Railway, and the other was the Lookout Mountain Park Funicular.

Although I can find no evidence to back me, I think the dance hall may have been atop Lookout Mountain rather than Castle Rock, or Table Rock as it also was known. People who were teen-agers in the 1890s have told me of riding the "interurban," a part of the Denver Tramway System, from Denver to Golden, and making the climb up Lookout Mountain.

Denver's mountain parks, which included Lookout Mountain Park, were formally opened on Aug. 27, 1913.

A newspaper account at the time said the Denver Chamber of Commerce had joined with the Denver Park Commission in taking members of the American Association of Park Superintendents (holding their 15th annual convention in Denver) over the newly constructed road to Lookout and Genesee mountain parks. They went up the new road, Colorado 21, and the Lookout Mountain Road.

The distance from the beginning of the new road to the summit of Lookout Mountain was reported as 4 miles, and the maximum grade was 6%.

"Once on top," said the article, "those who wished rode the funicular railway." The visitors also enjoyed a mountain trout fry, had their pictures taken on Wildcat Point and went on to visit Genesee Park.

The only instance I can find of anyone falling off Castle Rock was the sensational murder case in which 16-year-old William Eugene Wymer pushed or threw two younger boys off the cliff on April 3, 1943.

On that bright April day, Milo Flindt, 11, and Donald Mattas, 8, had taken the interurban from their motel homes in Lakewood to Golden. They straggled up the old cog railroad bed to the top of Castle Rock and enjoyed themselves throwing rocks and kicking cans. Then Wymer and his younger brother, Arthur, arrived.

The big boy spent a couple of hours bullying the youngsters, and finally ordered them to take off their shoes and stockings and a wristwatch. He dragged Milo to the cliff's edge and pushed him over. Then he turned on Donald, who was paralyzed with fright, and pushed him off the edge. Later, Wymer said:

"I did it to get some shoes for my little brother."

Wymer was picked up by police a few days later on another charge. He voluntarily confessed to the murders.

O. Otto Moore, who was later chief justice of the Colorado Supreme Court, was the attorney defending Wymer. He contended that Wymer's IQ was near the retarded range. The lad, he said, suffered from schizophrenia. He based his defense on the environment in which Wymer had been reared.

During his closing argument, Moore held up a pair of shoes with holes through the soles. They were the shoes of Wymer's little brother.

NEAR GOLDEN, COLO.

LOOKOUT MOUNTAIN PARK FUNICULAR

Tourists took the Lookout Mountain Park Funicular railway up the mountain near Golden about 1918. Visitors could partake of a mountain trout fry, be photographed and go on to Genesee Park.

The prosecution was handled by District Attorney Richard H. Simon. His closing argument attacked the testimony given by psychiatrists.

A jury in District Court in Golden on July 2, 1943, found Wymer guilty of first-degree murder in the death of Milo Flindt. The jurors had deliberated a little more than 6 hours. They fixed the penalty at life imprisonment.

As the verdict was read, a clap of thunder shook the courtroom and lightning highlighted the gaunt spire of Castle Rock on the edge of the town.

Wymer spent 17 years in the State Penitentiary at Canon City, then escaped from the prison farm where he was working in 1960. He was captured a few days later and returned to prison.

In 1963, Gov. John Love commuted Wymer's sentence to a minimum of 25 years. In his report, the governor said "Wymer is a good risk for parole . . . his conduct in the penitentiary has been good."

Wymer was paroled on July 21, 1968, according to Wayne K. Patterson, chairman of the parole board, who also was warden of the penitentiary during some of the years Wymer was there.

The prisoner left the penitentiary at that time, having served 25 years. He was discharged from parole in March 1974, when he was 47 years old.

January 10, 1982

The readers said . . .

MARYANNA Quaintance Johnson, who grew up in Golden, came by the office to tell us her father, Arthur D. Quaintance, a Denver attorney, and his brothers, Charles F. and Cregar Quaintance, contracted the building of the cog railway to the top of Castle Rock and also built the dance pavilion that opened May 17, 1913.

"It was very popular for people from Denver to ride the tramway to Golden, then walk over to the foot of South Table Mountain and take the cog railway to the top," Johnson said.

"There are so many stories about Castle Rock," she added. "I was up there a number of times as a child and I remember that they gave brightly colored Japanese paper parasols to the ladies to keep the sun off. People took care of their complexions then.

"And many were the Colorado School of Mines students who conned their parents into extra money for a field trip to gather specimens when actually the field trip was one up Castle Rock."

Johnson said her father also had leased some of the area on the rock to a soaring school, where people took off in gliders. Dangerous downdrafts ended that sport after only a short time.

"In 1927, the dance hall burned down," Johnson said. "We stood at our home down in Golden and watched it burn. I don't remember what started the fire. There's no water up there, and there's nearly always a high wind blowing. Any little fire easily could have been blown into a big one.

"Rails of the funicular were taken up in World War I to use the iron. I still walk up the old roadbed nearly every year to enjoy the beautiful view from the top."

Johnson also brought in a newspaper for Feb. 13, 1927, advertising "The Last Leap of Leaping Lena." In a stunt staged by the Denver Automobile Dealers Association and *The Denver Post*, 50 old cars the next day were to be dropped over the edge of the rock to a landing in a ravine 150 feet below. B.P. Quaintance of Golden, a director of Castle Mountain Inc., the company that owned the mountain, had given permission for the stunt, along with F.W. Beamer, who owned the land directly below.

Parking for 5,000 cars had been provided, and this Valentine Day stunt was being staged as the "grand opener" for the auto show starting that day in the Denver Auditorium.

Florence E. Wertz of Wheat Ridge also wrote about the landmark.

"I was born in Golden in the spring of 1921," she said, "and only remember most of the stories of Castle Rock from hearing my family talk about them. I do not remember hearing that anyone had fallen from the dance hall, but I do remember the murder case in 1943, as the whole town was in shock over it.

"Then Ralph Rohr's young son fell to his death from Castle Rock while up there climbing around looking for wild birds with his older brother in 1953."

Marnie Barnhardt of Lakewood wrote that during the 1920s she lived with her parents at the base of Golden's Castle Rock, about where the corner of 13th and Ford streets is now.

"There was a dance hall on top of the rock, and it was a wild and wooly place, as I remember," she said. "There was also a restaurant. I can remember people passing by our house to go up there. The place was closed down by a fire, I believe, in the late 1920s, and never reopened."

"One terribly scary thing I remember is the fiery cross the Ku Klux Klan burned up there. The Klansmen met up there, but drove up the 'back way' on a dirt road in Pleasant View. . . . I remember the night the Klan burned a cross in the front yard of the old St. Joseph's Catholic Church, which was at the foot of the rock."

Mrs. G.P.T. of Denver wrote: "We moved to Golden in 1916. I remember the funicular up Castle Rock. We used to climb up there as kids. I also remember the pavilion on top of the rock, and the night it burned in 1927. It lit up the whole sky — a sight I'll never forget.

"The Quaintances, who built the dance hall, also cut a road up South Table Mountain and rented donkeys for the ride to the top of Castle Rock. As a boy, my husband used to help with the donkey concession."

John Light of Golden, who was born near Idaho Springs in 1903, told us he knew about another dance hall, on Lookout Mountain, very well.

"I was a single man having a hard time getting along during the Depression," he said. "Because I was single, I couldn't get on welfare. I heard the town of Golden had bought the dance hall and wanted it torn down because it stood too close to the town reservoir. I put in the lowest bid and got the job of demolishing the dance hall.

"My bid was so low I couldn't afford help, so I tore the whole thing down by myself. It was about 44 feet by 90. It took me 2 months to tear it down, and I was paid $200, which was good money then. The dance hall on Castle Rock burned down in the late 1920s. I watched it from my place. You could see it real good."

From Arthur Lowther of Golden, we heard, "In 1922, I came to Golden with my parents who had bought a home at 16th and Ford streets. Castle Rock was directly east of our front door. ... Lookout Mountain was directly west of my boyhood back yard. My mother had been born and reared in the very same block (where) our home was located, and she had told me many tales about cog railway trips to the top of Castle Rock and Lookout Mountain. ...

"There definitely was a dance hall atop Castle Rock. As a boy under age 10, I climbed Castle Rock with another lad one Saturday morning to sweep out the dance hall. As our wages for the chore we were given a bottle of pop. I can still recall our delight at this reward. ...

"A long flight of concrete steps remains today on the back side of Castle Rock. These steps were used by the railway passengers after they got off the cog to complete their way to the top of Castle Rock. After the railway was removed, which was before my time, the dancers drove their Model T's up the back side of the rock. Remains of this roadway are still in evidence."

Another old-timer, Howard Carnagan of Golden, wrote:

"I came to Golden in 1920, and lived at the base of Castle Rock. It was not a cog railway to the top; it was a funicular, which means that there were two cars, one at the top, one at the bottom, connected with a 1-inch cable wrapped around a drum at the top, with a hoist to make it move. When one car came up, the other went down, and they met halfway.

"One car was named Douglas, after W.L. Douglas, who founded the shoe company. He first pegged shoes in Golden. The other was named for George M. Pullman, who invented the sleeping car. Pullman lived in a 2-story log cabin in Golden, which was demolished a few years ago to make room for a garage."

Carnagan said he and other boys would hike up Lookout Mountain to the funicular, find a flat rock and make a seat of it to slide down between the cables.

"It's a wonder we didn't break our legs when we put our feet down to slow us up if we were going too fast," he recalled.

Carnagan wrote that he heard the screaming from his home on April 3, 1943, the day Milo Flindt, 11, and Donald Mattas, 8, were pushed to their deaths off the top of Castle Rock by an older boy.

"I looked out the window and saw nothing," he said. "There was always a lot of this going on when kids played on top. The boys were pushed off around a bend where I couldn't see. ... "

The Coors brewery sits at the bottom of Castle Rock. At the top was a dance pavilion.

Bill Hoeper of Lafayette told us: "I used to live in Pleasant View on Table Mountain, and I've heard many stories about it. There was a dance hall on it, which burned in the late 1920s. There is a photo of this rock with smoke coming from the dance hall in the Golden Museum. . . .

"The Ku Klux Klan used to congregate on South Table Mountain and at one time burned a cross on top of the mountain. . . .

"I have heard that there were several suicides by persons jumping off the rock."

January 24, 1982

Bill Coors, chairman of the board of the Adolph Coors Co., also wrote:

"Having lived in the shadow of Castle rock most of my life, your article . . . recently brought back memories which may serve to fill in some historical gaps.

"Shortly after my grandfather, Adolph Coors, established his brewery just north of Castle Rock in 1873, he incorporated a picture of the rock into his trademark where it still resides.

"Some years later, Brough Quaintance, a prominent Golden citizen and friend of my grandfather, proposed a cable car railway up the shoulder of Castle Rock to transport guests to a proposed dance pavilion to be built atop the rock. The guests would travel to Golden via the Denver and interurban streetcar and meet the Castle Rock cable car at the East Golden Station just adjacent to the brewery.

"Quaintance had title to the rock, and my grandfather owned the north slope of South Table Mountain all the way up to and including the rimrocks.

"My grandfather agreed to the plan, and thereupon, Quaintance built his dance pavilion and the cable car access to it. The cable car consisted of a car at each end of a cable which was powered by a reversible bull wheel drive on top. As one car went up, the other car went down. As a small child, I can remember watching the cars go up and down.

"Sometime around 1920, the dance pavilion closed, and the cable cars shut down, never to run again . . . "

A guide with a megaphone described the sights to visitors riding the funicular railroad.

"Shortly thereafter, the Ku Klux Klan began using the mountain as headquarters for its operations around Denver. In that era, the Klan wielded a great deal of influence in . . . Colorado and was much feared by many people, who included my grandfather.

"Of Germanic origin, my grandfather, although a naturalized citizen, remained loyal to his homeland, Germany, during the early years of World War I. This did not sit well with some of the citizenry of the Golden community whose ethnic backgrounds were predominantly British. They were known as 'Cousin Jacks' then, and the name still sticks today.

"So my grandfather was persecuted as a German sympathizer and even was accused of being a German spy. In that the 'Klan was believed to be a solidly WASP organization, my grandmother firmly believed that the Klan was responsible for his persecution, so his fear and resentment of the Klan is understandable.

"When the Germans torpedoed the *Lusitania* and America went to war, Adolph Coors' allegiance to Germany came to an abrupt end. Overnight the official language of both family and brewery changed to English, and Germany, the enemy of his adopted country, became his enemy in every sense of the word.

"The Klan continued to flourish and wield sinister political influence upon Colorado. As a boy, I recall on many nights the burning of enormous fiery crosses on Castle Rock and watching ghoulish, shadowy figures dance around them. At times they used the pavilion on top.

"One notable summer afternoon in 1927, the pavilion went up in flames. It was an awesome sight, with the flames reaching up into the sky as high as the cliffs of the rock itself. I watched the fire from my family home on the brewery premises a full half-mile east of the center of Golden. Yet I could hear the jubilant shouts coming from the town as that resented structure on Castle Rock burned to the ground.

"It was rumored that some boys had sneaked up to the rocks and set the fire. But I have always doubted that rumor.

"The top of Castle Rock is accessible only from the east unless one is a technical rock climber. Those of us who had climbed to the top of South Table Mountain and approached Castle Rock from the east were aware of the armed guards who patrolled the Klan premises. Regardless, no miscreants ever were apprehended, and I don't believe anybody spent much time looking for them.

"The building was never rebuilt after the fire. The power of the Klan was waning and no evidence of it was ever again visible in the Golden area.

"A visit to the top of Castle Rock today reveals only a few faint vestiges of its past. Concrete foundations of the cable car railroad, a concrete stairway from the terminal to the top of the Rock and a few rusty steel tie rods embedded in the rock itself are all that remain."

April 4, 1982

Leadville Ice Palace melted many dreams

THE mild, sunny days of this winter of 1981-82 bring to mind the story of Leadville's celebrated Ice Palace, and its untimely fate.

During the summer of 1895, Leadville, which had been one of the richest towns in Colorado, was wallowing in gloom brought on by the deep skid in the price of silver. E.W. Senior, a real-estate agent, offered a solution.

Senior suggested that the town sponsor a 3-month winter carnival and build an ice palace to house the events. Senior was a persuasive man, and the townsfolk were ready to clutch at any straw. After all, handsome and successful ice palaces had been built in Montreal in 1883, and St. Paul, in 1894, so why not in Leadville?

Tingley S. Wood, a successful mining man, took charge of the project. He formed the Leadville Crystal Carnival Association and sold stock to raise the $20,000 needed to start work.

As Wood and his backers envisioned it, the Leadville Ice Palace would be far larger than any predecessors. Its ambitious promoters estimated that the carnival would bring in $5 for every $1 spent.

Western History Department, Denver Public Library

The remarkable Leadville Ice Palace was constructed in 1895. A total of 5,000 tons of block ice was used to build it. It was a financial failure, partly because spring came early in 1896.

C.E. Joy of St. Paul, who had built the ice palaces in Montreal and St. Paul, was brought in to construct the Leadville wonder. Five acres of land was leased on Leadville's Capitol Hill, between 7th and 8th streets. A wooden framework was erected for the interior.

Ice was quarried out of nearby lakes in blocks 5-by-2-by-2 feet, with the work directed by W. H. Cole of the Leadville Ice and Coal Co. Eighteen teams of horses hauled the blocks on sleds to the palace grounds. Stonecutters, at first, were employed to carve out the blocks of ice, but when they proved too slow, Canadian woodchoppers were imported to do the work.

When the supply of ice ran low in Leadville, it was quarried out of Palmer Lake between Castle Rock and Colorado Springs and shipped by the Denver and Rio Grande Railroad to Pueblo and the Arkansas Valley to Salida, then on to the building site.

The icy cornerstone was laid Nov. 25, 1895. A total of 5,000 tons of ice was used.

The enormous structure, 450 feet long by 350 feet wide, was designed to resemble a Norman castle, with turrets, towers and battlements. Two corner towers were 90 feet high. When completed, the Leadville Ice Palace was said to have been the largest ice structure ever built in America, and possibly the largest in the world.

The blocks of ice were piled one upon another, then drenched with water which froze and held the walls together. The roof and timbers were supported by heavy trusses to keep weight off the ice.

In front of the building stood a female allegorical figure, Lady Leadville, carved of ice and standing 19 feet high on a 12-foot pedestal. With one arm she pointed toward the mountains, which had supplied Leadville's wealth, and with the other, she held a tablet inscribed with $200,000,000, the amount taken from the mines in the area.

Disaster nearly overtook the project in early December during construction when springlike air wafted over the area and chinooks blew off the mountains. The ice structure was sprayed nightly with water from fire hoses and covered during the day with thousands of yards of canvas.

The palace contained several rooms, including a skating rink 190-by-80 feet, two ballrooms, both with pine floors and one with a restaurant.

The skating rink and ballrooms were rimmed with pillars of ice in which were frozen displays of Colorado products, such as cuts of beef, and even six bottles of Coors beer. The ice pillars were illuminated at night in a variety of colors through that new wonder of the age, electric lights.

New Year's Day 1896 saw the grand opening of the Ice Palace, with a costumed parade through town and many special events.

The evening was topped off with a ball, with music provided by the famous Fort Dodge Cowboy Band led by Jack St. Clair.

More ceremonies were held on Jan. 4 under the guidance of the Leadville Pioneer Society.

At the beginning, the Ice Palace gave every indication of being a success. Three railroads ran regular excursion trains to Leadville for the carnival and visitors could indulge in a number of winter sports.

Season tickets to the Ice Palace were sold for $25, but individual admissions were 50¢ for adults and 25¢ for children.

A poet of the day wrote:
"On a massive range where towering peaks
Hold white the font of the river's flow,
We have builded a house from the Frost King's freaks
And invite all the world to play in the snow."

Spring came early to Leadville in 1896. On March 1, water began to trickle down the palace walls, and out in front Lady Leadville started to sweat. The structure again was swathed in muslin to stave off deterioration, but to no avail. By April 1, the great palace was just one grand slush pile.

Final construction costs were tallied at $120,000, and far from bringing in $5 for every dollar spent, the Ice Palace had cost $10 to every dollar brought in. No attempt was made to rebuild it in following years.

But while the structure melted away in a few weeks, its memory has remained frozen in Colorado history for years.

January 31, 1982

Riding the rails
of Switzerland Trail

TOURISTS by the hundreds in the early years of this century made a thrilling trip on the Colorado and Northwestern Railroad on a line that snaked its way between Boulder, Ward and Eldora. The route was dubbed the Switzerland Trail of America.

A letter from Shirley and Jerry Todd of Lakewood asks for information about the Switzerland Trail.

The Switzerland Trail was the shortest of 1-day rail trips out of Denver, but it provided a superb view of the Rockies. From viewpoints along the route, the snow-covered mountains appeared extremely close.

The trail opened in 1883, when the Union Pacific built a line called the Greeley, Salt Lake and Pacific, starting in Boulder. This ambitious project stopped at the mining town of Sunset, about 12 miles from Boulder.

Books have been written about the Switzerland Trail. They include *The Switzerland Trail of America* by Forest Crossen.

Without going into the complicated railroad history retold in the books, we will mention that the tracks of the original Greeley, Salt Lake and Pacific were washed out in a flood in 1894.

Three years later, M.F. Leech, an adventurous businessman, started work on his Inter-Mountain Railway, over much of the old route. This railroad later was incorporated as the Colorado Northwestern Railroad.

Leech's line was chartered in 1897, with capital stock of $500,000. The first train ran from Boulder to Sunset on Feb. 18, 1898. By the end of May 1898, the road had been completed to Ward, a prosperous mining camp. The rail line extended west from Boulder and passed through Crisman, Salina, Copper Rock, Sunset and Dewdrop on the way to Ward. A branch from Sunset Junction to Eldora opened in the fall of 1899.

The line was a remarkable piece of engineering, under the direction of the chief engineer,

J.L. Frankenberger. The distance was 26½ miles from Boulder to Ward, but only 14 miles as the crow flies. The rails climbed 4,000 feet in that distance, with an average grade of 3½%. In places, the grade was much steeper, at some points rising 200 feet a mile.

Railroaders tell the story that it took 3 tons of coal to go to Ward from Boulder, but only 60 pounds for the return trip.

From Boulder, the line passed through the rugged canyons of Boulder Creek and Four Mile Creek, then Left Hand Creek with its precipitous walls and on into California Gulch.

The Colorado and Northwestern started as a freight line carrying goods to the mining towns, but passengers soon discovered its marvelous scenery. The line's management was quick to capitalize on that and began to publicize it as the Switzerland Trail of America.

Tourist excursions were offered, and the railroad company published a brochure offering information and photographs of points along the route. The trainmen made the trip as pleasant as possible and in passing, would point out highlights, such as famous mines. Long's Peak, Mount Audubon and the Arapahoe Peaks formed a part of the stunning view.

In his autobiography, the engineer, Frankenberger, says:

"From Summit the line began to ascend the mountains and at the top you could look down into the canyon and see the railroad tracks beside the creek and count tracks on six different grades below." This viewpoint was named Point Frankenberger.

Another favorite stopping place to let passengers enjoy the view was Mont Alto Park, just below Gold Hill. In its heyday, Mont Alto Park boasted a handsome sandstone fountain combined with a mountain indicator giving the names of peaks.

In fair weather, the little narrow-gauge trains

1901 tourists on the Switzerland Trail stopped at Camp Frances between Boulder and Ward. The trip from Boulder to Ward took 3 tons of coal, but only 60 pounds for the downhill return trip.

moved along smoothly over the Switzerland Trail, but it was a different story in winter. Engines often were snowbound, and double-header snowplows had to be put on to clear the track. Service was irregular.

The Denver Times of April 3, 1901, reported that an avalanche the day before had "swept two engines of the Colorado and Northwestern aside as if they had been pebbles." The train had pulled out just before telegraphed orders could be received ordering it to turn back. Four people in the double crew were killed and another was reported to be dying.

In 1909, Crossen tells us, the company's corporate name was changed to Denver, Boulder and Western. This was part of a joint operation in which the Colorado and Southern Railroad laid a third rail to Boulder to accommodate the narrow-gauge engines of the Colorado and Northwestern.

Under the Denver, Boulder and Western management, tourist excursion trains were made up in Denver, pulled by standard-gauge engines. At 15th and Water streets in Boulder, the narrow-gauge sightseeing cars were pulled off and at-

tached to narrow-gauge engines for the climb up the Rockies.

Problems, mainly with weather, proved a financial disaster to the Denver, Boulder and Western. The rail line made a small profit only 2 years, and the rest of the time, operated in the hole. In 1916, the company abandoned the daily line to Ward.

In August 1918, a flood washed away nearly all the track of the old Colorado Northwestern, effectively killing the operation. Nine months later the Public Utilities Commission issued an order to junk the line.

The rolling stock was sold, and the remaining track was torn up to be used in the aftermath of World War I. It was a sad ending to a courageous enterprise.

Vestiges of this pioneer wonder remain. It is possible to drive much of the old rail line in an automobile, although in some stretches it is very narrow. It has been washed out in spots, and in some places, there is no access where the line crosses private property.

February 28, 1982

Elephant trampled boy

MRS. George Bakewell Jr. of Denver writes: "Is there any truth in the story that an elephant killed someone at the old amusement park, Manhattan Beach, then was buried in what now is the parking lot of the Safeway store in Edgewater?"

Dear Mrs. Bakewell:

The tragedy you mentioned is described in the *Rocky Mountain News* of July 6, 1891.

The paper reported that the day before, a 6-year-old boy, George W. Eaton, had been trampled and instantly killed by Roger the elephant. For some time, Roger had been a favorite animal, providing rides for children at Manhattan Beach, an amusement park on the north shore of Sloans Lake.

Young George, whose father, Pressley Eaton, was a Union Pacific switchman, was riding with five other children in a box on the elephant's back when the tragedy occurred.

The paper reported that a balloon ascension, another regular feature at the park, was starting just as the elephant ride began. As the balloon started to rise, sway and shoot upward, it apparently frightened the elephant. The article described Roger as "a huge elephant, wild with the frenzy of fear."

Roger broke away from from his keeper, Fred King, breaking King's nose as he struck him with his trunk and started to run. The keeper, bleeding, tried to restrain the elephant and shouted to the crowd to keep back.

As the elephant thundered forward, the seat holding the children swayed and the children screamed and cried. The Eaton boy, who had stood up to watch the balloon ascension, was knocked off balance and fell to the ground, falling under one of Roger's tremendous feet.

"ROGERS" TERRIBLE CHARGE.

A drawing in the *News* on July 6, 1891, showed Roger the elephant on his deadly rampage.

The boy was crushed by the elephant's foot.

Roger then was quieted briefly by the keeper, and all but one child climbed from the box. Roger was made to kneel, and the last boy was lifted out.

It was not all over, however. The elephant, still excited, began to bellow and trumpet, and tried to free himself from the hooks and ropes that held him.

A book, *Edgewater Four Score*, by Judy Allison, reports that Edgewater old-timers say Roger was killed and buried in a former swamp located, not under the Safeway parking lot, but under the parking lot of the King Soopers store at West 20th Avenue and Depew Street. I can find nothing, however, to document this.

Agnes Putnam, 86, who has lived in Edgewater 83 years, said she was told that Roger the elephant was buried under the present King Soopers store, "but it happened before my time."

April 11, 1982

Faith healer left marks on the soul

FRANK Hogan's play, *Denver Messiah,* a lab project of the Denver Center Theatre Company, is based on one of the most unusual happenings in Denver history.

It is the story of Francis Schlatter, a shoemaker of Alsatian descent who held thousands spellbound in Denver as a "miracle man," a faith healer who accomplished remarkable cures.

The *Rocky Mountain News* on July 16, 1895, printed an account of the shoemaker who had reappeared in Pajarito, N.M., 2 years after he had left his shoe shop in Denver. Schlatter was healing the poor in that little town, and stories were told of miracles. Juliana Sedillo, a woman who had not moved her arms for 16 years went back to work in the fields after Schlatter prayed over her. A man blind for 3 years had regained his sight, and so on.

Edward L. Fox, a Denver businessman and politician as well as a man who knew a good thing when he saw it, journeyed to Pajarito and persuaded Schlatter to return to Denver and work his miracles in the city.

Fox lived in a modest white frame cottage at 625 Witter St., which research in city directories indicates would be in the 3200 block of Quivas Street. (Witter was changed to Quivas in 1904.)

A platform was built in front of the house, and a rail fence was erected to keep people in single file as they approached for Schlatter's healing. The faith healer was 5 feet 9 and of medium build. He had shoulder-length, slightly wavy brown hair, mustache and beard, giving him a Christlike appearance. Many said his most remarkable feature was his penetrating blue eyes.

Schlatter made no personal claims, but was widely heralded as "the new Messiah." When asked the direct question "Are you Christ?" he would reply, "Yes."

Denver never had seen anything like the reception given Schlatter. Crowds by the thousands flocked to see him or to be healed. Even Aimee Semple McPherson, the healing sensation of the 1920s, did not attract such crowds when she came to Denver.

After the first day of Schlatter's ministry, police were sent out to the Foxes' little house to keep order. By then the line of supplicants was 3 blocks long. As each approached, Schlatter would grasp him or her by the hand, say a prayer, and reach for the next in line.

The reported miracles were many. Some who had arrived on crutches flung them down and walked away. A tumor disappeared from the face of a Nebraska woman. A 12-year-old girl, blind in one eye, saw perfectly after a visit to Schlatter, it was reported. Judge J.W. Kerr of Pueblo said Schlatter had cured him of inflammatory rheumatism.

Daily stories of Schlatter and his miracles were played heavily in Denver newspapers and picked up by papers across the nation. Every train arriving in Denver was filled with the sick and disabled. For many, it was a last resort.

Those who were unable to come, Schlatter said, could receive treatment by sending a handkerchief, which he would bless and send back.

Mrs. E. Dickinson, wife of an officer of the Southern Pacific Railroad, arrived in a private car to be treated for deafness and general illness. Following her successful treatment, the Union Pacific allowed ill employees to travel at company expense to be treated by Schlatter.

Schlatter refused pay for his cures, and if money were left, he gave it to the poor. He also declined to take personal credit for the miracles.

"Don't thank me, thank the Father," he said. "It is through faith in Him that I work.

"The new Messiah" worked at healing 12 hours a day, but couldn't see everyone who came. Many built fires on the sidewalk and stayed all night.

The healer, with the help of the Fox family and other volunteers, spent his nights blessing

Francis Schlatter was a faith healer who made an enigmatic mark on Denver and the West.

the handkerchiefs coming in cartloads of mail — as many as 8,000 letters a day — and mailing them back.

Schlatter's story was told in bits and pieces and gradually patched together.

He said he had been apprenticed to a cobbler during his youth in Alsace-Lorraine. Schlatter's parents died when he was in his early 20s, and he came to America, eventually running his own shoe repair shop in Denver at 1845 Stout St.

One night as he sat at the bench repairing shoes, Schlatter said he heard a voice telling him to sell his business, give the proceeds to the poor and set out on a long journey. The voice told him to walk until he received the power to heal the sick.

Schlatter embarked on a program of physical conditioning, with long walks to the Denver suburbs and later the foothills. In July 1893, he left his boardinghouse in a heavy rainstorm with only $3.

His wanderings lasted 2 years, taking him on a cross-shaped trail from Topeka, Kan., to the West Coast and from Denver to Old Mexico. En route he endured terrible hardships, which are chronicled in a book, *The Life of the Harp in the Hand of the Harper,* which he dictated to Mrs. William S. Morley of Datil, N.M. (A few years ago it was reported that there are only three

copies of this book in existence, and two are owned by the Western History Department of the Denver Public Library.)

He was arrested in Hot Springs, Ark., as a vagrant, beaten with a rubber hose and jailed for several months. He also was jailed in Texas, and he crossed the Mojave Desert on foot without food or water.

The voice of the Father came to him throughout the journey, he said, and no matter how hungry or thirsty he might be, he would not eat nor drink until the Father gave him permission. He finished his 2-year pilgrimage with a 40-day fast.

A short time later, he began his healing ministry in Datil, where he was discovered by Edward Fox from Denver.

Although Schlatter refused payment, his Denver healings became tainted with commercialism. People began to take places in line early in the day and sell them to latecomers. Others had handkerchiefs printed with the healer's picture and sold them for $1 apiece. Vendors set up food and lemonade stands along the line. One man put up tents containing cots which he rented to people desiring a short rest.

All this distressed Schlatter. He also was disturbed that he was not endorsed by a number of Denver ministers and that he was referred to in some newspaper articles as a "monomaniac."

One morning on his pillow in the Fox cottage, a note was found. It said:

"My mission is finished. Father takes me away." Schlatter had ridden away in the night on a retired gray firehorse named Rowdy, which had been given to him by Fox.

When the waiting crowd heard the news, they were distraught. They tore up the fence and platform and carried them away in splinters. They even took shovelfuls of earth from the spot where Schlatter had stood.

A great search for the faith healer was launched by newspapers and hired detectives. He was often seen, but never found.

Near the end of the year, close to the meeting of the Gila and San Francisco rivers, a teamster who had suffered a broken leg reported being healed by a mysterious bearded stranger. It was believed to be Schlatter.

Later, according to Mrs. William Morley, Schlatter stayed several months on the Morley Ranch, and there dictated his manuscript. With the book done, he left.

Ten years later, a pile of bones thought to be Schlatter's was discovered under a tree in the Sierra Madre Mountains of Chihuahua, Mexico. The clues of identity included an old saddle with a Denver label and a Bible bearing Schlatter's name and a brass rod in a leather case always carried by Schlatter. He was believed to have died of starvation or exposure.

Many questioned the identification, among them Fox. It was Fox who asked where the wooden bead rosary and medals Schlatter always wore pinned to the inside of his jacket were.

Through the years the impostors pretending to be Schlatter appeared in various places. One claiming to be the faith healer was picked up for mail fraud in 1916 in New York. The bogus practitioners usually were spotted when they took money, because Schlatter always spurned payment.

A St. Louis newspaper reporter developed a story about an unclaimed body in a St. Louis funeral home. He believed the man who died in a St. Louis roominghouse in 1922 was Schlatter. But it was not proved, and the body was buried in a pauper's field.

Schlatter's fate as well as his life remain a mystery. The question remains: Did he actually work miracles? The late Joseph Emerson Smith, a widely respected Denver newspaperman who covered the Schlatter happenings for *The Denver Post*, was interviewed about it years later. He said:

"Faith moveth mountains. After 46 years, I still am unable to account otherwise for the healings I saw."

April 25, 1982

Four streetcars were overturned at East Colfax Avenue and Logan Street on Aug. 5, 1920, during the strike against the Denver Tramway Co. It was a dark page in Denver's labor history.

1920 trolley strike
left tracks of blood

THE contract negotiations between the Regional Transportation District and the Amalgamated Transit Union bring to mind the Denver Tramway Strike of 1920. Today's bargaining, with only occasional reference to a strike, is less colorful, but also far less dangerous than the confrontation of 62 years ago. Several readers have asked us to tell the story of that tumultuous period.

Several people were killed, a number were injured, streetcars were overturned and burned and the city was put under martial law as a result of the strike against the Denver Tramway Co. that began Aug. 1, 1920. At the time, Denver's population was 256,000.

A local of the Amalgamated Association of Street and Electric Railway Employees of America was formed in Denver in 1918. Labor and management got along until the spring of 1920, when the company announced that a raise of 10¢ an hour, bringing a motorman's salary to 58¢ an hour, would be dropped back to 48¢ an hour because of the company's financial straits. The workers countered by demanding 75¢ an hour.

After weeks of fruitless negotiations, the union called a strike to start Aug. 1, in violation of an injunction issued by Judge Greeley W. Whitehead. The long buildup, however, had given the company ample time to prepare.

John C. "Black Jack" Jerome, a professional strikebreaker who had broken a strike in San Francisco, was hired by the Tramway Co.

From the start, public sentiment was against the strike. An editorial in the *Rocky Mountain News* of Aug. 3, 1920, said in part:

"The demands of the men are liberally considered unreasonable. Seventy-five cents an hour for the work required by trainmen seems beyond good sense. The men so employed do not have to serve an apprenticeship — usually a couple of weeks' instruction is sufficient. The work is not tiring. The men can work all the year round if they so desire. . . . "

No streetcars ran on Aug. 1 or 2. By late in the day Aug. 2, more than 500 jitney buses were operating without licenses to carry passengers, and the papers reported "bicycles are more numerous than they have been since the height of the cycle craze."

The first strikebreaking car moved out of the Central barns at 3 p.m. Aug. 3, with Jerome at the controls. Hints of "lead pipes" and "brickbats" to be used against the strikebreakers were made as the first car prepared to come out.

Mayor Dewey C. Bailey urged that the cars be put in service at any cost, and promised "all possible protection and assistance to the Tramway Co. as long as it is making an honest effort to serve the people." Thirty-five special officers were sworn in and situated around the city to protect Tramway property. Every car that went out was to be protected every foot of its journey.

As the first streetcar moved out of the Central barns and into the downtown district, it was preceded by Chief of Police Hamilton Armstrong in an auto with Frank M. Downer, manager of safety. Other police cars followed. The streetcar made a round trip from downtown to East 11th Avenue and Humboldt Street.

Western History Department, Denver Public Library

Rampaging strikers burned two streetcars on Aug. 5, 1920. Military rule was instituted; strikebreakers were hired; the workers, who wanted 75¢ an hour, were humiliated and the union was broken.

By Aug. 4, there was continuous traffic over this line, and plans were to provide service over half the lines in the city the next day.

The worst trouble started Aug. 5. On that day, four streetcars were overturned, and windows were smashed at East Colfax Avenue and Logan Street. Bystanders were injured by flying bricks and other missiles.

Strikebreakers manning the cars fled into the Cathedral of the Immaculate Conception and were saved by priests who barred the doors.

Two more cars were wrecked and set afire at East 40th Avenue and Williams Street, near the East Side barns. At the South barns at South Broadway and Dakota Avenue, shots were fired from within and two people in the crowd outside were killed.

A mob, angry over editorials they felt supported the Tramway Co., marched on *The Denver Post* plant, shattered desks, demolished the offices of the publishers, Harry Tammen and Frederick Bonfils, smashed composing room machinery and tried unsuccessfully to damage the presses.

At the Central barns, the mob marched on the Tramway building, hurled bricks through the windows and a shot was fired, hitting a strikebreaker in the leg. The chief of police was struck in the head by a rock.

The rioting continued into the night, and at the end of it, two were dead, 33 injured and eight tram cars were wrecked.

When 300 members of the Trades and Labor Assembly marched on City Hall demanding that the mayor withdraw police protection from the strikebreakers, he refused, saying he would not allow 1,100 men to run the city because they chose to ignore the injunction.

On Aug. 7 at 1:20 a.m., infantry troops rumbled into Denver in trucks from Fort Logan, and military law took over at the police station, fire department and every city office. On the order of Maj. Gen. Leonard Wood, another 500 troops were on the way from Camp Funston, Kan. By then, six people had been killed.

By Aug. 10, 614 strikebreakers were operating 107 streetcars. The company announced that all former employees who did not reapply for their jobs by Aug. 12 would lose seniority.

Despite this, union-management negotiations dragged on for weeks.

Gradually, the momentum of the strike wound down, and the city returned to a semblance of normality. Military rule ended Sept. 9.

The strike ended Nov. 4, 1920, when the strikers voted almost unanimously to return to work.

That day, hundreds flocked to the Tramway Building to ask for their old jobs, but the company said they would be rehired on the basis of past performance and ability. Seniority would not be restored, and the employees hired during the emergency would not be dismissed to make way for the returnees.

"We have lost the strike," said Harold Silberg, the union president. "We could see no possible hope of gaining our demands. The company won, and we lost."

May 2, 1982

Georgetown Loop thrilled travelers

ONE of the most popular turn-of-the century tourist attractions in Colorado was the Georgetown Loop, with visitors coming from many parts of the world to ride the narrow-gauge train over its spectacular mileage.

Rocky Mountain Memories has received several requests asking for information on the loop, which will have its 100th anniversary in 1983.

The Georgetown Loop and the high trestle which formed a part of it were regarded in their day as one of the most marvelous engineering feats ever accomplished.

This bit of railroading, often ballyhooed as an "eighth wonder of the world," was built by the Union Pacific Railroad as an extension of a line into the mountains built by the Colorado Central Railroad. Narrow-gauge rails only 3 feet apart and sturdy little coal-burning engines built to run on them were chosen in preference to broad gauge for transportation into the mountains.

The line first was built from Golden to Black Hawk in 1872, and then extended to Central City in 1878. The Clear Creek County terminal was at Floyd Hill, and in 1877, it was stretched onward to Idaho Springs and Georgetown.

By 1884, after the Union Pacific had obtained a 50-year lease from Colorado Central, the famous Georgetown Loop was finished, to carry passengers, and millions in silver ore, between Georgetown and Silver Plume.

Georgetown's altitude is 8,507 feet, and Silver Plume's is 9,189. The spectacular stretch of railroad that connected them was the famous Georgetown Loop. Because of the narrow valley, called Devil's Gate, and the steep climb, the tracks made 14 curves in their 4½-mile journey between the towns, and at one point crossed over themselves creating the loop. This portion of the line was laid out by Robert Blickensderfer, an engineer.

The high trestle, called the Devil's Gate Viaduct, was the most sensational part of the line.

The trestle held a single narrow-gauge track built on a wide curve of steel supports rising 77 feet above the bed of Clear Creek for a distance of 303 feet.

Constructing the trestle had more than the usual problems, because riveters would take one look straight down, 70 or more feet, to the stream bed, pick up their pay and return to Denver.

The first man to take a train across the trestle was George Cooper of Idaho Springs, engineer of a work train that was used in building the trestle. Later train crews told of winds and blizzards that "darned near pushed us into the creek."

Passenger service began April 2, 1884. The fare was 35¢ from Georgetown to Silver Plume, and the running time was 25 minutes. With the completion of the line, tourists got more thrills than they had bargained for as the train crept over the high trestle, with a steep drop on either side. On some trains, passengers were let out, to walk ahead of the engine as it inched across the trestle.

While the Union Pacific operated the line, the rolling stock was furnished by Colorado Central. These little, two-coach trains became world famous. Pictures of the loop became a standard, along with Niagara Falls and Old Faithful, in geography books printed around 1900.

Excursion trains to the Georgetown Loop — as many as seven a day — operated regularly out of Denver. Passengers thrilled to coal-burning locomotives spewing out cinders and sending forth eerie whistles that echoed against the steep canyon walls. The trip from Denver to Silver Plume took 3 hours and 40 minutes.

Both Georgetown and Silver Plume were boomtowns when the rails came in. But in addition to the usual attractions, the railroad added another — an elaborate dance pavilion at Silver Plume. Day excursionists could visit the towns, climb the hills, bring their own picnics and

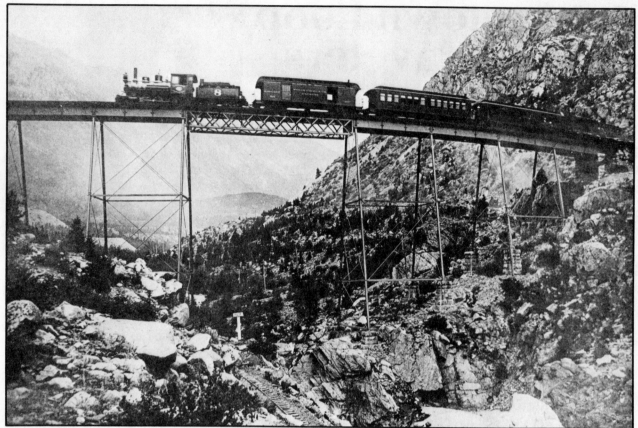

A steam engine pulling a passenger train crept across the spectacular trestle on the Georgetown Loop. Sometimes, passengers were allowed to walk across the trestle ahead of the train.

dance in the pavilion.

The line was acquired by the Colorado & Southern Railway in 1898, and operated by it until it was abandoned in 1937.

In 1939, the trestle was purchased from the Colorado & Southern by a Silver Plume mining and milling company for $450. The mining firm dismantled it and used the steel as supports in the mines. At the same time, the Georgetown railroad station was sold for $50.

May 9, 1982

The Loop was an engineering marvel, ballyhooed as the "eighth wonder of the world."

Digging up the roots of Memorial Day

OUR observance of Memorial Day brings to light a little-known fact.

Did you know that this great holiday, first set aside to honor the Civil War dead, was brought about by Gen. John Alexander Logan, for whom Colorado's Fort Logan is named?

Logan was a Civil War hero who distinguished himself in the siege of Vicksburg and received the Congressional Medal of Honor. He was called "the most distinguished volunteer officer of the Civil War." During the war he also spent some time in Colorado and had many friends in the state.

He was born in Murphysboro, Ill., Feb. 9, 1826, and studied law in Illinois. He was a representative in Congress from 1859 to 1861, when he resigned to join the Union Army as a private. He rose to the rank of major general and succeeded Gen. William T. Sherman as commander of the 115th Army Corps.

He was discharged from the Army in 1865, and returned to his home in Illinois. There he was elected to the U.S. Senate, serving from 1871 to 1877.

Logan was one of the organizers of the Grand Army of the Republic and served three terms as president. He conceived the idea of Decoration Day, as it was first named, and called on Union Army members to decorate the graves of Union soliders with flowers and wreaths.

The date of May 30 was chosen because it was the date of discharge of the last of the Union volunteers. Decoration Day first was observed in 1868, and in 1873, the May 30 date was made official by the state of New York.

For many years Memorial Day customarily was observed on May 30, but in 1971, federal law changed it to the last Monday in May. Through the years, the observance has been broadened to cover the servicemen of all wars, and civilians as well.

Some southern states do not observe Memorial Day, but observe their own day set aside in honor of Confederate veterans.

May 30, 1982

Rocky Mountain News

The stone grave markers at Fort Logan National Cemetery honor servicemen and women.

History marched through Fort Logan

A reader who liked our story May 30 on the beginnings of Memorial Day (designated through the efforts of Gen. John Alexander Logan), asked for information about the history of Fort Logan. The fort was named for Logan, a Civil War hero and Congressional Medal of Honor winner.

Fort Logan never was a frontier fort, but still, it has a colorful history. In its early years it was known as a "society post," famous for its dress parades, band concerts and fancy dress balls staged for the benefit of Denver visitors.

Some of our country's most famous soldiers were stationed at Fort Logan. President Eisen-

Western History Department, Denver Public Library

In 1918, tents filled Fort Logan, which was used as a receiving station for draftees and enlisted men who would fight in World War I. Some of America's most famous soldiers were stationed there.

Officers lived in these Victorian-style houses at Fort Logan in the 1890s, shortly after the fort was built. The commanding officer's house was a handsome building that cost $13,647 to build in 1891.

hower, early in his Army career, served a hitch at Fort Logan. And when Gen. Douglas MacArthur was a student at West Point, he spent vacation time at the fort because his father, Gen. Arthur MacArthur, was commander.

For many years, Fort Logan was the only garrisoned military post in Colorado. The site southwest of Denver near the foothills included 1,000 acres and 136 buildings, among them barracks, officers' quarters, administration buildings and warehouses. (It's now part of the city of Denver.)

The commanding officer's home, built in 1891, was a handsome building with stained-glass windows and fine woodwork. Fireplaces were faced with tile imported from France. The cost of building this house was $13,647.

Agitation for a fort near Denver began in 1886, when Secretary of War William C. Endicott pointed out a need for a concentration of Army forces at large rail intersections. Several Denver businessmen, mainly David Moffat, Walter S. Cheesman and Chester S. Morey, enlisted the aid of the chamber of commerce to bring pressure on Congress for the fort at Denver.

Colorado Sen. Henry M. Teller initiated a bill

for the fort and requested an appropriation of $250,000 to establish it. In Washington, Gen. Philip H. Sheridan, commanding general of the Army, said a post at Denver would be inexpensive compared with other posts scattered around the state and recommended shutting down most of the others in favor of the Denver site.

Teller's bill was passed by Congress, but the appropriation was cut to $100,000. On Feb. 17, 1887, President Grover Cleveland signed the bill for the fort near Denver, which by then was being called Fort Sheridan.

Shortly after the law passed, Sheridan came to Denver to select a site for the fort, and, after nearly choosing a spot near Sloans Lake, he designated a site 7.5 miles south of Denver, known as the Johnson Ranch, at the Morrison branch of the South Park Railroad. A subscription campaign to pay for the land was conducted by the same group that had pressed Congress to establish the fort.

On Oct. 25, 1887, Maj. George K. Brady assumed command of the fort and moved troops onto the reservation, housing them in tents. Temporary barracks were ready by December.

The fort, still called Fort Sheridan, was established Oct. 20, 1887, and, at that time, the government abandoned several other military posts in Colorado, including Forts Garland, Crawford, Lewis, Lyon and Uncompahgre.

At about the same time, a fort was being established in the Chicago area, and it was named Fort Logan, after Gen. John Alexander Logan, who was called "the most distinguished volunteer officer of the Civil War." Logan was a native of Murphysboro, Ill., so naming an Illinois fort after him seemed appropriate. The name plan was changed shortly after ground was broken for Fort Logan; up to then, the name had been unofficial.

Sheridan became ill, and, when he was practically on his death bed, he was asked by the secretary of war which post he preferred to have named after him. Believing that the Illinois installation was going to be the more important, he chose it. The Colorado post, by default, became Fort Logan.

On April 5, 1889, the Denver military post officially was designated Fort Logan. Logan had served in Denver and was well-liked in the community.

He had won a commission as a lieutenant in the war with Mexico, then studied law in Illinois and was elected to Congress. He resigned from Congress to join the Union Army as a private, but quickly rose to the rank of major general and succeeded Gen. William Tecumseh Sherman as commander of the 115th Army Corps.

Fort Logan was completed in 1894, being laid out around a 3.2-acre plot Sheridan had thought would make a good parade ground. Accommodations were provided for two troops of cavalry, eight companies of infantry, 28 officers, a headquarters staff and band.

The 7th Cavalry arrived at Fort Logan in 1889. It was the company that was sent overseas April 20, 1898, after the battleship Maine was blown up in Havana harbor.

By 1909, Fort Logan had become mainly a rest and recruiting center. During World War I, it was used as a receiving station for enlisted men and draftees.

One of its first society charity functions was a garden party on July 25, 1925. Proceeds went to the orphans of Army men. Socialites who competed in a riding event included Verner Z. Reed, Lafayette Hughes and Lawrence C. Phipps Jr.

During the 1920s, the fort was used largely as a center for reserve officers' training. Starting in 1927, it also was used for 30 days each summer as a citizens' military training camp.

By 1935, the fort had fallen into disrepair and was being referred to as "Fort Forgotten." The *Rocky Mountain News* waged a successful campaign for repair and restoration of the property.

Fort Logan enjoyed renewed activity with the start of World War II, when it became an Army Air Force clerical school associated with Lowry Air Force Base. Starting in January 1942, it also served once again as a reception center, and for 6 months after November 1945, it was a separation center.

Next, the Veterans Administration used the fort for hospital facilities for 5 years, until its hospital was completed in Denver.

Fort Logan was declared surplus property by the government in 1956. In 1960, 308 acres of fort land were deeded to the state for a mental health center, now renowned as Fort Logan Mental Health Center. Later, other acreage was sold to private developers.

June 13, 1982

Long-gone restaurants gave a taste to Denver

THE *Rocky Mountain News'* annual restaurant guide appeared in the paper the day this column was printed. An advance look at articles in the guide on some of the top eating spots started us thinking of the great and long-gone restaurants of an earlier Denver.

To reel off a few names, there was the Tortoni at 1541-1547 Arapahoe St.; the Manhattan, 1635 Larimer St.; George Watrous Restaurant, 1525-27 Curtis St.; Home Dairy Restaurant, 1620-1642 Welton St.; the five McVittie's Restaurants scattered around the downtown area during the 1920s and 1930s; Pell's Oyster House at 1514 Welton St.; and Hoff-Schroeder Cafeteria in the basement at 1545 Welton St.

Of those, the Manhattan stands alone, a restaurant that served presidents and nobility, as well as the gamut of Denver residents, from wealthy members of the Sacred 36 to some of the poorest transients.

When a rotund Englishman, Richard Pinhorn, arrived in Denver in 1892 and proclaimed he intended to establish a restaurant that would become world famous, he nearly was laughed out of town. But diners soon were flocking to the restaurant to gorge on the charcoal-broiled steaks, which were to become a Manhattan mainstay.

Pinhorn stopped in St. Louis on his way West and hired a chef, Chris Rapp, a German immigrant, who stayed with the Manhattan until it closed nearly 50 years later. At the top of the Manhattan menu Pinhorn listed a dinner of sirloin steak with fried onions, combination salad and french fries, adding:

"The meal for which the Manhattan always will be famous."

The Manhattan's tender steaks were celebrated, and Pinhorn bragged that the secret lay in the aging — hanging them until they nearly were blue. The restaurant's homemade salad dressings also were praised highly.

At the Manhattan, booths — they were tufted dark brown leather — lined the walls, with tables and chairs in the middle of the room. White cloths covered the tables, and waiters wore black trousers, white shirts and black ties. A small waiting room at the rear of the restaurant offered padded, leather-covered benches built into the walls to accommodate customers waiting to be seated.

Pinhorn was proud of his policy of giving "the very best for the lowest possible price." It was said he was content to make a profit of 1 cent a meal and still became a millionaire because of the Manhattan's great volume of business.

It wasn't long before Pinhorn's prediction came true. Carriages from Capitol Hill rolled along Larimer Street on Saturday and Sunday nights for dinner at the Manhattan, and the waiting line often was a half block long. Denver's "Unsinkable" Molly Brown was one of the regular customers, but reportedly not one of the meekest.

Meals at the Manhattan were hearty western fare, plain and good. There was no French cuisine with elaborate sauces at Pinhorn's restaurant. And, unusual in that day, the restaurant was open 24 hours a day.

In only a few years the Manhattan was almost as widely known as Delmonico's of New York. The restaurant was hailed as one of the important tourist attractions of the West.

Pinhorn eventually could boast that the Manhattan sold more charcoal-broiled steaks than any other restaurant in the world, and he never was challenged.

The restaurateur's success has been attributed to his personality and his love of people. Patrons enjoyed Pinhorn's practice of visiting tables to check on how customers were enjoying their meals.

His staff also found him to be thoughtful and compassionate, and most of his original employ-

Pell's Oyster House at 1514 Welton St. was one of Denver's best-known restaurants of the early days. Others that made a name for themselves included the Manhattan and the Tortoni.

ees were working at the restaurant when he died May 30, 1922. It was said he had a kind heart, and it was a legend of Larimer Street that no hungry man was turned away from the Manhattan.

In 1919, Pinhorn was cited publicly for keeping prices down despite the profiteering of World War I.

Pinhorn died of uremic poisoning at age 61 in his home at 1724 Lincoln St. After his death, Denver residents raised $2,500, and a granite fountain topped by a bronze cherub was placed

on the sidewalk in front of the Manhattan. The fountain was designed by a local artist, Paul Gregg, and a simple inscription said it was erected by Denverites in 1924 in memory of Pinhorn.

After several moves around town, the fountain stands in Larimer Square on the eastern side of Larimer Street.

In his will, Pinhorn appointed Joseph J. Walsh, later a judge, as his executor and trustee and authorized him to carry on the business for 2 years. At the end of the 2 years, the Manhattan was to be turned over to designated employees, including Eugene Navarro, executive chef, and John Winslow, head waiter, who each received a 25% interest. Certain interests were bequeathed to other longtime employees.

Pinhorn also designated 11 charities to receive some money from the restaurant's profits. These charitable interests ranged from Jewish and Catholic institutions to helping the blind and agencies aiding children and animals.

Without Pinhorn's personality and management, the Manhattan fell on hard times. Eventually, it faced bankruptcy and was sold by the estate in March 1938 to David Harlem, a real estate speculator.

On April 20, 1941, the Manhattan closed, after 45 years in business. The final day reminded personnel of the "good old days" as thousands came to enjoy a "last meal" at the Manhattan. Chef Rapp was there, and at day's end, Rapp said they had served 3,500 meals, mostly steak.

The restaurant later was reopened briefly, but the magic was gone. On May 28, 1947, when it was owned by W.C. Wallace, the Manhattan was sold at a federal auction for taxes of $3,500.

July 11, 1982

The readers said . . .

Western History Department, Denver Public Library

The Manhattan Restaurant, 1635 Larmier St., was a special place for long-ago Denverites.

THE column on early Denver restaurants brought in a number of letters. Joan Caruso writes that her father, William Elmer Ewing Sr., was a partner in the Manhattan Restaurant.

"After the restaurant was left to the employees, (after the death of the restaurant's founder, Richard Pinhorn) and they went bankrupt, it was sold back to the owners of the building, Joe Alpert, Dave Cook and a partner, William Elmer Ewing Sr., my father."

"It was reopened approximately 2 months after receivership and was a very successful operation all during World War II. All the traditions were maintained and the original employees' jobs were salvaged.

"We had five full-time bakers for 7 years, 35 waiters and waitresses. The restaurant was open on a 24-hour basis. The angel on the fountain outside the main entrance seemed to smile its approval of my father who, at the age of 7, had sold papers outside this very door and had stood looking inside at the display of delicious steaks that he couldn't afford to buy."

The restaurant had one chef who was 90 years old and worked every Saturday night frying steaks. Chris, Blackie and Frank, cooks, worked for the restaurant 30 to 40 years and stayed on.

"We never had a turnover of employees. They loved their jobs. Nate Rosenfeld worked the horseshoe counter for 40 years, morning shift. He was waiter No. 1.

"The Lighthouse Mission was next door, and any food that wasn't used off the line after lunch was taken next door immediately to feed the mission occupants.

"I started working for my father when I was 12. My first job was in the restaurant basement ironing white napkins 8 hours a day for 2 silver dollars. After that summer I worked in the pantry, cleaning vegetables and preparing them for salads, cleaning shrimp and packing lunches for soldiers on troop trains.

"We could accommodate 300 soliders from the trains at Union Station. They would march up to the restaurant four deep with officers in charge. The customers were always happy to oblige while our soldier boys ate.

"Tony Roberts was head waitress. She would fly around and with the help of other workers waited on 100 men with very little trouble. This took teamwork, a spirit that seemed to prevail in that era.

"My father later received an award from the United States government, signed by the president, for feeding soliders during World War II.

"When movie star John Payne was stationed at Lowry, he had dinner every Sunday at the restaurant for a few months. Among a few celebrities who dined there during the war were Dorothy Lamour, Jack Dempsey and Leo Carillo.

"My father kept the crew together for 7 years. He had a heart attack and his partners found a buyer for the restaurant in 1946. The Manhattan sold for $85,000, which was a lot of money in those days. When it was sold in 1946, the era was over.

"I feel William Elmer Ewing Sr. should get credit for making many people happy during this period, doing a great service to the old tradition in Denver."

August 8, 1982

David beats Goliath, wins the love of Utes

ONE of Colorado's most unusual stories, is brought to mind by a reader who asks for a history of Pagosa Springs, on the eastern edge of the San Juan Basin.

The story centers on the hot springs at Pagosa, which reputedly include the largest hot spring in the world. The spring is about 50-by-75 feet, and its depth never has been determined. At about 850 feet, measuring devices buoy up, and an accurate measurement never has been made.

The temperature of the sulfurous water as it boils out of the volcanic rock, is 153 degrees. One legend tells of an Indian brave who tried to swim across the spring but was scalded after he had gone only a few feet. Another story says a calf plunged into the steaming water to escape from dogs chasing it and lost its hide.

Many buildings of Pagosa Springs are heated by geothermal wells tapping into the underground water that's also the source of the spring.

The mineral content of Pagosa Springs, heavy

Western History Department, Denver Public Library

The great Pagosa hot spring, photographed in 1942, is the subject of many a legend. Its depth has never been measured; the temperature of the sulfurous water is 153 as it boils out of volcanic rock.

on sulfur, is said to be similar to the famous Czechoslovakian spring Karlsbad, and for many decades, it has been used for drinking and bathing by Indians and white men who believe it has curative power.

The name comes from an Indian word meaning "healing water." Long before white explorers came into the territory, the spring was prized by Ute and Navajo Indians and was the object of several battles for possession.

Depending on the outcome of battle, both tribes at times controlled the spring.

The unusual story of Pagosa Springs also involves a small white man, Col. Albert H. Pfeiffer, an Indian scout who became one of Kit Carson's most trusted aides.

Pfeiffer was born in the Netherlands. His father was a Lutheran minister, and his mother was descended from Scottish nobility. Pfeiffer set out for adventure in the American West when he was 22 and joined the Army under the command of Carson.

Carson soon learned that Pfeiffer, despite his small size, was capable of the most dangerous duty. He became a captain in the Abiquiu Mounted Volunteers of New Mexico and frequently was sent out to punish marauding Utes who were full of Taos Lightning, the powerful drink made at Rio Hondo, north of Taos.

Far from hating Pfeiffer, the Utes came to admire and respect the bold and fearless little white man, eventually making him a member of their tribe.

Not long after his arrival, Pfeiffer married a Spanish woman, Antonita, in Santa Fe. The bride's dress, of white satin and elaborately hand-embroidered in red roses in the local convent, was declared to be the most beautiful wedding dress ever seen in the region.

In 1863, when Pfeiffer was stationed at Fort MacRae, N.M., he, his bride and several servants went to bathe in some hot springs.

As they bathed, they heard shots and looked up to find a band of Apaches swooping down on them. Pfeiffer was wounded by an arrow that went through his body. His wife and servants were carried off by the Indians. Being an expert swimmer, Pfeiffer swam to safety in the Rio Grande, then hid in a canyon until it was safe to emerge.

Naked and barefoot, as well as seriously wounded, he stumbled and crawled 9 miles back to the fort. He lay near death for 2 months, unaware that his wife and servants had been found murdered.

When he recovered, the scout devoted much of the following few years shooting Apache and Comanche men and burning their tepees.

In 1865, Pfeiffer was appointed Indian agent and made a lieutenant colonel by President Andrew Johnson. He also homesteaded on the upper Rio Grande.

It was on the homestead one day in 1866 that Pfeiffer received a message to come to the aid of the Utes, his adopted tribesmen. Once again, they were at war with the Navajos, and the prize was the great Pagosa spring and the surrounding country.

After a few skirmishes, leaders of the two tribes conferred and agreed on a change of battle tactics. Each tribe would appoint a champion, and the two champions were to fight a duel to the death, which would determine ownership of the hot spring. At the same time, many lives would be saved.

As their champion, the Navajos sent out a Goliath who strutted and loudly boasted of his strength and skill. Little Pfeiffer, the David of this battle, agreed to represent the Utes if he could choose the weapons. That was agreed upon.

The Utes were surprised when their champion, who was an expert rifle shot, chose to fight the duel with Bowie knives.

The battle took place in the David Hersch pasture, about 7 miles southwest of the present town of Pagosa Springs. The air was crisp with tension as the two adversaries faced one another. When the fight was over, one man would be dead.

Accounts of the duel vary. Both men were stripped to the waist, and one story says Pfeiffer ended the contest almost instantly by taking deadly aim with his Bowie knife and throwing the knife straight into his opponent's heart. Another story is that the men slashed at one anoth-

Lt. George M. Wheeler, on an 1874 expedition, examined the mud — supposedly a cure-all.

Col. Albert H. Pheiffer was the David who fought a Goliath sent by the Navajos.

er briefly, but Pfeiffer, being far more skillful with the knife, quickly got the advantage and plunged the weapon into the Navajo champion's heart.

Either way, Pfeiffer was the victor, and the great Pagosa spring belonged to the Utes. He was revered by the Utes ever after, and the site still is marked by a large mound of rock.

In later years, Pfeiffer went into the cattle business with a couple of partners. The Utes let these white men use their winter grazing range when they learned that Pfeiffer was one of the owners.

Pfeiffer died April 6, 1881, on his homestead near Granger and was buried on the old Gredig Ranch near Del Norte.

In 1880, the president of the United States issued an order creating a townsite of 1 square mile that included the great Pagosa spring. The town was platted in 1883, and lots were sold to the highest bidders by the U.S. Land Office.

When the town of Pagosa Springs was laid out, the government moved the Utes to their reservation a few miles away.

August 22, 1982

TR loved the West, especially Colorado

NO United States president, with the possible exception of Dwight D. Eisenhower, loved the West as much as did Theodore Roosevelt. Roosevelt's western adventures take the spotlight with a question from a reader who would like to know about "Teddy's" visits to Colorado.

Roosevelt was sworn in as president when he was 42 after the assassination of William McKinley in 1901. He proved to be a president who was strongly interested in reclamation and preservation. He established 51 national bird reservations, five national parks and four big-game refuges.

The famous "Rough Rider" liked all the West, and Colorado was high on his list of favorites. That was despite a misadventure:

During a campaign stop in Victor in 1900, when he was running for vice president, he was struck across the chest by a heckler and his private railroad car was stoned as it pulled out of the mining town.

Two versions of how one of the world's most famous toys, the teddy bear, got its name say it happened in 1905 when President Roosevelt was hunting near Glenwood Springs. The story told by Lena Doose, a Glenwood historian, is that his daughter Alice who was staying with him at the Colorado Hotel, admired a bear pelt brought in, and decided to name it Teddy. Another Glenwood historian, Nellie Duffy, said Glenwood residents gave the president a toy bear they called Teddy after his successful hunt in the area.

Still another variation is that after the president's first bear kill made international news, an opportunistic toy manufacturer made a small stuffed bear and sent it to Alice. This supposedly became the prototype of the famous teddy bear.

It may be that those stories grew out of events surrounding the "birth" of the teddy bear three years earlier — 1902 when Roosevelt was on a mission to arbitrate a boundary dispute between Mississippi and Louisana. A small bear was cap-

tured and brought to camp for the president to shoot. Roosevelt refused, claiming the cub didn't have a chance to defend itself. The act of mercy was captured by political cartoonist Clifford Berryman, whose sketch of the incident appeared in eastern papers, and the teddy bear was born.

As a young man seeking good health, the future president in 1883 hunted and fished in the Badlands of the Dakotas, Yellowstone Park, the Bighorn Mountains and Jackson Hole in Wyoming and elsewhere in the Rocky Mountains. He also ran a cattle operation in the Dakotas for 3 years, proving to doubters that cattle could be raised there. The 70,416-acre Theodore Roosevelt National Memorial Park in western North Dakota contains part of his ranch plus scenic badlands.

He was just 28 when he left the West to make an independent run for mayor of New York City. The strength and self-reliance he had gained in the wide open spaces were of value to him then and for the rest of his life.

Roosevelt visited Colorado seven times during the early 1900s. His first trip, the campaign tour in 1900, when he still was governor of New York, started auspiciously. He was McKinley's vice presidential candidate on the Republican ticket.

"At every stop from Cheyenne to Denver the vice presidential candidate was cheered with rampant enthusiasm," reported one newspaper. A banner headline in the *Denver Times* when the Hero of San Juan Hill reached the capital said:

"Here's to Teddy! Thousands Cheer Him on His Tour."

Thousands turned out at the depot and lined the streets of Denver to see Roosevelt, who rode in to the strains of martial music and bugle calls. In three appearances in the city he addressed more than 20,000 people. In Florence, the continuous blowing of steam whistles greet-

Western History Department, Denver Public Library

Theodore Roosevelt tipped his hat as he campaigned for the vice presidency in front of the Brown Palace Hotel in September 1900. He also visited Colorado to hunt bears.

ed his train.

But it was different in Victor, where the majority supported William Jennings Bryan and the silver platform. In what was to become a national disgrace to Colorado, Roosevelt was insulted and came close to injury by a group that the *Denver Times* of Sept. 27, 1900, described as "a crowd of thugs and bruisers."

Roosevelt was on a campaign trip with Sen. Henry Cabot Lodge of Massachusetts, Sen. Henry Wolcott of Colorado and Frank C. Goudy, Colorado's Republican nominee for governor.

Through a ruse, the "toughs" managed to clear the Armory Hall of Roosevelt supporters and take the seats. Roosevelt arrived at the hall

behind the Rough Rider Band which led the way with a spirited march. It was virtually impossible for the candidate to speak, because of hecklers, and he left after an hour. A howling, drunken mob filled the streets, according to the newspaper.

"I'll make Roosevelt eat this banner," said a man carrying a Bryan sign. Although Roosevelt was surrounded by Rough Rider guards, the man pushed into the group and broke the sign pole over a Rough Rider's shoulder. One end of the stick flew off and hit Roosevelt on the shoulder. The man then managed to hit the candidate across the chest with the rest of the stick.

Cripple Creek's famous feisty postmaster,

Denny Sullivan, yelled: "Take that, you coward," and hit the attacker in the face. The blow knocked out four teeth and sent the man rolling in the mud. Some time later, Roosevelt presented Sullivan with what became his lifelong treasure, a red, white and blue ring containing a ruby, diamond and sapphire.

Other grabs were made at Roosevelt and there were attempts to pull the guards off their horses. The guards retaliated by riding down the banner bearers and taking their poles. It was a scene of general confusion and chaos. Two men were seen dueling with the two ends of a broken banner pole.

Roosevelt and the other speakers were rushed under guard to the train. Then the Rough Riders rushed the attachers, and the rowdies disappeared. As the train pulled out, the hecklers urged small boys to stone Roosevelt's car, which they did.

In nearby Cripple Creek, Roosevelt's reception was entirely different. He spoke in three halls, and said the reports: "Each was packed to full capacity by courteous, hospitable, refined, enthusiastic people."

In Leadville the hero of San Juan Hill was given a glorious welcome, and hundreds marched ahead of his carriage as he rode from the depot to the speakers' platform erected at the corner of Fifth and Harrison streets.

Pueblo staged one of the largest parades ever seen in southern Colorado in Roosevelt's honor.

At all these functions, Roosevelt, the consummate politician, "went right down among them and shook the hands of as many men, women and children as he could reach." During speeches, ever the showman, he held his Rough Rider hat and gestured with it.

As vice president-elect, Roosevelt returned to Colorado in January 1901 for a mountain-lion hunt with a noted guide, J.B. Goff. Of the 17 lions killed on the trip, Roosevelt accounted for 12 of them. One lion he bagged on that trip, according to official records, was one of the largest mountain lions ever killed with a rifle, with a skull measurement of 15¾ inches.

Two of Roosevelt's legendary hunting stories came out of the trip, which started from the Keystone Ranch near Meeker.

One story widely circulated by Goff was that Roosevelt, one day near twilight, wounded a lion that sprang over a large boulder and hid in a crevice facing a steep and dangerous drop. Determined to get the animal, Roosevelt insisted on hanging head down over the cliff while Goff held his feet and Roosevelt shot the lion between the eyes. Roosevelt later described this adventure in a two-part article in *Century Magazine.*

One of Roosevelt's hunting companions described another day when the fearless Teddy rushed in among several dogs that were attacking a mountain lion, apparently because it appeared that the lion was killing one of the dogs. With one hand Roosevelt rammed his rifle butt between the jaws of the lion, then finished off the animal with his knife.

Only a few months after that hunt, Theodore Roosevelt became president of the United States when McKinley was assassinated, being shot on Sept. 6, 1901 and dying 8 days later.

Roosevelt paid a return visit to Colorado in April 1903, in a combined campaign for re-election and pleasure trip.

He won re-election in 1904 and came back to Colorado on a bear-hunting trip in March 1905. In his honor, the train carrying him spewed red, white and blue smoke as it went over Ute Pass.

The Colorado Hotel at Glenwood Springs was turned into Roosevelt's White House during the hunt. His party was credited with killing 10 bears, with the president receiving credit for six of them. After the hunt, the participants relaxed in the hot springs pool at Glenwood.

This was the bear hunt that generated the stories of how the teddy bear got its name.

Roosevelt visited Colorado briefly again in August 1910, September 1912, and October 1918.

September 5, 1982

Pitiful lad's genius grew in a grimy prison

THE case of Jason Rocha, 15, who recently was sentenced to 12 years in prison for the fatal shooting of a schoolmate, Scott Darwin Michael, 13, brings to mind another case that is infamous in Colorado history.

It is the story of Antone Wood, who on Nov. 2, 1892, killed Joe Smith, 22, an employee of the state Fish Hatchery, because he wanted Smith's "pretty gold watch."

Antone's age always has been in question. He was reported to be 11 years old when the crime was committed, but the courts later decided he was at least 12.

On April 5, 1893, Antone was sentenced to serve 25 years of hard labor in the state penitentiary. At the time the sentence was pronounced, Antone, then 12, was the youngest person ever to serve time in the penitentiary.

He served almost half of his term.

It was a crisp fall day when Joe Smith and two companions, Alexander Baker and Harry Wyman, started on a rabbit hunt west of Brighton. Baker had an interest in a Denver hotel, and Wyman was a saloonkeeper at 31st and Market streets.

The trio left Denver about 4 a.m. with a horse and wagon. When they were 9 miles west of Brighton, at about 8 that morning, they parked the wagon, staked out the horse and continued on foot. A short time later, according to an account given later by Baker, they met "a young Pole," later identified as Antone.

"He asked the time and Smith pulled out his gold watch to tell him," Baker said.

The youth was carrying an old musket with a broken stock bound with wire and several rabbits tied with a cord were slung over his shoulder, Baker added. He said he lived in the neighborhood, and Smith asked him to show the visitors where to get rabbits. The boy agreed.

Colorado Historical Society

Antone Wood was only 11 or 12 when he killed a man with a gun that was as big as he was.

Smith started out with Antone, but Baker and Wyman had decided to go after ducks and took a different route. They agreed to meet at the wagon at 5 p.m.

A few minutes later, Baker and Wyman heard three shots and assumed Smith had found some rabbits.

Smith wasn't at the wagon when Baker and Wyman returned about 5 o'clock. They waited an hour, then started to search but found no clues to their friend.

They resumed the search by wagon the next morning and found Smith's body on a hillside.

His gun, watch and chain were missing. The coroner ruled that Smith had been shot in the back, according to a report in the *Denver Republican* of Nov. 5, 1892.

At the time the body was discovered, the boy's identity was not known. Two nights later, however, the home of a Polish dairy farmer in the vicinity was surrounded by sheriff's deputies while the family was at dinner. The father said his son, Antone, had gone to Elyria for the day.

The officers searched, however, and found Antone under a bed. Smith's gun was on the floor beside him. The gold watch was in Antone's pocket.

With little prompting, the boy told his story. He said he had wanted Smith's watch more than anything he'd seen, and as they walked along, he fired three shots into Smith's back.

With the watch and gun, he hurried home and confessed his crime to his father. His father advised him to keep the watch and gun out of sight, "or you will get into trouble."

"Yes, I'm sorry I killed him," Antone answered the sheriff, "but I wanted his pretty watch and gun, and I took them."

Antone's arrest as well as his trial, which began Feb. 27, 1893, became a national sensation. At the time he was the youngest person in the country to be tried for murder with robbery as a motive.

The youth was defended by Henry S. Jonston, John A. Deeweese and John A. Converse, who first tried to prove he shot Smith accidentally while aiming at a rabbit. The youth's confession, repeated at the trial, contradicted this.

The defense then tried to show the boy had been drinking, which led him to commit the crime without realizing what he was doing.

B.M. Malone, assistant district attorney, presented the testimony of teachers and doctors to show that Antone was a bright boy who could distinguish between right and wrong.

The jury deliberated 29 hours and cast 60 ballots without reaching a decision. A second trial started March 23, 1893. This time, after eight ballots, the jury reached a guilty verdict of second-degree murder.

Both parents testified that, at the time of the crime, Antone was not yet 12 — too young legally to be committed to the penitentiary. The judge, however, said evidence had established that the boy was older than 12.

The judge expressed regret at the youth of the prisoner, but added that he felt it was his duty to the community to sentence him to the penitentiary. He called Antone's act a "coldblooded, premeditated crime."

Antone's prison experience was unusual. A former college professor serving time offered to tutor the boy, and Antone proved to be something of a mathematical genius. In a year, he mastered a college course in math.

When he was 15, he began to study the violin with an excellent violinist-prisoner, and they soon were playing duets for prison entertainment. The youth also practiced drawing which always had been one of his principal interests.

Antone's progress in prison attracted renewed attention to him, and Madge Reynolds, wife of a Denver oilman, began a campaign for his release. Several women's clubs of Denver joined the crusade.

Elbert Hubbard, a wealthy Eastern author and philanthropist, petitioned for Antone to be paroled to Hubbard's Roycrofters Colony at East Aurora, N.Y. It was done, and Antone arrived at Hubbard's colony when he was 24 — after 12 years in jail — using a different name.

On June 2, 1906, he married the daughter of a New York judge who knew his past. And Oct. 15, 1906, Antone Wood was granted a full pardon. There is no record that he ever was in trouble again.

September 19, 1982

Mardi Gras of '95 put silver back in the city

OCTOBER brings to mind the days when Denver had an all-out celebration that was heralded as the Mardi Gras of the West. Denver's Festival of Mountain and Plain was patterned after the Mardi Gras, and when the festival made its debut in October 1895, it even borrowed floats from the New Orleans celebration.

A writer from *Harper's Magazine*, who covered the festival in its third year, reported somewhat breathlessly:

"The festival indicates the presence of a streak of spectacular gaiety in the American character not too well known in the East."

Colorado had been through some stringent times started by the Panic of 1893, which had seen the bottom drop out of the silver market and left many miners unemployed. This crisis was followed by a drought that caused many farmers to lose crops and cattle.

By 1895, when the picture was brightening, Colorado was ready for a celebration. Inspired by his wife, who had seen a flower festival in Colorado Springs, Maj. K.S. Hooper, a passenger agent for the Denver & Rio Grande Western Railroad, suggested putting on a huge festival. He managed to interest William N. Byers, publisher of the *Rocky Mountain News,* and Byers' editorials on the subject led to the organization of a festival committee.

Robert W. Speer, who later became one of Denver's outstanding mayors, was appointed director of the celebration, which was held Oct. 22-24. A contest was held to name the festival, and the winner, I.N. Stevens of Denver, received a prize of $10 for his suggestion.

Byers was shrewd enough to realize a bunch of amateurs couldn't put on the kind of festival envisioned. So, to run the event, he persuaded the committee to import a professional, J.H. Jordan of New Orleans, who had helped produce that year's Mardi Gras.

The festival was financed by Denver businessmen, but every individual was invited to share in the event. Counties from every corner of the state sent bands and floats, fire engines and rifle teams, as well as beauty queens.

Contests, races, parades, band concerts and balls were all a part of the celebration. The Denver Tramway Co. got 13 bands and staged a "trolley musicale." The electric company brought in 3,000 light bulbs from Menlo Park and strung them along 16th Street from Larimer Street to Broadway. Street booths were set up exhibiting various products.

Associated Cycle Clubs sponsored matched bicycle races and exhibitions, and held a parade. There were illegal prize fights and balloon ascensions, and bands of Indians camped around town. A group of Apaches had appointed 12 young men to act in a simulated stagecoach attack in City Park. They promised to stop short of scalping.

The guest of honor for that first Festival of Mountain and Plain was George A. Jackson, a Georgia mule skinner, who along with John Gregory, made the first big gold discoveries in Colorado. The queen of the festival was a Denver debutante, Sally Comberger.

Other young ladies from prominent families, who acted as queen either of the festival or of the grand ball over several years, included Louise Hughes, Mabel Gilluly, Katherine Foster Symes, Lillian Hurd and Blanche A. Wright.

The main viewpoint for parades and festival events was the square block bounded by East 16th and East Colfax avenues, Broadway and Lincoln Street (the block that now is the site of the RTD transfer station and office building). An outdoor ball also was held on the site as the climax of the festivities. By 1899, a grandstand seating 10,000 was erected on the block to accommodate festival viewers.

Jordan advised his Denver employers that a

grand ball was a necessity for such a festival, and the Slaves of the Silver Serpent Ball was born, inspired by Colorado's silver interests.

A debutante was chosen queen of the ball, and her identity was kept secret until the night of the celebration. The queen's bodyguard consisted of 100 carefully chosen young men from select circles, "mounted on handsomely caparisoned steeds."

The ball was preceded by a nighttime parade, illuminated by calcium and flaring gasoline torches. King Carnival led the parade in a coach drawn by six white horses. The keynote was sounded by a group of citizens, of whom only the legs were visible, as they pranced along the parade route covered by the giant framework of the Silver Serpent.

The Festival of Mountain and Plain became an annual event until 1900, when it was postponed until 1901 to make a really gigantic celebration for the first year of the new century. The Silver Serpent Ball, however, was held in 1900, in the capitol, with dancing in the corridors.

The festival of 1901 was not a success. Businessmen didn't support it, and attendance dropped.

A revival eventually was promoted and the final Festival of Mountain and Plain was held in 1912. Ruth Boettcher Humphreys was queen.

About 60,000 visitors came to Denver for the festival in 1912, and special events included a mock battle in City Park staged by state and federal troops.

One nighttime parade featured floats, each decorated with 500 to 1,000 lights. A staged fire at Colfax and Broadway was put out in spectacular style by the Denver Fire Department.

The grand finale was the casting of oil on the waters of City Park Lake, with fire set to the oil and a final bursting of explosives in the water.

The city-sponsored festival ended in 1912, due to lack of financial support.

In recent years the idea has been revived occasionally. For several years a Festival of Mountain and Plain was staged on the campus of Colorado Women's College. In 1983, the Festival of Mountain and Plain ... Taste of Colorado celebration started in Civic Center and has been continued annually. But there never has been anything to match the original Festival of Mountain and Plain.

October 3, 1982

Rocky Mountain News

Mrs. Elizabeth Graff Klein drove her friends in a float for the Festival of Mountain and Plain in the 1890s. It was known as the Mardi Gras of the West, and it's been revived in recent years.

The big snow of 1913

OLD-TIMERS who were in Denver nearly 70 years ago still talk about the "big snow" of 1913. A couple, perhaps reminded by the first snow flurries a few days ago, have asked us to refresh their memories of that historic storm.

The *Rocky Mountain News* on Dec. 2, 1913, reported:

"The curtain has risen on the first scene of the first act of the *Winter's Tale* featuring the shivery householder shoveling the sleet and snow from the sidewalk. ... The weatherman says Denver and the state will feel the grip of winter for several days."

Little did that long-ago reporter guess what an understatement that was. The curtain was going up all right — on a storm drama that lasted several days. From Dec. 1 through Dec. 5, 1913, 45.7 inches of snow fell on Denver, making it the biggest storm in the city and state in 28 years, since 1885.

(The Christmas Blizzard of 1982 — 40 days after this column orginally was printed — didn't come close, as far as total snow measurement goes. In the city limits, 24 inches of snow fell in 24 hours. But that was enough to set one record: It was the heaviest one-day accumulation since April 1885.)

Starting Dec. 1, 1913, snow fell intermittently for three days, piling up 8 inches. This snow lay on the ground, packed and icy, when the big storm started around 6 a.m. Dec. 4. Early-morning flurries had turned into a blizzard by midafternoon. During Dec. 4-5, 37.4 inches of snow fell on top of the 8 inches on the ground.

Streetcars, which were responsible for much of the city's transportation, were out of commission Dec. 4. The tieup began about 11:30 a.m., and by 5 p.m. every line in the city had stopped running. A number of cars were derailed. By noon Dec. 5, only sleighs and homemade wagon sleds remained serviceable.

On the first day, it became apparent that downtown workers would have little chance of getting home, if home was more than a few blocks away. Some businesses dismissed employees early.

Downtown department stores did not permit their female workers to go home. Daniels & Fisher rented the Claxton Hotel for its clerks, and Charles MacAllister Willcox, one of the store's executives, sent a 12-pound box of candy to them. Dinner and breakfast also were provided. The Denver Dry Goods Co. sent its female clerks to the Plaza Hotel and the Francestan. The telephone company billeted 300 female operators at the Auditorium Hotel.

The Denver Club, the Denver Athletic Club and the University Club were filled. The City Auditorium and the jail were used to shelter hundreds of men, women, and children.

Many people spent the night in Curtis Street movie houses. Downtown drugstores did a thriving business in toothbrushes and hairbrushes, and saloons had a field day.

The adventure was greeted with a certain joy of the unexpected and scores of parties flourished downtown that night. Telephone lines survived the storm, so that those stranded at work could telephone their worried families.

On the first day, taxicabs were rushed beyond capacity, and an extra 200 autos were pressed into service. It was estimated that cabs that day had carried nearly 4,000 people. By the next day, automobiles were "almost as useless as airships," according to one newspaper account. An effort was made to keep trolley tracks clear, but by the time one end was clear, the other was closed in. Horsedrawn vehicles made the best headway.

The storm's fury hit Denver, but the central part of the state also was affected severely. By Dec. 5, no trains were running in and out of Denver; no streetcars were operating; schools were closed; there were few deliveries, even of such necessities as coal; and mail was not getting in or out.

Every effort was made to deliver coal, which had to be delivered by four- and even six-horse teams, instead of the usual two, and loads were cut in half to facilitate delivery. Even then, many went without fuel.

With the weight of the snow, roofs of a number of buildings collapsed. Among these was the roof of Calvary Baptist Church at East 16th Avenue and Downing Street, which dropped into its basement.

The highway department and the Denver Tramway Co. marshaled all possible forces for snow removal. The highway department had 200 special "snowmen" and 65 horse teams on the payroll for snow removal. To this was added a specially built snowplow with 20 Army mules to pull it. This group worked throughout the nights clearing paths to outlying sections of the city.

In addition to its equipment, the city requisitioned 29 dump and four beet wagons from Fort Collins. It was reported that 600 to 800 wagon loads of snow were removed to clear one block.

John A. Beeler, general manager of the Denver Tramway Co., took personal command of the company's snow fighters, directing the removal at various locations. Nearly 1,000 men hired by the Tramway Co. were fighting the snow, and teams of horses pulling wagons dumped their loads of snow in Civic Center, making a mountain of snow. Even though men received only $2.50 and teams $5 per day for the work, clearing the snow cost the Tramway Co. $10,000 per day.

Where shovels were ineffective, workers used picks to dig snow and ice out of the streetcar tracks.

An interurban car with a party of six women, four children and two men was marooned near Golden and was rescued by 24 Colorado School of Mines students using shovels and burros. The rescue party dug through snow 4 to 12 feet deep.

At Monaco Parkway and East Colfax Avenue, according to the Dec. 6 *Rocky Mountain News*, a trolley car had been stranded for 2 days with a conductor and motorman aboard.

The second day of the storm, it was reported that Jay P. Treat, president of Colorado Woman's College, had succeeded in getting supplies to the college "where about 60 young women are still imprisoned."

Craig Colony, the tubercular sanitarium, was running out of coal, but coal in sacks was hauled 2 blocks on foot from the streetcar line.

On Dec. 7 the News reported:

"Through drifts of snow to their armpits in many instances, attaches of the outlying charitable institutions and hospitals fought their way to freedom yesterday and returned carrying provisions for the storm-beleaguered institutions."

Firefighting was another problem aggravated by the storm. Firemen wrenched fire extinguishers from trucks and traveled to the scene of several blazes on foot.

By Dec. 7, downtown streets had been cleared and the main tram lines were running. Coal deliveries, however, still were far behind, and it was estimated that many people would not receive fuel before Dec. 9.

Because many were running out of food, Mayor J.M. Perkins asked grocers to keep their stores open on Dec. 7 so householders could replenish their supplies. Wholesale houses spent the day trying to equip the stores for the additional business.

By Dec. 9, the city was almost back to normal.

Most necessary deliveries were being made, and schools, except Gilpin, had reopened. Gilpin remained closed because of the danger of snowslides from the roof.

In a few weeks the historic snow was gone, but it was never to be forgotten.

November 14, 1982

The readers said . . .

GEORGE H. Riggle of Denver was inspired to write after reading the column about the 1913 snowstorm.

"Indeed, I remember that big snow all too well," wrote Riggle. "I was 9 at the time, and living with my folks in north Denver at West 31st Avenue and Hooker Street. My brother and I were attending Boulevard School at (West) 23rd Avenue and Federal Boulevard at the time.

"The students were all sent home after the second day (Dec. 5, 1913) of the big snow. I can remember that the walks were all shoveled out way over our heads, and we had a ball building forts and tunneling into the deep snow.

"My father was stranded downtown the first night, but came home a couple of days later after working on a shoveling gang for the Denver Tramway Co.

"After about a week, things got back pretty much to normal except that it seemed to me that an awful lot of snow remained on the ground for a very long time . . .

"Two years later we moved to south Denver where I have lived ever since, with the exception of 4 years when I was overseas in India and Burma during World War II."

December 19, 1982

Rocky Mountain News

The Daniels & Fisher Tower on 16th Street stuck out of the storm during the big snow of 1913. Men could still cross Welton Street during the early hours of the storm that left 45.7 inches of snow.

Rocky Mountain News

The hero Bryan Untiedt was carried off the plane at Lamar where he and other children were hospitalized. When he recovered, he spent several days as a guest at the White House.

Bus tragedy made Colorado boy a hero

FEW events in Colorado history have garnered as many national headlines as the "Towner Bus Tragedy."

One of our readers has asked us to tell this story that started on the snowy day of March 26, 1931. And why not? It's a dramatic story, filled with pathos and pioneer pluck. The incident made a national hero of a 12-year-old schoolboy.

Early on that Thursday morning, Carl Miller, 33, was making his schoolbus rounds across the prairie of Colorado's southeastern plains, picking up children destined for the Pleasant Hill schoolhouse. The school was 10 miles south of Towner in Kiowa County, about 2 miles from the Kansas border and 24 miles north of Holly.

The *Rocky Mountain News* that day reported

that 76 mph winds were driving a storm from the Northwest with such violence that travel in eastern Colorado was virtually impossible.

As Miller and his load of 20 children approached Pleasant Hill, a blizzard was raging, making it difficult for him to hold his bus on the road. It was 9 a.m., and the teacher, Maude Moser, and principal, F.R. Freiday, decided it would be best to send the children home.

Realizing the danger of being on the prairie in a blizzard with a bus full of children, Miller protested, but he was persuaded to leave with his young passengers.

Visibility was zero as he put the bus in gear and drove out of the schoolyard. He had traveled about 7 miles when the storm became so bad he decided to turn back. He took a little-used road as a shortcut and had gone almost 5 miles when, unable to see the road, he drove into a ditch. He couldn't get the bus started again.

During the first few hours of being stranded, the children were cheerful, even gleeful over the unexpected turn of events. As time passed, they got cold, and then drowsy.

Fearing they would drop off into a never-ending sleep, Miller tried to keep them moving, telling them to stay awake and pray. At one point he lay on the floor at the front of the bus and told the children to huddle next to him to keep warm.

At 6 a.m. Friday, 21 hours after they got stuck, Miller set out afoot, hoping to find help. One of the children left behind was his daughter, Mary, 9, who was near death.

"God bless you, children," Miller said as he left. "We may never see each other again."

The driver's frozen body was found on Saturday in a wheat field, about 3 miles southeast of the bus.

When Miller left, one of the boys, 12-year-old Bryan Untiedt, took over, making the children march inside the bus, leading them in games and singing and giving some of his clothing to younger ones. Stories of his heroism were told later by surviving children.

When rescue finally came, Bryan was found swinging the arms of a younger child. His own hands and feet were frozen.

Rocky Mountain News

Bryan Untiedt carried his box camera as he toured Washington on his visit to the president.

Rocky Mountain News

Bryan Untiedt as an adult. He became a contractor and he died in Aurora in 1977, age 59.

At about 6:30 p.m. Friday, almost 33 hours after the bus was stranded, help arrived. The search had been hampered because the bus was off the main highway, not where rescuers were looking for it. H.A. Untiedt, father of four children on the bus, and Dave Stonebreaker, who had two daughters aboard, discovered the bus.

The rescuers found the children huddled in the front of the vehicle because the rear was filled with snow. Three children — Robert Brown, 11, Louise Stonebreaker, 14, and Kenneth Johnson, 9 — were dead. Bryan asked to be the last to leave the bus. When he finally was lifted out, he collapsed. He remained unconscious for three hours.

The children were moved by horse and wagon to the Andrew Reinert farmhouse only half a mile away. The storm had blotted out the sight of the house, and no one had known that warmth and food were so near. At the farm, Orlo Untiedt, 7, Bryan's brother, and Mary Miller, 9, the driver's daughter, soon died.

After the children were located, two planes were sent to carry them to the hospital at Lamar. One, a Fokker cabin plane, was owned by Denver socialite Al Humphreys and flown by Eddie Brooks.

As the stories of dedication and bravery filtered out to the world, Bryan Untiedt became a national hero.

On April 29, 1931, Bryan Untiedt went to the White House at the invitation of President Herbert Hoover. Two Secret Service agents escorted him to Washington, and he stayed several days with the Hoovers.

The young hero left high school after 2 years to help his family earn a living during the days of the dust storms. During World War II he served 2½ years in the Navy Seabees. After the war he became a partner in the Denver contracting firm of Untiedt and Forsberg.

He died in Aurora in 1977 at age 59.

A granite monument in March 1962 was placed alongside the gravel road where the schoolbus was stalled during the blizzard. Money for the monument was raised by the Lions Clubs of Towner and Holly.

December 5, 1982

The readers said . . .

SOME interesting comments from Virgil Untiedt of Commerce City followed our Dec. 5, 1982, column on the Towner Bus Tragedy of 1931, in which five children and the bus driver died in a blizzard near Towner on Colorado's eastern plains.

Untiedt is a brother of the late Bryan Untiedt, the 12-year-old hero of the tragedy. Bryan's quick thinking and unselfish acts brought him national recognition.

"Who could ever forget that storm?" said Untiedt, a retired truck-transport driver. "I had another brother, Orlo Untiedt, only 7, who died when the school bus was stranded. I was 11 at the time. I would have been on the bus that day except that I stayed home from school because I had tonsillitis."

After news of the tragedy and Bryan's heroism had gone around the world, all sorts of unusual attention was lavished on Bryan and the others, Untiedt said.

"Our whole family was brought to Denver, and housed in the Brown Palace Hotel for a week," he recalled. "Denver Buick furnished cars and drivers to take us around town, and we ate in a different place every day."

One of the restaurants where they dined was McVittie's.

"The owner's daughter, who was about our age, presented each of us with a nice little watch engraved on the back with our names, and 'from June McVittie,' " Untiedt said. *"The Denver Post gave each survivor a commemorative gold medal."*

Bryan, as we've chronicled before, went to Washington to spend several days with President Hoover and his family.

"Over the years, as I would sign in at hotels or motels while I was in the trucking business, people would read my name and immediately inquire if I knew anything about the bus tragedy," Untiedt said. "Our name is unusual and it became synonymous with the tragedy because of Bryan."

A retired United Airlines pilot, J.D. Hutchinson of Evergreen, also wrote us about the Towner tragedy. He said:

"I sent your article on the Towner tragedy to Eddie Brooks, a famous aviator of the 1920s in Colorado. He now lives with his wife, Nelle, in Balboa, Calif. I have been corresponding with him on some aviation historical material.

"Brooks was Albert E. Humphreys' personal pilot in a big, expensive Fokker cabin airplane, probably the largest plane in this part of the country at that time, 1928-31. Most of the airplanes, (there weren't many then) were the standard, small two-seater World War I type, like the popular Eaglerock."

The plane, owned by Humphreys and flown by Brooks, was one of two that went to the rescue of the youngsters trapped in the stranded bus, flying them to hospitals. In his letter to Hutchinson, Brooks wrote:

"On the morning of March 26, 1931, I was flying for Al Humphreys. I got a call to see if I could go to Towner and get the kids to the hospital at Lamar.

"While we were warming up the Fokker, *The Denver Post* sent out a reporter and photographer. Then two Western Airlines mechanics wearing flying suits and boots and carrying shovels showed up to go along and help out, as we didn't know what we would find.

"We were able to land at the farmhouse where the children had been taken and loaded up the worst cases, about six at a time, to take to the hospital. The parents raised the question of expense, as they were in sad financial condition. The *Post* reporter assured them that the *Post* had made all the hospital arrangements and would pay all expenses.

"We made two trips, and by then some of the local pilots had heard about it, and they finished up the transportation of the last children and the families, and we headed for home. . . . We didn't know the public impact until the papers came out the next day.

"I was later awarded a plaque and $100 by one of the news services for the best story of the year. I have long since lost the plaque and spent the $100."

March 6, 1983

Mint robber tripped on hollow-leg scheme

EARLY in 1920, it was discovered that the Denver Mint didn't have all the gold it should have. Somehow, gold bullion was disappearing. No one knew how it was vanishing or where it was going.

Nothing was said to the employees, but one night a worker in the mint refinery saw Orville Harrington, a longtime and trusted employee, slip a gold bar off a tray. Harrington, however, returned the bar to the tray a few minutes later.

But the other employee reported the incident, and the Denver office of the Secret Service set a watch on Harrington's modest house at 1485 S. University Blvd.

A news story of two female accident victims who were having such a hilarious time as patients in a Colorado Springs hospital until marijuana was discovered hidden in one woman's wooden leg reminded Helen Black of Denver of the long-ago mint robbery.

At the time of the robbery, Black was a reporter at the *Rocky Mountain News*, assigned to cover the incident.

The Secret Service operative who was watching Harrington's home reported that each evening after work, Harrington went to his back yard, carrying a shovel.

On Feb. 5, 1920, before Harrington reported for work, a piece of gold valued at $1,400 was placed near his work area. When Harrington finished work at 11:30 p.m., the gold was missing. Rowland K. Goddard, director of the Secret Service in Denver, accompanied by another agent, accosted Harrington at 15th Street and Court Place, as he waited for a streetcar.

The Secret Service men escorted Harrington back to the mint and searched him. They found the gold in his vest pocket. Harrington walked with a peculiar limp, and because of this, the sag in his vest went undetected as he passed through inspection.

Before the investigation was finished, it was revealed $81,400 was missing from the mint.

Rocky Mountain News

Orville Harrington stole gold from the Denver Mint by stashing it in this wooden leg.

Harrington was taken to his home where he disclosed the hiding places of the bullion. Most of the gold was found hidden behind bricks that were removed, then replaced, in a basement wall.

After he stored what he could in the basement, Harrington turned to the back yard. More gold was found hidden under the cement walk.

Although he was trapped with the gold in his vest, Harrington ordinarily concealed his valuable loot more ingeniously.

When he was hunting as a teen-ager, a gun exploded and shattered his hip. The sciatic nerve, damaged in the accident, pained him so much, he said, that he had three toes amputated and then his foot and part of his leg.

He was fitted with an artificial leg and foot. Through the years, he underwent several operations. During one recovery period, he met a nurse, Lydia Melton, who became his wife.

In January 1920, when he began his plan to steal thousands from the Denver Mint, Harrington stowed most of the loot in his hollow artificial leg. The bullion he took was in anodes, hardened into bars about 7-by-1-by-3½ inches. One anode was a perfect fit for his hollow leg. Fifty-three anodes were taken, most of them carried out one at a time in the artificial limb.

Harrington was a surprising candidate for theft. He was an honor graduate of the Colorado School of Mines, class of 1898; belonged to a fraternity; and was manager and editor of the college magazine. He was a trusted employee of the mint for years and nightly handled gold valued at from $1 million to $5 million.

He was regarded as a family man. He and his wife had done most of the building of their home, and their 10 lots of land were a showplace of fruit trees, a vegetable garden and an outstanding flower garden. Harrington did most of the yard work and took great pride in it.

At the time Harrington was arrested, the couple had a 4-year-old daughter and an 11-month-old son. The infant was ill with pneumonia.

Harrington's salary was $4 a shift, and his wife blamed the frustration of the job for his actions. In a brief interview with Black the day after the robbery, Lydia Harrington said because of the limitations of his wooden leg her husband could not obtain work as a mining engineer and never could command the salary "his brains and education entitled him to."

He once took a 2-year leave of absence from the mint and worked in mining in South America and Cuba. They liked Cuba, Lydia Harrington said, and it was their hope to return someday.

Harrington's wife had no knowledge of the thefts and assumed Harrington's forays into the basement and the back yard were simply a part of the puttering he did around the house.

Harrington later revealed his scheme to get rid of the stolen gold was to lease an abandoned mine in the Cripple Creek area, melt down the gold with a mixture of native metals and gradually sell it back to the mint as newly mined.

On May 12, 1920, Harrington pleaded guilty to a charge of embezzlement before Judge Robert E. Lewis in Federal District Court. Despite his attorney's plea for leniency, Harrington was sentenced to serve 10 years in the Federal Penitentiary at Leavenworth, Kan.

He was paroled 3½ years later and got a job with the city of Denver, overseeing street-paving crews.

Three years later, when he was 50 and apparently rankling over a fate that had given him a lesser station in life than he thought he deserved, Harrington gave up his job and walked out on his wife and children. He told his wife he was going to Arizona where there were better work opportunities. A few weeks later, she received reports of him in Denver, but the family never was reunited.

Left with no income and little money, Lydia Harrington rented her home and lived in the well-equipped chicken coop in the back yard. She put her children in an orphanage and went to work as a governess.

Some years later, it was reported that Harrington died at the home of a sister in New York.

December 26, 1982

Chapter 3

'Rattlesnake Kate' earned her name

LULA Bayles of Denver writes that she enjoyed the story of the Towner bus tragedy that appeared in *Rocky Mountain Memories.*

"It reminded me of some of my own childhood experiences in the snow," she said.

"When we lived at Fort Lupton, my brother and I went to school in Vollmer, 3 miles away. On bad, snowy days, my mother would wrap our legs in newspapers, and we would ride an old, sway-backed, white horse named Walt to school. Walt would wait at school all day, to take us home in the late afternoon.

"Now I have a question I hope you can answer for me. Do you know anything about a woman called 'Rattlesnake Kate'? I think she lived around Melvin in the mid-1920s. I remember my parents telling of her bravery."

Dear Mrs. Bayles:

"Rattlesnake Kate" earned her name the hard way on Oct. 28, 1925. Kate's real name was Katherine Slaughterback., She homesteaded 640 acres of dry land in 1923 in the Four Way area east of Ione, but as the years passed, pieces were lost to hard times and taxes until she had just 80 acres left.

There was a lake on Kate's property, and on the fateful day, she heard duck hunters' guns. She knew there probably would be wounded ducks in the area, so she saddled her horse, put her 3-year-old son, Ernie, in front of her on the horse, and went out to look for duck for dinner. As usual, she carried her rifle.

As she went to open the gate to the pond, she saw a rattlesnake. She shot its head off. Then there were three more. She killed them also.

The rustling of rattlers grew louder, and Kate found herself surrounded by nearly 2 dozen snakes. She took a stake off a "No Hunting" sign and started clubbing them.

More snakes appeared from all directions, and Kate kept flailing away. She kept at the exhausting job for nearly 2 hours until she killed all the snakes. While Kate was killing the rattlers, Ernie cried and the horse trembled.

Reporters who were called to the scene strung the snakes along a fence and counted 140. Kate later skinned the snakes and pieced them together to make a dress. The last I heard, the dress was in the Greeley Municipal Museum.

Kate lived for years in a converted chicken coop. But in 1952, she moved a 4-room shack onto her property and began renovating it. She did the roofing, made general carpentry repairs and poured concrete. She hoped to have the job done early in February 1957.

While she did this construction work, she barely subsisted. She had goats and chickens that supplied her with protein and her garden gave her fresh vegetables. She raised hay for her livestock and corn to sell.

She weighed 97 pounds, and regularly lifted bales of hay weighing 90 pounds when she was past 60.

"I'm not lonely," she said in an interview. "I have a lot of people who drop in."

Kate died in October 1969 at Weld County Hospital. She was 75.

January 9, 1983

Rocky Mountain News

Katherine Slaughterback was a homesteader who once went for ducks, but found snakes.

Mary Lathrop thrived as a woman of firsts

A longtime Denver lawyer, Estelle Hadley, has a question.

"I read and appreciated your story of the Towner bus tragedy," writes Hadley. "I recall that the night before the bus got stranded, my husband and I were on our way from our law offices in the Equitable Building to our home near Golden, about midnight. The wind was so strong it shook our car as we were crossing the Colfax viaduct. The next morning the blizzard hit Towner.

"Since you invite historical questions, I have one. Will you dig into the career of Mary Lathrop? She was practicing law when I was in law school in the late 1920s."

Dear Mrs. Hadley:

It happens that I do know of Mary Lathrop, but not in the way you might think. I first heard of her through my grandmother, who was Lathrop's neighbor when she lived in a block of terraces at 522 E. 18th Ave. in Denver.

Mary Florence Lathrop was an unusual character for her time. She had many "firsts" to her credit — first woman to start a law practice in Denver, first female member of the Colorado Bar Association, first female member of the Denver Bar Association, and, in 1918, the first woman admitted to membership in the American Bar Association.

In 1898, she became the first woman admitted to the U.S. Courts of Colorado, and she was the first woman to argue a case before the Supreme Court of Colorado. The case that came before the Colorado Supreme Court involved the George W. Clayton will, in which $2.5 million was left to establish a college for orphan boys.

The will was attacked by T.S. Clayton. But the case, which was won by Lathrop, resulted in the law of charitable bequests in Colorado. With diligent research, Lathrop built her winning case on a regulation dating from the time Colorado was a part of the Louisiana Purchase.

Lathrop, who was 5 feet tall and weighed about 100 pounds, worked mainly in probate and real-estate law. From the start of her career, she refused to handle divorce cases. She was outspoken and often militant, and resented being called a "woman lawyer."

"I'm either a lawyer or I'm not," she told people who made such a remark. "Don't drag my being a woman into it."

Lathrop was born in Philadelphia on Dec. 10, 1865.

Rocky Mountain News

Mary Lathrop began her law career at age 31 after graduating from the University of Denver.

She started a professional career as a newspaperwoman on the *Philadelphia Press* when she was 19.

During the year she worked on the newspaper, she specialized in industrial stories. Through her articles on the conditions in fabric mills in Pennsylvania, she promoted child-labor laws in the state in 1884.

Impressed with her work, Samuel S. McClure, head of the McClure Syndicate, persuaded her to leave the *Press* and work for him. Then came a series of adventures most modern-day reporters never experience.

Lathrop was sent West, where she traveled in buckboards and stagecoaches to cover stories. She reported on Indian troubles, cattle wars and gold discoveries. She was sent to cover a riot in Cripple Creek when troublemakers threatened to lynch any newspaperman.

She went to San Francisco to report on a race war involving attacks on Chinese laborers and later received a decoration from the Chinese government for helping to end the trouble. She was sent to China when it was considered unsafe for a woman to travel there alone.

Her unflagging pace, however, affected her health. On doctor's orders, she came to live in Colorado when she contracted tuberculosis after a bout with double pneumonia.

In Colorado she decided on a change of career and studied law. She received her bachelor of law degree from the University of Denver in 1896, when she was 31. She had finished the prescribed 3-year course in 18 months, and she did it with a record-setting grade average of 96.

In those early years, men in the profession did not welcome her, she recalled later. During the first 10 years she practiced she said, male attorneys often referred to her as "that damn woman."

One counsel refused to try a case because his opponent was a woman. Lathrop promptly asked for a judgment by default and was granted it.

Always a patriot, she was active in World War I bond drives and the State Speakers Bureau. With the coming of World War II, she became the darling of many soldiers through her custom of entertaining at least a dozen soldiers at dinner every Saturday in the Cosmopolitan Hotel. Special parties on Thanksgiving, Christmas and the Fourth of July saw the number expanded to 100.

"I don't bother with officers," she said. "I have a high opinion of the GI." At the end of the war, it was estimated she had entertained about 14,000 soldiers. For this, the Veterans of Foreign Wars honored her with the Distinguished Citizenship Medal.

In 1940, Lathrop was named "Woman of the Year" by the Business and Professional Women's Club, and in 1946, she was named Denver's First Lady of the Year by Beta Sigma Phi women's organization. The University of Denver awarded her an honorary doctorate in law, as well as its Founders Day Medal.

When she died in 1951, Mary Lathrop left a substantial estate, and valuable changes in Colorado's probate laws, which she had fought to have enacted.

January 23, 1983

Political mockery
stared out of painting

AN intriguing portrait of Denver's City Council painted in the 1930s is the subject of a letter from J.R. of Denver. She writes:

"In the late 1930s, I worked at the Umbrella Shop, located at 515 15th St. It was owned by Mr. and Mrs. William Capella. Next door to us was Harry's Florist, and beyond that was the Colorado Art Shop.

"I am wondering what happened to a large picture which was displayed in the art shop window. The picture had (members of) the city council hanging by strings around their necks,

From left: H.W. Risley, A.A. Blakley, H. Rosenthal, L. Straub, C.P. Harrington; O.N. Anderson, C.M. Stafford, H.N. Webster, W. Knight. Clerk Georgia Cox is at doorway; Mayor Stapleton wears wings.

and a sign said: 'This picture is worth $10,000.' The city taxed the artist on the $10,000, and there was quite a row about it in the papers.

"I am wondering what happened to that painting. Can you tell me?"

Once again our readers must come to the rescue. I have been unable to find the original painting or even to locate a photocopy of it.

But let me tell you a little about it. The second coming of Rembrandt couldn't have caused much more hullabaloo than that picture.

The artist was Donald I. Griffith, a native of Jamestown, N.Y., who had studied at the Cleveland School of Art where he won several awards in painting and sculpture. One of his Denver works, begun in 1936 as a Works Progress Administration art project, was the mural for the clinical amphitheater of University Hospital, then Colorado General.

The big to-do started Aug. 26, 1938, when the *Rocky Mountain News* printed an article that began:

"The most costly painting currently offered for sale in Denver hangs in the window of a 15th Street art shop ... priced at $10,000."

According to the *News,* the painting was a satirical study of Denver's nine city councilmen and the mayor, as they were seen in the unflattering eyes of the artist. Councilmen pictured were Harry W. Risley; A.A. Blakley, president; Harry Rosenthal; Louis Straub; C. Paul Harrington; Oskar N. Anderson; C.M. Stafford; Harold N. Webster; and William Knight. Benjamin F. Stapleton was mayor.

Clerk Georgia E. Cox was shown in the background of the council chambers, and the head of the mayor was depicted flying down to replace the eagle on the medallion hanging behind the council president. Councilmen were in various unflattering poses. Anderson and Stafford were shown only as heads hanging by strings.

The trouble, the *News* said, began several years before, with the death of Vaso L. Chucovich, Denver gambling figure. Chucovich, a great admirer of the late Mayor Robert W. Speer, left $10,000 in his will to be used for a memorial to Speer.

Chucovich's estate executors, two nephews,

first offered the commission to a Yugoslavian sculptor. Public protest about allowing the money to leave the country changed that, and the executors invited 30 sculptors to submit models. Griffith was among the 14 who accepted.

"The public was never permitted to see the ... sculptural ideas submitted," charged Griffith. "A packed committee of judges awarded the job to Arnold Ronnebeck, a Denver sculptor.

"We knew it was a cut-and-dried deal and appealed to the council to take a hand to ensure fair play. President Risley said none of the models submitted were any good, and eventually Ronnebeck withdrew his."

About this time, Griffith conceived his idea of a painting to be called "The City Council," and persuaded the unsuspecting council members to pose for sketches.

Griffith priced the painting with the announcement that he usually charged $1,500 for a portrait, but felt $10,000 was appropriate for the painting with the mayor and nine councilmen.

On Aug. 29, 1938, the *News* said, "Council kicked the artist in the pocketbook for his audacity." It passed a resolution calling on Frank E. Wilson, manager of revenue, to assess the painting on the basis of Griffith's $10,000 evaluation.

The manager of revenue, however, ruled that it was too late that year to tax the painting. That apparently ended the matter, and no more was said about it.

Now we'd like to know what happened to the painting.

If someone can help us locate the original or a good copy of it, we would like to publish it.

February 6, 1983

The readers said . . .

WE really doubted that we'd locate a copy of the satirical painting of the Denver City Council that created such a stir when Donald I. Griffith painted it in 1938. But two readers telephoned to say they have copies of it, autographed by the artist.

And then we got a letter from Griffith himself. He's living in Las Vegas, Nev., and may be reached at 205 E. Harmon Ave., Las Vegas 89109.

To recap the story, Griffith made the unflattering painting of the council after he had failed to get a commission to do a memorial to Mayor Robert W. Speer. The job went instead to Arnold Ronnebeck, a sculptor, and Griffith retaliated with the painting.

The artist put a $10,000 valuation on the painting, and city council tried to have it taxed $385 on that price, but the matter was postponed.

Griffith sent along a photo of the painting, with this letter:

"Regarding the case of the missing painting: The original which Mrs. J.R. asked about is 3-by-4 feet, oil on canvas. I remember her very well next door in the Umbrella Shop. The painting has hung in my office all these years and is of continual interest to those who see it.

"You have a rare gift for phrasing — 'the second coming of Rembrandt' — is a classic. His knock-down and drag-out over his painting, 'The Night Watch,' is a monument to man's injured vanity. My controversy with the city council ended after the municipal election in 1939. I ran against Lou Straub. He was re-elected.

"The matter of the memorial to Mayor Speer ended when the bequest was used toward building a children's wing to Denver General Hospital.

"As to the artist who 'disappeared':

"After Pearl Harbor in 1941, I worked as an engineer for the Rocky Mountain Arsenal, Climax Molybdenum, Silver Engineering and Stearns-Roger. I established the American Engineering Co. of Colorado in 1944, became a registered engineer in 1946 and a licensed architect in 1959.

"Because of the failing health of my wife, Gladys, we moved to Las Vegas in 1960, and I bcame a Nevada resident in 1966. I still paint and do sculpture in silver and bronze. I exhibit frequently in Las Vegas Art Museum shows and am continuing my architectural practice in Denver.

"Thank you for refreshing a memory. No one was really damaged by my painting. Some feel-

ings of pride were hurt — maybe. At the time, due to the depressed conditions of the '30s, everyone packed a short fuse and did not hesitate to light it.

"The day the *Rocky Mountain News* flashed the story on the front page, Aug. 16, 1938, crowds blocked traffic (streetcars and all) in front of the Colorado Art Shop on 15th Street, where the painting hung in the window."

Many thanks to Griffith for writing. It's a treat to hear the end of the story.

Our first telephone call concerning the painting came from Ben Wayne of 1285 Albion St., a retired druggist, who said Griffith was a regular customer when Wayne ran a drugstore at 17th and Lawrence streets. He offered to let us reproduce a copy of the painting, which was autographed by Griffith.

Our second caller with a photo of the painting was Anne Pace of 13661 E. Marina Drive, Aurora. Pace got the picture from her mother-in-law, Lea Robinson, to whom the artist gave it.

A third call came from Fred Bartlett of 800 Washington St., retired director of the Fine Arts Center in Colorado Springs. Bartlett said:

"I was working at the Denver Art Museum at the time all the controversy arose over the awarding of the bequest to create a memorial to the late Mayor Robert W. Speer. The selection was in the hands of the Denver Art Commission, of which Ann Evans was a member.

"Because Vaso L. Chucovich, donor of the money for the memorial, was Yugoslavian, first choice for creating the memorial went to Ivan Mestrovic, a world-famous Yugoslavian sculptor. Everyone on the committee was happy with the choice, but then a hassle started about keeping the money at home and employing an American sculptor.

"The leader in this dispute was Arnold Ronnebeck. You said the award later went to Ronnebeck. That is a mistake. The job of creating the Speer Memorial went to his wife, Louise Emerson Ronnebeck. The outcome was that she did a fresco mural for the new children's wing of Denver General Hospital."

February 20, 1983

And then . . . the deed was done

IN the early days of the West, legal hangings took place in public, on almost any handy tree. A holiday air usually marked such events as scores of people turned out for the festivities.

Andrew Koch of Lakewood has asked *Rocky Mountain Memories* for a story of the last public hanging in Denver.

"My grandfather mentioned this," he said, "but I don't know any of the details. He thought it was downtown, somewhere near the present location of the Denver Mint."

Dear Mr. Koch:

The crime that preceded the last public hanging in Denver was the fatal shooting of a horse-car driver, Joseph Whitnah, on the night of May 19, 1886. Sam Howe, a veteran Denver detective, recalled the killing in a newspaper article a few years later:

"At first, the crime was a great mystery," Howe recounted. "Whitnah guided the horse and streetcar onto the turntable at Colfax and Broadway around 10 p.m. and was found there by police about 30 minutes later, shot through the heart.

"F.O. Peterson, a blacksmith who heard the shots and said he saw a man running away from the car, was first arrested . . . but was released a short time later."

Whitnah was described as a cleancut young man of excellent reputation, whose wife was expecting their first child. Robbery was a possible motive, but the cash box on the streetcar had not been taken.

The murder was solved when Larry Foutz told police two "toughs" had asked him to help them rob a streetcar driver. He got too drunk to accompany them, he said. They later told Foutz they had fired at Whitnah when he didn't obey their order to throw up his hands, and he began to scream. After the shooting they ran, without searching for the cash box.

The killers identified by Foutz were Andrew Green and John Withers. Withers confessed to the crime, turned state's evidence and was sentenced to life in the Colorado state penitentiary. Green was arrested and held for trial.

Reports of the crime aroused great feeling in Denver and, on May 26, 1886, a lynch mob stormed the county jail where Green was held. He was spared, thanks to quick action by Sheriff Frederick Cramer and his deputies. But the danger of a lynching resulted in the calling of a special grand jury, which set a date for a speedy trial.

A jury found Green guilty of first-degree murder on June 25, 1886. His execution by hanging was scheduled for July 27.

The day before the execution, a *Rocky Mountain News* reporter interviewed Green at length, at the doomed man's request. Green said he had been born June 15, 1862, on a farm 9 miles from Lexington, Ky. As a boy, he had shot, but not killed, his father, he said, because his father was going to beat him. He had stolen money to buy the gun. As he grew up, he committed other crimes and had served time in prison.

Green topped off his story by saying he felt the Denver judge had been prejudiced by public opinion and had railroaded the trial. His last request was for a copy of the *News* containing his interview.

The hanging, with all the elements of a vaudeville show, started at 1 p.m. A crude scaffold, with a platform but no steps, had been erected along Cherry Creek "midway between the Broadway and Colfax bridges."

A firsthand account of the event appears in a book by L. Vernon Briggs, *Arizona and New Mexico, 1882, California 1886.* Briggs was on his way from Boston to California in 1886 when he stopped in Denver. On the morning of July 27, he wrote, he found "a general appearance of a holiday in Denver."

"Shops were closed, and men and women,

babes in arms and children all were hurrying to Cherry Creek Bottom." Briggs said he found a crowd of 15,000 to 20,000 waiting to see the hanging.

"Many of the women present were well-dressed and looked like ladies," Briggs continued. "All the small boys in town appeared to be there."

When Green stepped lightly onto the scaffold, Sheriff Cramer read the death warrant. Then the Rev. William Gray of Zion Baptist Church, which Green occasionally had attended, read several passages from the Bible.

A choir from Zion Baptist surrounded the scaffold and sang several hymns, including *Why Not Tonight?* and *Nearer My God to Thee.* The prisoner joined in the singing.

At last, Green was called upon for his final words. He stepped forward to unroll a sheaf of papers and read his life's story, which he had been writing for several days. The reading took about 20 minutes and, in it, Green confessed his crime, stating that he was guilty of murder, but not in the first degree.

He warned youths to avoid bad company, adding, "Whiskey and such companions as him, that hang around the GAR Saloon, are the reason I stand on the gows today."

At the end of the speech, according to Briggs, the sheriff put a cap over Green's face and adjusted the rope. The prisoner all the while continued singing with the choir.

"At last he called out, 'Farewell, everybody!' " Briggs wrote, "and the rope was cut . . . releasing a weight which jerked him into the air."

That was the end of such barbarism in Denver. Future executions took place in penal institutions, out of public view.

May 1, 1983

Vigilantes burned ugly mark on history

A reader, J.W.B. of Denver, asked about a Colorado criminal who was burned at the stake.

"My mother told me a little of this story," he wrote. "Apparently a young black man was burned at the stake by a vigilante committee after he attacked a white girl. But I don't know where or when this took place. As far as I've heard, it was a unique incident in Colorado history. Do you know the story?"

Dear J.W.B.:

For many years, a blackened piece of railroad iron, which had been hammered firmly into the ground, stood on the prairie near Limon, a grim and grisly reminder of a dark page of western history.

The story began on the afternoon of Nov. 8, 1900, when 12-year-old Louise Frost did not return to her ranch home from school in Limon a few miles away. When the horse she had been driving came in alone pulling Louise's little cart, her father, John W. Frost, a widely known Lincoln County sheepman, led a search for the girl. She last had been seen at the Limon post office, where she had picked up a few letters and periodicals addressed to her family.

A short time later the battered child was found lying in the woods near Lake Siding, 14 miles west of Hugo, some distance from the road. She had been kicked and clubbed and her body was covered with knife wounds. Her skull was fractured. She was alive when searchers found her, but she died at midnight, never able to describe her attacker.

The cruel crime aroused the public throughout the state and even the nation. Bloodhounds were brought in from Cañon City, and riders on horseback combed the countryside looking for clues. Sheriff John W. Freeman was joined by 50 to 100 men looking for the "fiend."

"Mob mania," as one newspaper described it, gripped Denver and surrounding counties. A law providing for capital punishment had been re pealed in 1897, but men standing in knots on street corners decided that the killer, when found, must be lynched.

Eventually, a bloodstained handkerchief and a pocketknife found near the scene led investigators to a black family named Porter who lived in a boxcar near Limon. The father, Preston Porter Sr., worked for the railroad. He and his two teenage sons, Preston Porter Jr. and Arthur, were arrested in Denver by police Capt. Hamilton Armstrong 2 nights after the killing.

Suspicion was directed mainly at the two youths, who several years before had been sentenced to the Kansas State Reformatory for an attack on a white girl. Finally, it was decided that Preston Jr. was the killer. For one thing, his shoes fit footprints found at the scene of the slaying.

After hours of grilling by the police, Preston Porter Jr. screamed, "I did it."

News of the confession spread rapidly over the Colorado prairie.

That night, Lincoln County ranchers met at Limon and formed a vigilante committee. Meanwhile, in Denver, hundreds surrounded the jail at 14th and Larimer streets, and it appeared that the Lincoln County men might never get a chance to lynch Porter.

Gov. Charles S. Thomas tried to reason with the mob, saying that Porter should have a proper trial, but added he doubted that he would.

No mention ever was made, however, of calling out the state militia to protect the prisoner.

Authorities hoped to hold Porter in jail in Arapahoe County instead of returning him to Lincoln County. However, a group of men headed by William Clifford, a rancher, visited Denver, and Clifford told authorities:

"If you do not bring that black brute back to the county in which he committed the crime, we will bring an army of men with Winchesters to

The *Denver Times* told the story of the lynching of Preston Porter Jr. in 1900 with 3-inch-high head-lines printed in red ink. The victim was called John Porter in some news accounts.

Denver, and we will kill all resistance and batter the jails to dust."

A short time later, it was decided that Porter would be returned. Sheriff Freeman asked for a chance to get the youth into jail at Hugo. "And then my duty as an officer is done," he said.

On the night of Nov. 15, a vigilante committee of about 100 men met in the Knights of Pythias Hall at Limon, preparing to avenge the death of Louise Frost. They were reported to be respected citizens of four counties.

Reporters were invited to attend the meeting as long as they did not use names in their articles. At the meeting, they decided that Porter should be hanged on the Rock Island Bridge, spanning the Big Sandy River.

Freeman left Denver with the prisoner in a buggy at 11:45 a.m. Nov. 16, and drove to Magnolia Station, 11 miles east of Denver. There the pair boarded a Union Pacific train for Hugo, where Porter was to be jailed.

The vigilantes, however, were determined that Porter never would reach his destination. Every passenger train was stopped and searched at Limon. When the train with Porter aboard was found, several men smashed open the locked door into the car holding him, overpowered the sheriff and seized the prisoner.

The sheriff said later: "I did not feel like killing someone to defend Porter, who was sure to be hanged anyway."

The vigilantes threw a noose over Porter's head as he screamed: "Don't take me," and others held his feet as he was carried from the train at Lake Siding. He was only about 5 feet tall and weighed less than 100 pounds.

The prisoner, with the rope around his neck, was marched 1½ miles along a dusty road to the spot of Louise's death, still marked by bloodstains. As he walked, he tore pages from a Bible he had been reading and distributed them to souvenir hunters.

At the scene of the slaying, the vigilantes debated nearly 2 hours whether to hang the youth or burn him at the stake. Some wanted to first mutilate him.

Louise's father objected to mutilation but demanded that Porter be burned.

A railroad iron was driven into the ground, and the men spread out to gather wood to pile around it. Oil was poured over the wood, and chains were brought to fasten Porter to the rail.

It was nearly 6 p.m., almost dark, when the chain was wrapped around the accused youth's feet and lifted to go around his chest and fasten him to the rail. The dead girl's father was invited to light the wood. As he picked up a brand and approached the stake, Frost said:

"Gentlemen, I can touch this match without a shake of my hand." A dozen others helped him light other sections of the wood.

One newspaper reported that hundreds came to the execution, and " . . . it was a holiday for five counties." An enterprising telegrapher had set up a temporary station by tapping in on a telephone pole, and the dots and dashes of his message provided an undercurrent of the event.

As the flames reached him, the prisoner screamed and pleaded for someone to shoot him. One man stepped forward to do it, but was stopped.

"Let him take his time dying," called someone from the crowd.

Porter stopped screaming and probably died in about 10 minutes, but the onlookers waited until only a few charred bones were left. These bones later were put in a box and buried on the spot. The crowd repaired to local restaurants and taverns, which did a big business that night.

The next morning's *Denver Times'* banner headline screamed, "Death in Flames," in red letters 3 inches high, bordered with a drawing of flames.

The vigilante action aroused as much public distaste as the crime that precipitated it. The following Sunday, ministers around the nation spoke against it in their sermons.

The governor ordered an assistant district attorney in Arapahoe County to take action against the men who had burned Porter, but no one seemed to know who they were.

The story of the lynching of Preston Porter, Jr., also is included in *Where the Wagons Rolled*, a Lincoln County history written by Mary Liz Owen and Dale Cooley.

June 12, 1983

Woodbury built a mansion serene

ONE of the big rewards of this column is the letters from readers with some great memories.

Lorna M. Shire of Wheat Ridge wrote:

"The Victorian house referred to in your article June 2, 1983, about the Zang Brewing Co. was not the *Brewmeister's* house. That house was built for Elizabeth Zang, as a bride, by her father, Philip Zang. It was not a house, but a lesser mansion.

"It was across the street from the mansion of Philip A. Zang, and quite beautiful originally. Not as pretentious as the big mansion, but tastefully and beautifully appointed. Quiet and serene.

"The present Zang Brewing Co. Restaurant was a rundown corner bar for all kinds of men. It was called the Rocky Mountain Bar.

"You see, I grew up in the Zang mansion. I played in every part of it, from the cellar to the garret. It was in its original state when my grandmother, Mary Jane Moffitt, bought it. She died there in 1944.

"She also bought the mansion across the street and a small house to the north of the big mansion. She owned more than half a block there.

"My father took it over when my grandmother died. Dad sold the main mansion to the state so the Valley Highway (Interstate 25) could run through there.

"I was there the night the brewery burned. All hands were on deck because cinders as large as plates were landing on the roof, ground, everywhere. Dad and grandfather were on the roof with garden hoses. The brewery fire started because a florist was storing baby's breath in there, and some transient set fire to it.

"Grandmother's real dream was (buying) the mansion called Woodbury Court (which stood on the hill alongside the Continental Denver Hotel), but the owners never would agree on her price. All the beautiful antiques and paintings, etc.

were scattered when they razed the house. A lot of valuable artifacts were bulldozed into the ground.

"I don't wonder that grandmother yearned to own the Woodbury mansion at 2501 Woodbury Court. It was a beautiful place. I visited it several times as a child when it was owned by Bill and Anna Gresham. The house sat high and alone, on 2 acres of land, and was partly surrounded by a stone wall. The interior contained magnificent hand-carved woodwork, solid silver and gold-plated knobs and pulls on the doors and windows and a stunning Tiffany window."

Our thanks to Mrs. Shire for writing. The story of Roger Williams Woodbury, who built the Woodbury Mansion, was the stuff of novels. He descended from a colonist who settled in Massachusetts in 1628 but as a child, labored in a cotton mill in Manchester, N.H., working his way through the public schools.

He learned typesetting at the *Manchester Mirror*, and by the time he was 19, was foreman of the composing room. He served in the Civil War, rising from private to captain.

Seeking still more adventure after the war, he came to Colorado in 1866, and tried mining in Summit County. He was unsuccessful, and within a few months, he was working as a compositor at the *Golden Transcript*. From Golden, he moved to the *Denver Daily Tribune*. Before long he became city editor, then managing editor and finally, part owner of the *Tribune*.

Woodbury sold his interest in 1872 to purchase the *Daily Times*, and he pushed the *Times* to such rapid growth that less than 7 years later he built a 4-story building on Lawrence Street near 16th Street to house the paper. The *Times* later was incorporated into the *Rocky Mountain News*, but not before Woodbury had become a wealthy man.

Woodbury married Anna M. Koons in 1870 and built the mansion on Woodbury Court for her.

Roger W. Woodbury built his mansion on West 25th Avenue in the 1870s. It stood high and alone on 2 acres of land. It eventually was vandalized and demolished in 1966.

Woodbury had become a force in the Denver community by then. He helped promote the first railroad into Denver, was instrumental in raising tax funds for the building of Denver's first high school, the old Arapahoe Street School, and is given credit for naming Colorado the Centennial State.

The Woodburys were known for gracious entertaining. Many celebrated Denver visitors were guests at the mansion.

Woodbury died in 1903, not long after his wife's death. It was said that he never entered the mansion after she died.

The house was inherited by the Woodburys' son, Frank, who died in 1935. It was sold then to the Greshams. Anna Gresham died after a few years there, and Bill Gresham stayed on in the mansion for some years. The grand old house was sold to Del E. Webb associates in the mid-1950s. The firm had built the nearby Continental-Denver Hotel.

Left vacant, the house and carriage house were vandalized, and in March 1966, the Woodbury mansion was demolished.

Roger Williams Woodbury is remembered not only for the house he built, but also for the Woodbury Branch Library named after him, a building at the University of Colorado named for him and for the Woodbury Oratorical Contest and award he established at East High School.

June 26, 1983

Religion's P.T. Barnum

A couple of routine news stories about a young evangelist appearing at the People's Tabernacle in Denver appeared in the *Rocky Mountain News* in 1921.

Browsing through the paper, city editor Ray Colvin paused and turned to his teen-age reporter, Helen Black.

"Helen, go down to the tabernacle," he ordered, "and see if you can get a feature out of what's going on there." In less than 2 hours, the young reporter dashed back into the news office, breathless with excitement.

"They're turning cartwheels in the aisles down there," she exclaimed. "That woman is amazing."

"That woman" was Aimee Semple McPherson. A little-known evangelist, she was to become a world celebrity. Her first big leap into headlines came in Denver, when Black's story was splashed over the *News'* front page with an eight-column banner headline.

"Stick with her," Colvin told Black. "We want a story every day." With the excitement stirred up by the *News, The Denver Post* and the *Denver Express* also leaped into the story. Two other reporters, Frances Wayne of the *Post* and Eileen O'Connor of the *Express*, were assigned to write about McPherson.

As Black described her 62 years later, the young evangelist was a "buxom brunet, with a beautiful figure and face."

"She wore a nurse's white uniform and a blue cape," Black recalled. "She was simple, and she was sweet. She had the greatest charisma of anyone I ever knew. Even the police assigned to guard her were enamored. She also was the most naive person I ever knew; she would do anything you asked her to."

On her first visit to Denver, McPherson was young, and had two young children, Black said.

The evangelist stayed at the Brown Palace Hotel with her mother, Minnie B. Kennedy, and her two children, Roberta Semple and Rolf McPherson.

Aimee Semple McPherson had a flair for the dramatic that served her well as an evangelist.

McPherson was born Oct. 9, 1890, on a farm in Ontario. As a girl, she dreamed of becoming an actress, and this flair for the dramatic served her well when she became an evangelist.

She changed her ambition when, still in her teens, she married Robert Semple, a missionary, and discovered she had a talent for preaching.

She accompanied Semple on a mission to China, and he died in Hong Kong, leaving her with a small daughter. She was then 19.

McPherson returned to the United States and resumed preaching. She married Howard S. McPherson, a bookkeeper, in 1912, and they had a son. The marriage was short-lived, and they separated, but were not divorced until 1931. With the breakup, she began a frenzied preaching-and-healing tour across the country. Her first visit to Denver was in 1921.

In Denver, Helen Black, with the brashness of a young reporter, began to tell McPherson what to do, with the idea of producing a fresh new story every day. She suggested that patients be brought in from a hospital to be treated, and 114 were carried in on cots. "Practically all" were cured, Aimee said in later reminiscences.

With publicity from all three papers, the People's Tabernacle soon was too small, and Aimee and her followers transferred the meetings to the City Auditorium.

They also made a healing tour through Denver's Chinatown. One healing involved a blind Chinese who regained his sight. The way he ran laughing and shouting out of the healing session made the evangelist suspect him of being a fraud.

An investigation disclosed that he had been blind almost from childhood, and Aimee commented: "It truly was a divine healing."

Black also suggested a "Sermon on the Mount," using Lookout Mountain as the site. Aimee liked the idea.

With ample newspaper publicity to help, McPherson did her preaching from the mountaintop before a crowd of thousands.

Later, at a "Children's Day" in the People's Tabernacle so many people showed up that they packed the streets. Police forced a way through for the blind, and for those on crutches and stretchers.

In her article the next day, Frances Wayne told the story of one mother who emerged from the healing session joyously exclaiming that her child had had a lump on the throat, "but now it's gone. Glory to God!"

When she wasn't healing, McPherson was preaching, with a dramatic simplicity even children could understand. She encouraged her listeners to shout out their "amens" and "hallelujahs" to emphasize her message, and it was a lively good time of audience participation. It wasn't long before skeptics dubbed her "the P.T. Barnum of religion."

During that first Denver visit, 12,000 were converted to Sister Aimee's Foursquare Gospel Church. Later, several Foursquare Gospel Churches were built in Denver. Some of them remain. She also said several years later the walls of her famous Angelus Temple in Los Angeles had been built with donations from the people of Denver.

As time passed and her fame grew, the evangelist changed. The rather plump brunet became a model-slim redhead, and her sermons took on an even more theatrical flair, with hand-painted scenic backdrops prepared for each one.

Scandal also touched Sister Aimee's life. She vanished in 1926 while surf bathing in California. She was believed to have drowned, but she reappeared 88 days later with a story of being kidnapped and held prisoner in the desert by a couple known only as "Steve" and "Rosie."

Coincidentally, the engineer for her radio station mysteriously was missing during the same time. An expensive, exhaustive hunt was launched during the time McPherson was believed drowned, and two men lost their lives in the search.

When McPherson reappeared, in Douglas, Ariz., neither her clothing nor shoes showed the ravages of the long trek through the desert she claimed to have made in her escape. Gossip about the matter was rampant.

McPherson returned to Denver several times and always was well-received. In 1937, she brought a convention of several thousand to the city, as she said, to show her gratitude to Den-

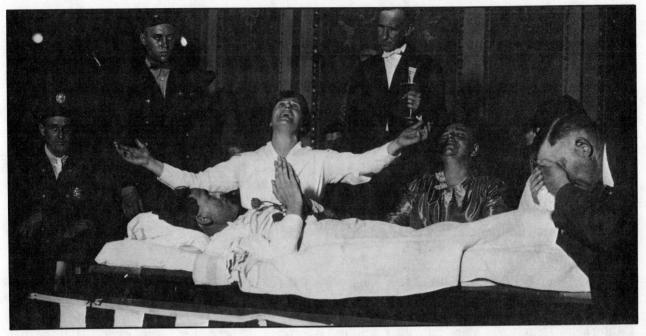

Aimee Semple McPherson prayed with a sick man during a Denver appearance. She founded the Church of the Foursquare Gospel, which later was led by her son Rolf Kennedy McPherson.

ver.

She died in 1944, in an Oakland, Calif., hotel room after taking an overdose of sleeping powders. She was 54.

August 7, 1983

The readers said . . .

FROM a surprise party, a group of eager women and some small cement bags, a temple arose in Denver many years ago.

That story was relayed in the following letter from Roberta Semple Salter of New York City:

"A Denver friend just sent me a clipping of your nostalgic story about my mother, Aimee Semple McPherson, and her evangelistic meetings in your city.

"Yes, those were fabulous days! I shall always remember the stars in Mother's eyes when she returned from her first trip. She told us children about the enormous crowds that came to hear her preach."

" 'And they were such warm-hearted people,'

she said. 'Look what they sent you.' It was a big box of toys: a bicycle for my brother Rolf, a fantastic doll, as large as a 2-year-old child, for me, and Indian suits for both of us. We were overwhelmed.

"The next June (1922) when Aimee returned to Denver, she sent for us at the end of the school year.

" 'The people want to meet you,' she explained. As we came in through the stage door of the huge Denver Auditorium mother hesitated and said:

" 'I think the people are planning some kind of surprise. Every time I come in they suddenly stop talking.' Then she took our hands and led us out to the center of the stage. She smiled at the audience and said:

" 'These are my children.'

"Suddenly, as if that were a signal, the air was filled with swirling, fluttering rose petals descending from high above our heads and falling at our feet. The crowd rose to its feet and cheered. In a moment we were standing ankle-deep in rose petals.

"Believe me, nothing — not even the ticker-tape parades in New York — was more thrilling and beautiful. We learned later that for a week before we children were to arrive in Denver, the congregation had been collecting blossoms from their gardens. They were placed in a wide canvas sling and hoisted high over the stage.

"At a signal, a rope was released, and down fluttered the fabulous rose tribute to our mother, a magnificent gesture. I was 11½ years old then. ... Now I'm 73, but Denver will always have a special place in my memory, as it always had in Aimee's heart.

"Indeed, yes, the people of Denver did 'build the walls of Angelus Temple' (in Los Angeles). It happened like this:

"A committee asked her to remain in Denver. 'If you do, we'll build you a church,' (the congregation said). Mother explained that she had already started to raise funds to build in Southern California. 'Then we'll help you. Just tell us how,' (the congregation told her).

"Mother figured that each bag of cement needed would cost, including labor, $1. But how to write that many receipts. Minnie Kennedy, her mother, had an idea.

"We'll get the ladies to make miniature cement bags (like the Bull Durham tobacco pouches) and stuff them with cotton. We'll give everyone who donates a dollar a tiny cement bag for a receipt.

"Eager ladies set up their sewing machines and the job was done. Thousands of cement bags were donated — enough to build the walls of Angelus Temple. Somewhere in Denver attics, I'm sure, there must be a few of these little bags tucked away as souvenirs.

"Aimee never forgot. Whenever she told the story of her life and how the Angelus Temple was built, she always told her congregation, 'And these walls are the gift of the people of Denver.'

"But that is not the end of the story. The Church of the Foursquare Gospel is still flourishing today, 60 years later, under the leadership of her son, Dr. Rolf Kennedy McPherson, my brother. There are now over 1,100 branch churches, with mission stations in 46 countries.

"Thank you for bringing back so many happy memories."

August 7, 1983

'King of Jazz' started in Denver

ONE of the most famous celebrities to come out of Denver was Paul Whiteman — the "king of jazz."

Mrs. Edwin Scott of Denver asked for information on Whiteman's years in Denver for the Paul Whiteman Library at Williams College, Williamstown, Mass.

Whiteman was born in Denver March 28, 1891, the only son of Wilberforce J. Whiteman, director of music for the Denver Public Schools, and Elfrieda Whiteman, a soprano-about-town.

Even though his fame rested on jazz, Whiteman's classical music background showed through. He was the first American musician to orchestrate jazz, and the first to hire symphony musicians for his band.

The Whiteman organization included such later noted musicians as Ferde Grofe, who played the piano and did the arrangements, Tommy Dorsey, Benny Goodman and Henry Busse, who played the trumpet and was assistant conductor.

Whiteman's famous theme song, *Rhapsody in Blue,* was composed by George Gershwin, a young musician he commissioned for the job.

In an interview years after he had achieved national fame, Whiteman said his parents were disappointed at his early lack of interest in music.

His father gave Whiteman a violin when he was 3. Although he studied for several years, he had little interest in the instrument. His father, a believer in discipline, regularly locked him in the sewing room to practice. But one day, furious at being locked in, young Paul smashed his violin over the sewing machine.

That didn't end his musical career. In addition to receiving a new instrument, this time a viola, he was assigned a summer of lawn cutting and odd jobs to pay for the broken violin.

Paul also studied singing with his mother and was the boy soprano in the choir his father conducted at Trinity Methodist Church.

He was a poor student, he admitted years later, but enjoyed playing football. As a result,

Whiteman with his fans and family: parents at his right and his sister Fern Smith at his left.

Rocky Mountain News

Paul Whiteman was the son of musicians, but he showed little early interest in music.

he went to "every high school in Denver — East, West, North, South and Manual." He briefly attended the University of Denver where, he said, he took "physics, football and my lunch."

Whiteman became an accomplished violist, and joined the musicians union while still in high school. He played in the Denver Civic Symphony Orchestra, in Rafaelo Cavallo's Orchestra at the Brown Palace Hotel and at the old Manhattan Beach amusement park. At one time, he would finish his stint at the Brown and hurry across Broadway to play in the pit of the Broadway Theater.

The young musician earned still more money by driving one of Denver's first taxicabs.

Paul Whiteman left Denver in 1915, to play at the World's Fair in San Francisco, and discovered jazz on the Barbary Coast. He was captivated by its "spirit of abandon," and conceived the idea of combining it with the precision of a symphony.

After leading a Navy band through World War I, Whiteman returned to his West Coast band. His new style adding strings and sweetness to jazz, was "symphonic jazz." By 1920, Whiteman and his band were featured at the Palais Royale in New York.

The King of Jazz owed his first recording contract with Victor Records to George Morrison of Denver. Morrison had his own jazz band then appearing in New York. Victor asked Morrison to record for the company, but he was under contract to Columbia and had to refuse.

Instead he recommended "a young boy who's a pretty good musician. His name is Paul Whiteman."

Victor hired Whiteman. By 1921, the Whiteman recording of *Whispering* had sold 1 million copies.

Whiteman always was thoughtful of his parents. In 1924, he purchased a home for them — 320 acres in Arapahoe County which he named the Black-and-White Ranch. Everything possible on the ranch was black-and-white, including Poland-China hogs, Holstein cattle and Plymouth Rock chickens. The place was noted for its flower gardens.

The band leader enjoyed wearing ranch clothes and relaxing with his parents on their Colorado property. His second marriage, to actress Margaret Livingston, took place there Aug. 18, 1931.

Whiteman made several professional visits to Denver in later years, once in 1956, when the Denver Public Schools dedicated its music week to his father and named the Whiteman Elementary School at East Fourth Avenue and Newport Street after the elder Whiteman.

The King of Jazz appeared at Lakeside Amusement Park in 1942, in a Red Rocks concert in 1954, and at the Denver Hilton, now the Radisson, in 1960.

He died Dec. 29, 1967, at another of his homes, near Doylestown, Pa.

November 27, 1983

Chapter 4

Denver Mint robbers got away with murder

TWO readers have asked about Denver's "crime of the century."

Although usually referred to as the Great Mint Robbery, it was actually a holdup of a Federal Reserve Bank truck parked in front of the Denver Mint.

It was 10:30 on a sunny Monday morning, Dec. 18, 1922, when a Federal Reserve Bank van pulled up at the curb in front of the mint at West Colfax Avenue and Delaware Street. Two guards

Rocky Mountain News

News photographer Harry M. Rhoads took this shot at the mint robbery of 1922. Nobody ever arrested was in the holdup of the Federal Reserve Bank truck, but some of the money was recovered.

waiting at an entrance hurried down the steps and tossed packages of currency into the back of the van and then turned to re-enter the building. The money being transferred came to $200,000.

As one of the guards, Charles T. Linton, was closing the iron grille doors at the rear of the van, a black Buick touring car with side curtains pulled up beside the truck.

Three of four bandits, according to witnesses, yelled "Hands up!" and opened fire. As Linton turned, he was hit with a blast from a sawed-off shotgun. He died in a hospital 3 hours later.

While two of the holdup men stood guard behind telephone poles across the street and shot at the mint entrance, a third removed 10 boxes of new $5 federal reserve banknotes from the Kansas City Federal Reserve Bank. Each box contained five packets of $4,000 each. (Packets of $5 bills were chosen in preference to bills of larger denomination, which were left behind.)

A fourth robber stayed behind the wheel, covering the driver of the bank truck.

As the shooting started, an electric alarm was sounded inside the mint, and 30 employees opened fire from the building.

At a signal from the driver, three of the robbers leaped for the car as it careened along East Colfax Avenue. One, believed to be badly wounded, sagged on the running board, and his companions pulled him inside.

As the car sped away, one of the mint guards, Pete Kiedinger, stepped out the front door, took aim, shot and wounded the leader in the cheek. A third robber was thought to be wounded in the arm because he had dropped his shotgun in front of the mint.

F.H. Hindel of the state Auto Theft Department was nearby and gave chase. At Bannock Street the getaway car nearly hit a truck, which leaped the curb and knocked over a fire hydrant.

Hindel was blocked by traffic at Broadway and lost the escaping robbers. They last were seen turning south onto Pearl Street. Several witnesses gave authorities various license plate numbers for the bandits' car. None of them checked out.

Police Chief H. Rugg Williams and Rowland K. Goddard, Secret Service chief in Denver,

concluded that the bandits had inside information on the money transfer. The Friday before, a coded telegram had been received at the mint from the U.S. comptroller's office in Washington, ordering the payment of the $200,000 to the Federal Reserve Bank.

Federal officers within a 400-mile radius were ordered to be on the lookout for the robbers. Almost every Denver police officer was put on the job.

Roads were guarded and trains watched. A $5,000 reward was posted for information leading to arrest of the bandit, but no information was forthcoming.

Twenty-three days after the robbery, the getaway car containing the frozen body of one of the robbers was found by a plumber in a rented garage of a Capitol Hill residence.

The dead man was identified as Nicholas Trainor, alias J.S. Sloan, a member of the Peters Street Gang that had operated in St. Paul, Minn. The car had been stolen for the crime. None of Trainor's confederates was around. Trainor was buried in Riverside Cemetery.

Sometime later, $5 bills from the robbery started showing up around the country and were traced to St. Paul. About the same time, a Cincinnati banker who had gone to St. Paul in an effort to recover some stolen securities reported that he had been offered $80,000 of the Denver Mint money at 60¢ on the dollar.

A plan was developed to trap the bandits with the banker's help, but the banker, apparently thrilled at his role, talked too much to a newspaper, and the trap never was sprung.

The Secret Service said that $79,000 of the stolen money was recovered in St. Paul. It was believed that the bandits had received $50,000 from a fence for the stolen currency.

No one was ever arrested in connection with the crime.

January 15, 1984

The readers said . . .

PHYLLIS Klink of Denver writes: "At the time (of the robbery, December 1922), I lived at 1620 Clarkson St. in the Alta Vista apartments. I was visiting a friend, Sally Fisher, in her home at the corner of East 17th Avenue and Clarkson Street when I was told to go home, and Sally was sent to dinner with her aunt. In the parlor were many men with rifles.

"Later that evening, I was playing in front of the apartment when a man ran down the street yelling, 'Children go home. Children go home.' We all scattered. One woman who had come after her boy yelled 'The Germans are coming.' I guess she thought the war had started again.

"A neighbor who lived across the alley on Emerson Street had come to take his son home and just made it across the alley when the first shots were heard. A car was going down the alley with another chasing it and shooting. They said it was the mint robbers, and there were also a woman and baby in the car.

"Being a child at the time, I don't remember more, but my sister and girlfriend went to see the dead robber at the morgue where he was on display after he was found frozen in a garage a few blocks away."

February 5, 1984

Mildred H. Earhart of Denver writes:

"At the time of the Denver Mint robbery in December 1922, my home was at 2932 Columbine St., and I was a day student at Colorado Woman's College. One of my classmates, Billie Pierce, who lived on Capitol Hill, drove to the college each morning. I would walk to East Colfax and York Street, where she would pick me up.

"One morning she did not come by, so eventually I boarded a streetcar to get to college. No one heard from Billie Pierce all day. A phone call that evening disclosed that her car had been stolen from in front of her house that morning.

Police had found no trace of it.

"A month later, when police were called to open a locked garage in east Denver, on which a month's rent was due, they found Billie's car inside with the dead bandit in it.

"The insurance company replaced the car, and the mystery of the bandit who had been shot in the mint robbery was solved."

Carl A. Wagner of Denver writes:

"I was a senior at the old South High School in December 1922, when a student messenger stuck his head in the door of our room to call out, 'The mint was robbed.'

"The next month I graduated and started as an apprentice at the old Midwest Electric Co., 1310 Tremont Place. The back end of the place was toward the mint. From the day of the robbery on, the boss of Midwest Electric kept a deer rifle around to help protect the mint.

"From the second floor of a cheap hotel across Tremont Place, the robbers evidently studied the precise times of the Federal Reserve money truck and the guards' routine. The robbers fled with the loot in a Richenbacher 'hat-in-the-ring' touring car. I don't know how many mint employees were killed or wounded.

"The old *Denver Express* newspaper which stood near the present site of the *Rocky Mountain News* scored an exclusive scoop. The reporters could just look out the front window and watch it happen.

"Maybe someday you might run the old-time story about the mint employee who walked out of the mint with gold in his wooden leg and buried it in his basement wall."

(That is the story of Orville Harrington, the mint robber with an artificial leg, that appears elsewhere in this volume.)

March 4, 1984

Tabor opera curtain dropped into dishonor

THE famous drop curtain from the old Tabor Opera House at 16th and Curtis streets is the subject of a question from Blanche Boshinski of Denver. She writes:

"When I came to Denver to attend DU, it was a thrill to see that curtain which was shown only on special occasions after the Tabor became a movie house. I am wondering what became of the curtain when the Tabor was torn down?"

Dear Blanche Boshinski:

The curtain — with its mysterious scene of a ruined city, vines twining over fallen pillars and a jaguar crouching in the ruins — thrilled viewers for years.

It first was shown Sept. 5, 1881, to a crowd at the Tabor's opening night. As the years passed, several stories grew up around the painting.

A nationally famous Denver writer, Will Irwin, said in a magazine article in 1922 that "a wandering painter — some say a German, others a Bohemian — arrived in Denver at the time the theater was being completed and was en-

The Tabor Opera House curtain showed a mysterious scene of a ruined city, vines tangled around fallen pillars and a jaguar crouching in the ruins. The curtain itself fell into ruin and was burned.

112 *Rocky Mountain Memories*

gaged to decorate the drop curtain. He painted superbly, suggestively, a ruined palace ... and underneath, the lines, from the Charles Kingsley poem, *Old and New*:

" 'So fleet the works of men, back to their Earth again;

" 'Ancient and holy things fade like a dream.' "

The truth appears to be that the Tabor curtain was painted by Robert Hopkin, a member of the Detroit Art Institute, who was paid $20,000 for the job. Hopkin, a native of Edinburgh, Scotland, was hired by the Sullivan Scenic & Decorative Co. of Chicago, which H.A.W. Tabor commissioned to decorate his opera house.

In an interview in November 1922, Charles S. Hathaway, a friend of Hopkin, said the artist tore away a portion of his home so he would have a wall large enough to work on the curtain.

It was said that Hopkin never repeated his success. A curtain he painted for the Columbia Theater in Chicago was a failure.

In later years, the Tabor curtain was backed with sturdy canvas to help preserve it. Because of the actors' wish to "count the house," a tiny peephole was poked in the curtain.

During the theater's last years, the curtain was shown only in the summer, twice a week, for tourists.

When the grand old opera house was torn down in 1964, the curtain was donated to the Central City Opera House Association, but the curtain was too large for the stage, and cutting it down would have ruined the design. So, it was stored in the old Knights of Pythias Building, along with a number of used opera sets which remained there undisturbed for 18 years.

The K of P building had a leaky roof, but Central City had no funds for maintenance and no other place to store the curtain, according to Glen Arko, general manager for the association. When the Knights of Pythias building was cleaned out after its sale (in 1982), the Tabor curtain was discovered mildewed and in poor condition.

"The curtain was shot when we got it, and ripped along one side when we took it down from the Tabor," recalled Frank Gates, for many years a Central City scenic designer, now a consultant to the association.

The remains of the famous Tabor Opera House curtain, along with several ruined opera sets, were hauled to the Central City dump and burned, Gates said.

January 29, 1984

Camp Weld proved Gilpin's Waterloo

MRS. Edward R. Saul of Edgewater writes: "One of my friends, a Denver native, and her father, who is 75 and has lived here most of his life, were telling me about a stockade under the 16th Street Viaduct from which soldiers kept an eye on the Indians camped along the river. They said it was torn out in 1952 or 1953. My husband, who has lived in Denver 67 years, says he can't remember such a stockade.

"Can you shed any light on this? Was there or wasn't there such a stockade?"

Dear Mrs. Saul:
Your friends probably are thinking of Camp Weld. This camp was located under the present Eighth Avenue viaduct, at about West Eighth Avenue and Umatilla Street.

Camp Weld proved the undoing of Colorado's first territorial governor, William Gilpin. And the camp helped defeat Confederate forces at Glorieta Pass.

The building of Camp Weld was authorized by Gilpin, appointed territorial governor in May 1861 by President Lincoln. Civil War sentiment in Colorado was about two-thirds in favor of the Union, and Gilpin organized the 1st Colorado Regiment of Volunteers to fight for the Union.

Barracks were needed for the soldiers, so Gilpin issued $40,000 in drafts to cover the construction of Camp Weld, named for Lewis L. Weld, first secretary of Colorado Territory. Because of the public's trust in Gilpin, the drafts passed from hand to hand like currency.

When they finally reached Washington, however, the drafts were rejected, bringing disaster to many Denver merchants. Ill feeling against Gilpin grew so great that he made a trip to Washington, hoping to straighten out the mess.

The matter came to the attention of the president's cabinet, but in early in 1862 it decided to remove Gilpin as soon as a successor could be found. John Evans was named territorial governor in May 1862.

After Evans' inauguration, a large portion of the drafts was paid by Washington.

Camp Weld was built
The camp included quarters for soldiers and officers, a guard house and hospital situated around a square.

Omnibuses plied the road between Denver and the camp, and the military post was the scene of numerous elaborate dinners given by the officers, as well as full-dress balls which included many townsfolk.

It was from Camp Weld that on Feb. 22, 1862, the 1st Colorado Volunteers marched toward New Mexico and the Battle of Glorieta Pass. The 2-day battle routed Confederate Gen. H.H. Sibley, who had made a triumphant march northward through Texas, with the intention of capturing the Colorado gold fields.

Another regiment of Colorado volunteers out of Camp Weld was formed to serve in Missouri. Camp Weld also had a cavalry unit that scouted for Indians east of Denver.

Col. John M. Chivington and his men were dispatched from the camp for the encounter at Sand Creek in December 1864. Between 400 and 500 Indians were slaughtered in that engagement which has gone down in history as "the Sand Creek massacre."

Camp Weld was damaged badly by two fires. As a result, the post was not used much after the spring of 1865.

Elisha Millison, a soldier at the camp, discovered that the land never had been properly assigned to the government. He filed a homestead entry to 40 acres and acquired title to the property. He and his wife lived there the rest of their lives.

February 12, 1984

'Bloody Bridles' Waite had a tongue of silver

COLORADO'S governors have been a distinguished and colorful lot. None was more so than Davis Hansen Waite, a populist, with the intriguing nickname of "Bloody Bridles."

Waite, who served in 1893-1895, was Colorado's eighth elected governor. He waged the famous "City Hall War."

He certainly was imaginative, and when Colorado and its mines were suffering from the Panic of 1893, he conceived a plan for the state to buy the output of the state's silver mines, ship the silver to Mexico and have dollars made for use only in Colorado. The dollars were to be made in Mexico to circumvent federal laws concerning coinage.

The press and public soon were referring to Waite's "fandango dollars." Legislative opposition was so great that the coins never materialized.

Waite also gained attention for his support of women's suffrage. In one speech he said:

"About 8 years ago, a law was passed giving to the women of Colorado the right to vote at school district elections, and in as much as, since that time, the heavens have not fallen and the efficiency of the public schools has been greatly improved, I recommend a law extending to the women of Colorado the right of suffrage at all municipal elections." (The general women's suffrage bill was passed by the legislature in April 1893, and approved by the voters in November).

Waite was a tall, lean New York native with a luxurious beard. Before he became Colorado's governor at age 68, he had worked as a lawyer, merchant, legislator, had been principal of a Missouri high school and edited a newspaper in Ashcroft.

An article in *Harper's Weekly* July 29, 1893, called him "an accident in politics . . . the leader of a forlorn hope." He was elected governor of Colorado on the Populist ticket, the article said, because of the unpopular Republican stand on

silver and the fact that the Democrats had withdrawn from the election. At the time, Colorado

Western History Department, Denver Public Library

Davis Hansen Waite was elected Colorado's governor on the Populist ticket in 1892.

was producing about 40% of the nation's silver.

Waite's famous "bloody bridles speech" was made July 1, 1893, in Denver to the state Silver League.

He started by saying that legislation decreasing the value of silver, as compared with gold, "beats that celebrated compromise which the devil proposed to Jesus Christ on the mountain."

Rather than surrender the rights of the silver interests to the corporations, he said, ". . . it is better, infinitely better, that blood should flow to the horses' bridles." The Associated Press wired across the country that Waite had declared war on the government. No blood flowed, but Waite was known forever after as "Bloody Bridles."

The "City Hall War" came closer to bloodshed. Waite, who was vehemently opposed to gambling, had appointed the members of the Fire and Police Board with the understanding that they would put a stop to that vice.

When two of the board members, Jackson Orr and D.J. Martin, ignored his instructions, Waite charged them in January 1894 with malfeasance in office, charging that they gave police protection to a notorious gambling den. They denied the charge, refused to resign and demanded a full hearing. Soon, Denver's Board of Public Works was drawn into the controversy.

On March 7, Waite isued orders for the forcible removal of Orr and Martin and the public works board.

Armed officers, sheriffs deputies and volunteers barricaded themselves in City Hall, ready to stave off the troops mustered by Waite.

The governor had ordered out the Denver companies of the Infantry Militia and the Chaffee Light Artillery, which arrived with two Gatling guns and two field pieces. In addition, U.S. troops were stationed in reserve at Union Station.

Despite the danger, sightseers jammed the streets in front of the City Hall, anxious to see the action.

Waite's maneuver proved to be bluster and bluff. A committee appointed by the Denver Chamber of Commerce urged both sides to submit the controversy to the state Supreme Court. Both agreed, and the troops marched away.

Eventually the court ruled that the governor had full control of the fire and police boards, so Waite won without firing a shot.

"Bloody Bridles" Waite was defeated in 1894, when he ran for his second term. Ironically, it was the first election in which women had the vote.

February 19, 1984

Arabian horses on the Lazy V-V

A VESTA Mauzey of Denver wonders about the Arabian horses that were bred and trained on what later became the Caribou Ranch near Nederland.

Dear Mrs. Mauzey: When the Arabian horses were romping through meadows at the foot of snow-covered peaks, the ranch was known as the Lazy V-V. The property, 4 miles outside Nederland, was owned by Lynn W. Van Vleet, president of the Trinidad Bean and Elevator Co.

Van Vleet didn't neglect the bean business, but the horses were his first love.

He became fascinated with the beauty and endurance of Arabian horses, and he wanted to try raising them in the United States. When his romance with Arabians began, he purchased what had been the Tom Tucker Ranch for Boys. His son, Wayne Van Vleet, recalled:

"When we first brought the Arabs to Colorado in the 1930s, there were none, and people were desirous of seeing them. In the period from 1908 to 1938, there were fewer than 2,000 purebred

Rocky Mountain News

Lynn W. Van Vleet's Arabian horses galloped around the show corral at his ranch near Nederland. He started the ranch in 1938 with 29 horses; by 1951, there were 285. Sunday shows began in 1939.

registered Arab horses in the United States. Now there are close to 400,000.

"Most of the horses in those days were from famous mares and few people worked them. We worked ours on cattle and used them on trail rides. They were bred by desert tribesmen to be useful, not just ornamental."

Van Vleet started his Arabian stud ranch in 1938 with 29 horses. By 1951, he had 285 horses, and they were sold to buyers all over the United States, Canada, Mexico and South America.

Because his neighbors and Denver friends were curious about the handsome horses, Van Vleet in 1939 started free Sunday shows.

He built a show ring rimmed with log rails to present the horses and put in bleachers for an audience of 2,000.

Within 10 years, the crowds at the Sunday horse shows had grown to about 3,500. Celebrities who came to view the horses included Emir Abdul Ilah, regent of Iraq.

The show featured the horses in dressage exercises, plus cutting, and pulling buggies. Van Vleet nearly always presided at the microphone,

describing the horses and explaining their stunts. One of the most famous performers was a stallion named Rifage, Van Vleet's personal horse.

The finale was a colorful make-believe desert raid, with riders wearing Arabian costumes and carrying spears, urging the horses into full gallop around the ring.

Van Vleet sold the ranch in 1951 to George Warren Barnes of Houston, and it has changed hands several times since.

Van Vleet moved the horses to Arapahoe Ranch, a mile east of Boulder. The cattle were moved to nearby Meadow Brook Ranch, also owned by Van Vleet, and some of the horses were kept there to work the cattle.

"The horses are on Meadow Brook Ranch now," said Wayne Van Vleet, "and we're still raising them."

(The studio burned in 1985, and even in late 1986, Guercio hadn't decided whether it ever would be used again as a recording studio.)

March 18, 1984

The house in the background is the old Virginia Dale stage stop. The barn in the foreground is no longer standing. Its station manager of the 1860s, Captain Jack Slade, was an infamous outlaw.

Stagecoach stop was gunman's lair

STAGECOACH stops were interesting places in the Old West, offering a refuge to travelers — some of whom stayed a few days; others, a few weeks.

One of the most famous of Colorado's stage stops was Virginia Dale in an area known as the Black Hills, about 40 miles northwest of Fort Collins. It was established in 1862 on the Overland line's main route for covered wagons heading for California. At times up to 100 wagons were encamped there.

Virginia Dale was noted not only for its beautiful setting, but also for a certain aura of danger. It was rumored that the station manager, Joseph A. "Captain Jack" Slade, was the leader of an outlaw gang.

By many, Slade was regarded as a dangerous killer, quick on the draw. It was said that he had killed at least two or as many as 26 people.

It is known that he did kill at least two. He killed for the first time when he was 13, using a stone to kill a man at his home in southern Illinois. His distressed father sent him to Texas

to avoid prosecution and more scandal.

Slade was 30 when he was appointed division agent for the stage line and he established Virginia Dale. He built the stone fireplace at the station with his own hands.

Slade replaced Jules Reni, a Frenchman for whom Julesburg was named. Reni was fired by the company, and, in his wrath, tried to kill Slade with a shotgun.

Lying on the floor, mortally wounded, onlookers believed, Slade raised himself and said to Reni: "You ————————, I'll live to wear your ears on my watch chain." And he did.

With the help of henchmen some months later, Slade captured Reni and tied him to a post outside overnight. The next morning, according to various accounts, Slade shot and killed Reni without giving him a chance. He then cut off the dead man's ears, dried them and wore them as a watchfob.

Sometime before, Slade had received rather loose permission from the military to protect himself in the event that Reni returned, and thus avoided prosecution.

As a division superintendent, Slade enjoyed an enviable reputation. His employers regarded him as one of their best. With him in charge, the stages and mail got through on time. Or at least they did for a time; it later was rumored that Slade was the leader of a gang who robbed shipments going through his post.

Liquor was sold at the stage stop, and Virginia Dale, named for Slade's wife, became a meeting place for some of the West's toughest characters. No one knew for sure, but Slade's wife was regarded as a "fancy woman." A record of their marriage never was found, and although she stuck with him for years, she was thought to be a common-law wife.

A mile northeast of the station is Table Mountain, with a rim of shale and cliffs that made it difficult, but not impossible, to climb. There was a lake on top, with abundant grass for horses, and the place became a robbers' roost.

Slade was thought to be the leader of the gang that hung out on the mountain, because they always seemed to know when a valuable shipment, such as gold or liquor, was going through.

Once, the gang held up the stage and rode off with $60,000 in government gold being shipped to Fort Laramie, Wyo.

The empty strong box that had held the gold was found dumped in a creek, but the bandits — who later were caught — were believed to have buried the gold on Table Mountain.

Also leading to the belief that Slade was in on the robberies was that he was known to have a geat deal of money when he finally left Virginia Dale.

The stage company abandoned the route and the station after the Union Pacific brought the railroad through to Cheyenne.

The station now is owned by the Virginia Dale Woman's Club and has become a restoration project of the Fort Collins Historical Society.

May 6, 1984

1880 riots made victims of Chinese

ONE of the darkest pages of Colorado history was written in Denver on Oct. 31, 1880, when the "Chinese Riots" took place.

Actually, the Chinese didn't riot at all. The trouble was caused by a band of liquored-up whites.

Many Chinese were brought to America in the 1870s to work on railroads and do other menial and hazardous work. Many moved east to Denver after a sojourn in the California gold fields. Others came to Colorado from the Caribbean, where they had been imported by the Spanish.

Denver had a colony of 3,000 Chinese, mainly in the area of Blake and Wazee streets between 15th and 20th streets. Denver's famous "Hop Alley" lay between Market and Blake streets, near 20th Street, and was an area of narrow cubby holes, dingy entrances and underground passages.

The industry of the Chinese was a cause of jealousy and hatred among other workers.

Chinese did most of Denver's laundry work, finishing the job with round irons heated by charcoal.

One version of the "riots" is that the trouble started with a miner over a 10¢ difference in a laundry bill. There are many other versions.

The *Rocky Mountain News,* which held to the story of the laundry squabble, reported that mobs stormed through the area, wrecking Chinese businesses and beating the occupants.

The city had no police chief at the time, but Mayor Richard Sopris called on the fire department to use hoses to disperse the mob. By then the mob was so angry that it turned on the firefighters, confronting some with knives, and the firefighters retreated.

One elderly Chinese, Ling Sing, was captured by the rioters about 6 p.m. and lynched from a lamp post in front of the Markham Hotel. He was cut down and died a short time later in a doctor's office.

By dark, the mob was breaking into the houses of the Chinese on Blake and Wazee streets, and throwing out personal effects.

Along with its bloodthirsty characters, the episode had a few heroes. Officer Ryan, first name not reported, was a huge man who carried a Chinese businessman under his arm out of the man's place of business to protect him from the rioters.

Jim Moon, a gambler who was calling for his laundry when the mob approached, pulled both guns and threatened the crowd, which backed off.

After the hosing failed to quell the mob, Gen. David J. Cook was appointed temporary chief of police. He picked 15 men and, with Sheriff Michael Spangler, assembled a large force of deputies. These were assisted by the Chaffee Light Artillery and the Governor's Guard, which had been called out as the mob thickened.

All saloons were closed, and rope barricades were set up to keep people out of the area. Fifty ringleaders were jailed. By 10 p.m. the town was quiet again.

May 20, 1984

Western History Department, Denver Public Library

Denver's Chinese community centered in "Hop Alley" between Market and Blake streets.

Bloody murder in St. Elizabeth's

AN old Denver crime story is the subject of a letter from Philip F. Belmont Jr. of Englewood. He would like to read the story of the murder of the Rev. Leo Heinrichs, the Franciscan priest who was killed in St. Elizabeth's Church 75 years ago.

It was Sunday, Feb. 23, 1908, when Father Heinrichs, 40, walked down the aisle of St. Elizabeth's Catholic Church at 11th and Curtis streets. He was the sixth pastor and had been there only a few months.

While church bells were chiming, calling worshipers to the 6 a.m. Mass, a man emerged from a rooming house at 16th and Blake streets and hurried toward the church. He was Giuseppe Alio, (or Alia, the name is given two ways), a Sicilian native who spoke no English.

Alio slipped into an aisle seat six rows from the Communion rail.

After Mass, Father Leo offered Communion. Alio, 50, stepped up to the rail, knelt and received the wafer from Heinrichs. He then leaped to his feet, spat out the sacred host and with a wild yell, shot Father Leo through the heart.

The priest fell, clutching the ciborium.

All was chaos.

Alio, brandishing the gun over his head, vaulted over the pews toward the rear of the church. Women screamed, cried and fainted. The Rev. Eusebius Schlingmann, the senior pastor, knelt to help Heinrichs.

As the killer rushed for the door, he was stopped by Patrolman David Cronin who had been assisting at the Mass. Cronin wrenched the gun from him and held him. The priests and brothers of St. Elizabeth's Monastery surrounded the pair to protect the killer from the enraged mob.

An account in the *Rocky Mountain News* by a young reporter named Alfred Damon Runyon reported that Cronin dragged Alio into a carriage and headed for the police station. Angry

The Rev. Leo Heinrichs was killed by a madman as he offered Holy Communion in 1908.

citizens ran alongside calling names and spitting at the killer.

Through an interpreter, the killer told his story:

He was a shoemaker who had moved from Sicily to Milan, Italy, where he was connected with an anarchist organization.

He and his wife had gone to a Presbyterian mission in Sicily. The Catholic priest there threatened them with excommunication if they continued. His wife was frightened and returned to the Catholic Church, but Alio continued to attend the Presbyterian mission. Because of this, his wife left him.

They had three children, and Alio accused the priest of breaking up his home. The priest, he insisted, was Father Leo.

The story could not possibly have been true, since Leo Heinrichs had left Cologne, Germany, when he was 16, to come to the United States. He never had been in Italy.

Most believe Alio was mentally ill, an illness brought on by some difficulty with a Roman Catholic clergyman. His crime was not against Father Leo, but against the priesthood.

Father Leo's funeral cortege Feb. 26 was the largest ever seen in Denver until then. It was witnessed by thousands who lined the sidewalks as the body was taken to Union Station to be put on a train for Paterson, N.J., and the monastery where Heinrichs had studied for the priesthood. Gov. Henry A. Buchtel and Mayor Robert W. Speer attended the funeral.

At Alio's trial in West Side Court, March 10, experts testified that the killer was sane. Three days later he was found guilty, and Judge Greeley H. Whitford sentenced him to hang. Alio was hanged July 15, 1908.

After the killing, St. Elizabeth's was reconsecrated. The church stands on the Auraria campus, and a plaque on the east wall near the door recalls Heinrich's violent death.

June 3, 1984

Killing of priest linked to a vast conspiracy

THE murder of the Rev. Leo Heinrichs was part of a conspiracy, said Kay Martin, secretary at St. Elizabeth's Catholic Church, recalling the priest's death during a Mass at the historic church at 11th and Curtis streets.

It was Feb. 23, 1908, when Giuseppe Alio stepped up to receive Communion and shot the priest in the heart. Alio was first believed to be a member of an anarchist organization, but later was believed to be suffering from a grudge against priests.

"We have a lot of material about the killing in our archives," said Martin in a call to the *Rocky Mountain News* after the June 3, 1984, *Rocky Mountain Memories* column about the killing. "There are conflicting stories, but we think Father Leo's killing was part of a conspiracy."

Martin said she and the pastor, the Rev. Len Schreiner, had found in the church attic the vestments Father Leo was wearing when he was shot.

A notebook written in a tiny Spencerian script contained some of the priest's study notes. Yellowed newspaper clippings gave details of the crime.

One account in the *Denver Times* quoted Alio after his arrest:

Rocky Mountain News

A bullet hole is still visible in the vestment the priest was wearing as he was shot at the altar.

"I had nothing against this particular man. I had decided to kill four priests. They are all alike, a hypocritical outfit who take bread from the mouth of the poor while they roll in luxury. . . . I had murder in my heart. . . . I would do something for the cause — something that would make me great."

Alio said he had mistaken Heinrich for a priest he knew in Italy. During this same time, several priests were murdered by Spanish anarchists, lending credence to the theory that Alio's crime was part of a conspiracy.

Mary Bennett of Denver said her grandfather was the Captain Cronin of the Denver Police Department who was attending church at the time, chased down Alio and arrested him. But Cronin's first name, she said, was Daniel not David.

"After the article appeared, I heard from people I haven't heard from in years," Bennett said. "It gives me such pride to go down to St. Elizabeth's and say a prayer there and think about my grandfather."

Cronin, a patrolman at the time of the killing, she said, was very athletic. When the murderer vaulted over the church pews in his run for the door, Cronin vaulted after him. J.E. Quigley, another parishioner, tackled and threw Alio at the church door and enabled Cronin to catch up.

Newspaper reports commented on Cronin's athletic ability. He had established local records for the 100-yard dash, 120-yard hurdles and broad jump, among others, so pew jumping came easily. A sports writer said:

"When he (Cronin) entered the games at the Caledonian Picnic, it was the custom to hand him first prize without further parley." Cronin also was captain and anchor man on the police tug-of-war team.

July 1, 1984

Rocky Mountain News

The Denver Times of Feb. 24, 1908, told the lurid story of the murder of the Rev. Leo Heinrichs at the altar of St. Elizabeth's Catholic Church. He died with a prayer on his lips, the headline said.

Picking the hills clean

COLORADO'S state flower, the blue and white columbine, is dancing in the breeze in the high country.

That brings to mind an incident of columbine picking from the summer of 1911. The story is told in the booklet *Rails Among the Peaks,* written many years ago by Jessie Moore Crum.

Silverton, renowned for its columbines at the time, received a request for large quantities of the flowers to decorate a hall for a national convention in Denver.

Otto Mears, railroad magnate, volunteered to run a train from his Silverton-Northern Railroad Co. to carry the blossom pickers into remote mountain meadows and bring back the flowers.

Railroad men donated their services to run the "Columbine Special," and a hardware merchant provided washtubs in which the blossoms were carried.

Many residents of Denver and Silverton participated in the columbine hunt, and it was estimated that on a trip between Silverton and Animas Forks, 25,000 blossoms were picked.

Packed in washtubs filled with water, the flowers started out of Silverton on flat cars and were transferred to boxcars at Alamosa. When they reached Denver they were displayed downtown.

Today, such a stunt is prohibited, but Coloradans in 1911 stripped the hills and meadows of columbines with a clear conscience.

July 22, 1984

Rocky Mountain News

Columbines were picked around Silverton in 1911 and brought to Denver in the Columbine Special to decorate a hall for a national convention. Otto Mears, the small man at center, supplied the train.

Prospector found a little fame

MARY G. Jordan of Denver asks about the man who posed for the statue of the miner that crowned the Mining Exchange Building at 15th and Arapahoe streets. She writes:

"I have heard that Winfield Scott Stratton, who made a fortune in Cripple Creek, posed for this famous statue of the prospector. Is that correct?"

No, Winfield Scott Stratton was not the man who posed for the miner's statue. The miner's statue was modeled after a photo of John William Straughn, whose distinguished appearance brought him many requests to be photographed.

The statue was saved when the Mining Exchange Building was torn down some years ago and now stands in the front courtyard of Brooks Towers on 15th Street. Today's passers-by get a much better look at the miner's statue than when it stood atop the building.

Rocky Mountain Memories was lucky enough to locate one of Straughn's granddaughters, Ethel M. Perkins of Boulder, who told us some of his story.

Straughn was born Feb. 4, 1842, on a farm in Putnam County, Ind. He had only a grammar school education. With the start of the Civil War, he enlisted in the Indiana Volunteer Infantry and ended, slightly wounded, as a second lieutenant.

He married Sarah E. Kennedy at Greencastle, Ind., Sept. 7, 1865, and they had five children.

After his marriage, Straughn worked for awhile as coroner and deputy sheriff in Dodge City, Kan.

Straughn and his family moved to Colorado after 1884. He did some prospecting and operated a blacksmith and wheelwright shop in Black Hawk.

Straughn was a distinguished-looking man, tall and straight, with a flowing beard and long hair. He usually wore a long-tailed coat of black broadcloth, with high boots. His appearance earned him the nickname of Colonel, and visitors

Western History Department, Denver Public Library

John William Straughn posed for this picture that was the model for the statue of a miner.

to Denver often stopped him on the street and asked to photograph him.

When the Mining Exchange Building was built in 1891-92, a statue of a miner was deemed appropriate for the top of it. Straughn was asked to pose for a full-length picture, and this photo provided the model for the sculpture done by Alphonse Pelzer, who was employed by W.H. Mullens, metal contractor of Salem, Ohio.

The statue was the final touch to a building which cost $450,000 and was the first structure devoted exclusively to mining activities.

The 7-story building was built of red stone and pressed brick, with a square tower and a red-tile roof. A stock exchange was housed on the second floor, with an observation balcony above. The seventh floor had a cafe with clubrooms.

The main-floor entrance had an archway with the life-sized head of a bull on one side and of a bear on the other, carved in red sandstone.

These have been saved and are included in some of the walls of Larimer Square.

The miner's statue, placed 165 feet above the sidewalk, was 12 feet high, of sheet copper finished to resemble antique brass.

In 1893, the portrait of Straughn, which preceded the sculpture, was shown at the Chicago World's Fair with the title, *Typical Prospector*.

Straughn lived his last years in failing health, according to his granddaughter. She recalls that he once said, "I have made a failure of everything from a financial side that I have ever undertaken, down to posing as a prospector."

In addition to Perkins, Straughn has four living granddaughters: Edith Smith of Boulder, Carol Phillips of Fort Collins, Carma Newton of Lakewood and Dorothy Malkow of Renton, Wash.

September 2, 1984

Trekking along the Boulder glacier

BOULDER is the only city in the United States that derives part of its water supply from a glacier.

In 1905, the city bought the lakes fed by Arapaho glacier, the largest in Colorado. In 1919, Congress passed a bill allowing Boulder to buy land in the area, including the glacier. For years, Boulder got all of its water from the glacier. Now, the water supply is augmented by the Big Thompson River.

Boulder's ownership of Arapaho glacier spawned an unusual Chamber of Commerce promotion — an annual trek to the glacier that gave thousands of people lifelong memories.

The idea began with the University of Colorado, which sponsored a few expeditions to the glacier in the 1920s, said Lawrence Paddock, a local historian who is editor of the *Boulder Camera*. Eben Fine, secretary of the Boulder Chamber of Commerce, and A. Gayle Waldrop, then CU professor of journalism, began the trips.

But the Chamber of Commerce inaugurated the large trips that brought the city national attention in 1938. Francis W. Reich, secretary of the Boulder Chamber of Commerce in the 1930s and '40s, and Reuben Olson, chairman of the hikes to the glacier, are credited with making the idea a success, Paddock said.

As many as 700 people from every state and several foreign countries made the trip to the glacier each year, usually on the first Sunday in August.

The journey was 7 miles round trip, on a gently graded trail through mountain meadows covered with wildflowers and other typical alpine growth. The altitude of the hike ranged from 10,000 to 12,006 feet.

Hikers started at 20-minute intervals in groups of 100 to 150, with escorts from the Colorado Mountain Club, Rocky Mountain Climbers Club and Rocky Mountain Rescue Group at front and rear of each group, Paddock said. Climbers ranged in age from babies to 81. In 1957, Texan Jack Bain made the climb on crutches.

The hikers met at Boulder's Highland School at 5 a.m. and went by motor caravan, led by the State Highway Patrol, to a base camp at 10,020 feet.

At the base, Boulder businessmen served fruit juice, scrambled eggs, sausage, pancakes and coffee.

The climb and return took about 4 hours. Climbers carried their lunches and beverages and had a snack when they reached the saddle of the Arapahoe Peaks, overlooking the glacier. Wind and rains frequently made life miserable on the trail.

One sparkplug of the treks was Dr. Howard Heuston of Boulder who rode horseback up and down the trail offering encouragement, first aid when needed and an occasional candy bar to the faltering few. Heuston could be identified by his heavy yellow slicker.

During the 38 years the trip was made, the only first aid ever needed was for an occasional blister.

After resting at the saddle and having lunch, most climbers would start down the trail to calls of the leaders to "Now blow," mountaineering language for "Take a breather," and "Now go."

A few lingered at the glacier to climb to the top while others climbed onto the ice, sat on gunnysacks and glissaded down the icy slope.

The glacier covers 100 acres, is about a mile long and 400 feet deep and moves 11 to 27 feet a year

When climbers returned to base camp they were treated to a hot meal, usually beef stew with biscuits and coffee served by the Chamber of Commerce. In 1969, the registration fee for the trip, which included guides, breakfast and dinner, was $2.50.

The trips gradually became so popular and

attracted such large crowds that they had to be limited to the first 600 who signed up, Paddock said.

The climbs were canceled after 1976. Changes in personnel, increasing costs and the project's unwieldy growth played a part in halting the treks, Paddock said.

What a pity! As one who made a couple of glacier climbs, I know what a memorable experience it was.

September 9, 1984

Hikers in 1961 made their way up to the base of Arapaho glacier near Boulder. The Chamber of Commerce sponsored the annual treks to the glacier, source of some of the city's water.

Columbus Day started in Denver

COLUMBUS Day, celebrated for years on Oct. 12, a few years ago was changed by Congress to the second Monday of October to accommodate those who like 3-day weekends.

Traditionalists may complain about such revision of history. But the fact that we celebrate Columbus Day at all is the work of a persevering and dedicated Italian printer, Angelo Noce, who organized Denver's north side Italians into a lobby that convinced the Colorado General Assembly that Christopher Columbus was a man worthy of a day, like Washington or Lincoln.

Columbus wasn't just an Italian hero, Noce argued; all Americans owe him a lot.

Noce was born in 1848 in Genoa, Italy, Columbus' birthplace, and that may have fueled his zeal. He came to America with his parents and attended St. Mary's College in San Francisco, then moved to Denver and started a printing business. Noce also served as a deputy sheriff for a time, as a constable and a clerk in the legislature.

Thanks to the efforts of Noce, Denver's Italian community celebrated Columbus Day regularly on Oct. 12, anniversary of the discovery of America, but the rest of the city paid little attention to it. Noce kept agitating, however, and in 1905, a bill was introduced in the legislature by Casimiro Barela, a senator of Spanish descent.

In 1907, the bill passed, making Colorado the first state to celebrate Columbus Day. Far from satisfied, the little Genoan from Denver started lobbying from state to state to see that everyone had a Columbus Day. He delegated his wife to carry the campaign to women's groups.

By the time Noce died in 1922, 35 states had adopted his idea and were celebrating Oct. 12 as Columbus Day.

Meanwhile, Noce also persuaded his friend Mayor Robert W. Speer to name a north Denver park after Columbus, and a mountain peak had been named Columbus.

By 1967, 38 states had designated Oct. 12 as a holiday. Congress made it a national holiday in 1968.

Pueblo also scored a first in the name of Columbus. Hector Chiariglion of Pueblo started the annual observance of Columbus Day there long before it became a state holiday. For many years he also was president of the National Columbian Federation.

Columbo F. Delliquadri of Pueblo, a delegate to the first annual meeting of the Columbian Federation in Chicago in 1892, appealed to the other delegates to start a fund for a monument to Columbus. By 1905, Pueblo had the first American statue of Columbus which was placed on a parkway in front of McClelland Library. The sculptor was Italian Pietro Piai.

In June 1970, Denver got a statue in honor of Columbus, a modernistic creation of circles representing the world, with a figure of Columbus in the center.

The artist is William Joseph of Denver, and the sculpture was given by Alfred P. Adamo of Detroit, who in his youth in Denver had caught the Columbus fever from Noce. Adamo, who once worked as a janitor in the state capitol, also gave a 29-inch statue of the explorer to the Colorado Historical Society Museum.

October 7, 1984

Hero of a train wreck loved his wife, indeed

A monument along the South Platte River near Dome Rock carries the intriguing inscription: "Tell my wife I died thinking of her." One reader asked for more information, and others came through.

The monument honors William "Billy" Westall, and one of the first with that information was Frances B. Rizzari of Golden. Other answers came from Florence Bilderback of Wheat Ridge, L.M. Meeker of Denver, Frank Humes of Westminster and G. King of Buffalo Creek. The story also is told in M.C. Poor's book, *Denver, South Park and Pacific.*

King said the monument stands in the area that will be flooded by Two Forks Dam, if the dam is built.

Westall was an engineer for the Denver, South Park & Pacific Railroad. Like the captain of a ship, he went down with his train.

It was the afternoon of Aug. 28, 1898, and Westall was at the helm of a seven-car excursion train on its way to Denver carrying 450 passengers. An afternoon cloudburst had dampened the crowd's spirits.

As the engine rounded a curve near Dome Rock, Westall saw the track covered with a pile of sand and gravel washed down by the cloudburst.

Rather than jump to safety, Westall and his fireman, Joseph Nichols, tried to stop the train. They slowed it and prevented a disaster.

As the engine struck and overturned, Nichols was thrown clear and landed unhurt. No passengers were injured. But Westall was pinned in the wreckage.

He died 12 hours later as Nichols held him. His last words were, "Tell my wife I died thinking of her."

These words are engraved on the 10-foot-tall granite monument that marks the site of the wreck near Dome Rock. The monument was erected in South Platte Canyon on Sept. 5, 1899,

by the American Order of United Workmen, and carries the letters AOUW and other notations.

Westall's friends and admirers supplied the money.

October 21, 1984

Rocky Mountain News

Monument to Billy Westall who died in 1898 says: "Tell my wife I died thinking of her."

Denver had a heroine in the Civil War

WE were amazed to get a letter from Mrs. P.A.J. Kerley of Rownhams, Hampshire, England. She asked:

"How many of your readers have ever heard of Sadie Likens, let alone know where the fountain commemorating this great heroine of the Civil War was erected 60 years ago?

"Sadie Likens was one of the first in her field — Denver's first police matron (1884), Denver's first woman's libber, surely, and yet not a woman to be gainsaid for her devotion to others.

"From the battle of Shiloh onward she devoted her life to the care of firstly, the wounded, and subsequently, the relatives and orphans of the deceased.

"Let's see a big photograph of the fountain which can be found on the corner of East Colfax and Broadway in the grounds of the state capitol. Sadie deserves a resounding tribute to her tremendous selflessness."

Mrs. Kerley doesn't explain her interest in Likens. However, we are grateful to her for calling attention to someone who was a distinguished individual in Colorado history.

Sadie Likens was the first Colorado woman to have a public memorial in her honor raised by popular subscription.

In connection with her work as Denver's first police matron, Baker and Hafen's *History of Colorado* says:

"Her great work was demonstrating beyond cavil that wherever women are held in subjection, a woman should be. Until she was installed in a pitifully inadequate little place upstairs and at the rear of the city jail, there was no place to put a lost child, a woman void of offense, held as a witness or for investigation, except a place known as 'the hospital cell' adjacent to the 'dark cells.'

"Ordinary women prisoners were locked up in half-a-dozen cells next to the male prisoners where they could converse back and forth. Un-

Rocky Mountain News

Fountain dedicated to Sadie Likens is at southeast corner of Colfax Avenue and Broadway.

speakable abuses took place. Even with this proof . . . it was some time before a woman matron was installed in the county jail, where the need was less."

Likens was believed to have been the second police matron in the nation. The first was appointed in Chicago at the insistence of the Chicago Woman's Club.

Likens was born July 14, 1840, in Trenton, Ohio, the daughter of Moses Morehouse, a widely known minister.

Her life was fairly routine until the early days of the Civil War when she lost her husband, two brothers and four nephews in the conflict.

She then enlisted to aid the wounded in the battle of Shiloh and later was transferred from battlefield to battlefield, helping the injured. At the end of the war, she returned briefly to her home in Cincinnati, and then moved to Denver.

In Denver she was one of the organizers of the Woman's Relief Corps, an auxiliary to the Grand Army of the Republic.

With the start of the Spanish-American War she again became active, caring for the wounded and helping veterans. She went on to help those who needed her during World War I.

Likens' first interest was veterans' organiza-tions, but she also gave her services to the causes of women and children. She helped organize the Denver Cottage Home and the Florence Crittenton Home for unwed mothers. She helped found the Girls Friendly Club and the Denver Orphans Home and was involved in the Old Ladies Home.

She was active in many veterans' organizations and the Women's Christian Temperance Union.

With all this, Likens still had time to rear four children.

She died July 30, 1920, at the home of a daughter, Mrs. J.H. Haggerty.

In 1923, veterans in the Denver area voted Likens the most deserving heroine of the Civil War, and a campaign was started to erect a memorial in her honor. The legislature approved placing a memorial fountain on the capitol grounds.

Contributions for the fountain came from individuals, the Woman's Relief Corps, the Grand Army Ladies, Sons and Daughters of Veterans and the WCTU. The fountain was set on the Capitol grounds in 1923.

October 28, 1984

Did Boxer Rebellion start in Denver?

Rocky Mountain News

The Great Wall of China is regarded by many as mankind's greatest building enterprise.

Denver has had a full share of hoaxes perpetrated by sharp schemers in its 125-year history, but perhaps none had the repercussions of the Great Wall scam dreamed up by a quartet of Denver newsmen.

Myldred Jorgensen of Denver asked us to tell the story.

It's one of those wild tales we'll probably never be sure is true. As far as we can trace it, the story first appeared in print in *The North American Review* in 1939.

In 1899, Denver had four daily papers — the *Rocky Mountain News, The Denver Post, Denver Republican* and *Denver Times.*

As the story goes, it was a dull Saturday night in Denver, and four reporters, one from each paper, were assigned to cover the area around Union Station. The four are said to have been Al Stevens, Jack Tournay, John Lewis and Hal Wilshire.

These four newsmen met in the station, and all complained that they had found no news for their Sunday papers. They repaired to the nearby Oxford Hotel bar to consider the problem.

Stevens, fearing to go back to the office with nothing, said he was going to invent a story. The others liked the idea and also decided to fake a news item.

As they discussed the idea, they agreed it was better to share in one big news item, which they all would swear was true, than to come up with four weak stories. Several local possibilities were considered and discarded, because they could be checked too easily.

The four plotters decided it was best to have a foreign locale for their fiction. After rejecting several ideas, they seized upon a brainstorm by

Lewis. He suggested that they invent a tale about tearing down the Great Wall of China.

After drinking beer, the four plotters went back to their offices with a story that a party of engineers from New York had been in Denver that day, en route to China. These experts were going to inspect the wall with the idea of razing it at the lowest possible cost.

The engineers' firm had been hired by the rulers of China who had decided to raze the Great Wall as a symbol to the world that China welcomed trade.

The great Wall of China was started in the third century B.C. and meandered along 3,700 miles of China's northern border. It was 20 feet high and wide enough for five horses to walk abreast. It had more than 25,000 lookout towers, each 40 feet high.

To give the story authenticity, the reporters left the Oxford and went down the street to the Windsor Hotel, Denver's best, and wheedled the help of the night clerk into "registering" the engineers with fictitious names. The clerk was sworn to secrecy and promised to answer all inquiries with the statement that the engineers had left the next morning for China.

Wilshire's city editor, John Charles Mason, was so impressed with the story that he scheduled it for the front page, although he was disappointed that it wasn't an exclusive. The story ran with a headline that the Great Chinese Wall was doomed.

Similar articles and headlines ran in the three other newspapers.

The story was picked up by the wire services and was run all over the world. Two weeks later an eastern newspaper came out with an interview with a wealthy Chinese who confirmed the article.

China, at the time, had a secret society, the Boxers, whose purpose was to drive out foreigners. When the story about the wall reached China, it incensed the Boxers, some accounts said. Newspapers next carried stories that "western barbarians," missionaries and other foreigners had been massacred and embassies attacked. It's unclear whether the Denver story provoked the attacks.

In retaliation, 12,000 troops composed of British, French, Russian, Japanese and American forces marched on Peking. Many were slaughtered in the short-lived rebellion.

Several years later, reporter Wilshire was assigned to cover a speech at Trinity Church by Methodist Bishop Henry W. Warren, who was talking about his recent tour through China.

Warren warned his listeners of the power of the printed word.

"Bad news and false news pick up fuel and eventually blaze devastatingly," he said. "As an example of the havoc that can be wrought, take the Boxer Rebellion. The spark that set off the tinder in that war was struck in a town in western Kansas or Nebraska (it was really Colorado, as Wilshire knew) by three (four) reporters who concocted and printed a wild yarn for what reason I have never been able to find out, that the huge, sacred Chinese Wall was to be razed by American engineers, and the country would be thrown wide open to hated foreigners.

"This pure canard reached China, and the newspapers there printed it with shouting headlines and editorial comment. Denial did no good. The Boxers, already incensed, believed the yarn, and there was no stopping them.

"It was the last straw, and hell broke loose to the horror of the world. All this from a sensational but untrue story."

Fortunately, the minister's story fell on somewhat skeptical ears, and the congregation had a hard time believing that anything so serious as the Boxer Rebellion could have come from a prank by four Denver reporters.

Wilshire slipped out of the church without comment.

November 4, 1984

Wyatt Earp's Colorado connection

MOST of us have heard of Wyatt Earp, one of the West's most famous gunslingers. He's most often associated with the gunfight at the OK corral, probably the most celebrated gunfight in frontier history, which took place Oct. 26, 1881, in Tombstone, Ariz.

But he also racked up a little history in Colorado.

Earp was born in Monmouth, Ill., in 1848. As a young man he was a buffalo hunter, rode shotgun on stagecoaches, was an assistant marshal in Dodge City, Kan., in 1878 and '79, and gradually blasted and gambled his way through the gold camps of Colorado, Arizona and Alaska.

He arrived in the Gunnison area in June 1882, as a newspaper account at the time said, "about two jumps ahead of police officers from Tombstone."

Earp was accompanied by his brother, Warren Earp, Texas George, Big Tip and John Henry "Doc" Holliday, all quick-on-the-draw men who had been involved with him in the fighting on the streets of Tombstone.

They rented the second floor of a downtown building to open a faro bank and beer garden. A barber shop and saloon owned by Ernest F. Bieble occupied the ground floor.

Wyatt Earp, according to reports at the time, was considered good-looking, with a drooping mustache curled at the ends. He wore two guns high under his arms but was quiet and well-behaved if not provoked. However, Bat Masterson and Wild Bill Hickok said they regarded Earp as the greatest gunfighter ever.

With a reputation like his, he was sure to attract the attention of Sid Byers, Gunnison's town marshal, and Joseph Blackstock and Judd Riley, members of the police force. The lawmen, however, had no confrontations with Earp because he never fired his pistols while he was in Gunnison; no one challenged him to the draw.

In a story published in the *Rocky Mountain News* in 1960, Adela Rogers St. Johns recalled an interview with Wyatt Earp when he was 80. The formula for being a successful gunslinger, he told her, was:

"Stay calm, keep your mouth shut and take your time ... don't figger to pull the trigger but once."

Discussing the gunfight at the OK corral, in which three cattle rustlers were killed and two others jailed, he told St. Johns:

"It took about 30 seconds." It took longer than that when Randolph Scott and Hugh O'Brian played Earp in the movies and on TV.

The faro venture in Gunnison lasted about a year. Then the gang split up and left town. Earp was in and out of Colorado for the next 5 years. At times, he worked as a gambler in Trinidad, Silverton, Aspen and Denver.

In Denver, he dealt faro for Ed Chase and Ed Gaylord at the Arcade. He lived at the same boarding house as Bat Masterson, who also was dealing at the Arcade.

Earp eventually settled in San Francisco. He went to California in 1891 after an Arizona murder warrant was issued for him. He was charged with shooting three men he blamed for killing his brother, Morgan.

In California he sometimes worked as a consultant for 1920s movies on the Old West, and he became a friend of western stars Bill Hart and Tom Mix and of fighter Jack Dempsey.

Earp died with his boots off in 1929, at the age of 81. His body was cremated, and his ashes were placed near those of his in-laws, the Marcus family, in Eternity Cemetery on a hillside south of San Francisco. His wife, Josephine, who died in 1944, shares the tombstone.

Doc Holliday died of tuberculosis in Glenwood Springs Nov. 8, 1887, and was buried there.

November 11, 1984

Ex-slave made, lost fortunes in Denver

IF you happen some night or noon to dine in Denver's east Indian restaurant, the Tandoor at 1514 Blake St., you might like to think about Barney L. Ford, the mulatto pioneer who built the building in 1863.

Ford was a businessman, politician and civil rights leader, a long journey from his birth as a slave in Stafford, Va., Jan. 22, 1822.

He made and lost several fortunes in Nicaragua, Wyoming, California and Colorado. At times his assets were listed as greater than those of such Denver luminaries as A.B. Daniels, of department store fame, real estate developer Walter Cheesman and railroad magnate David Moffatt.

Ford, the son of a slave and a white plantation owner who educated him, had dark skin, blue eyes and dark reddish-brown hair.

He was christened only as Barney. In Chicago, after he had run away, he named himself "Launcelot Ford" after a steam engine of that name.

In his teens, Ford was sold to a man who put him to work in the gold fields of Auraria, Ga., where he caught "gold fever."

Sent north on an errand, Ford escaped in Quincy, Ill., and went to Chicago. There, he met H.O. Wagoner, a free black who ran a livery stable and was active in the underground railroad, helping slaves escape.

Ford learned to be a barber, worked as a steward in a wealthy household and married Julia Lyoni.

The California gold rush stirred Ford's gold fever, and he and Julia headed west, via ship through Nicaragua. Ford grew ill in Nicaragua and remained to launch his first business, a small hotel and restaurant.

A few years later, the couple returned to Chicago, where Ford helped Wagoner with the underground railroad.

But the Colorado gold boom lured him West once more. He arrived in Denver in May 1860

Western History Department, Denver Public Library

Barney Ford, businessman, politician and civil rights leader, is well-remembered in Denver.

and filed two claims near Central City. But white men seized them under a law that barred blacks from filing mining claims.

Moving on to Summit County, Ford and two other blacks struck gold on a hill that came to be called "Nigger Hill." In 1964, the Board of Geographic Names changed the name to Barney Ford Hill.

When Ford returned to Denver, he opened a barbershop on Blake Street but lost it in the April 1863 fire.

Luther Kountze, of Kountze Brothers Banking, refused to lend Ford $1,000 to rebuild, but instead, lent him $9,000 to support a good business. Kountze's only security was Ford's reputation for honesty and dependability, but he charged 25% interest.

Ford built the structure at 1514 Blake St. and opened the People's Restaurant on the ground floor, a bar on the second floor and a barbershop in the basement.

The restaurant was advertised as offering "the most choice and delicate luxuries of Colorado and the East," with "oyster suppers to order."

Ford paid back the $9,000 within 90 days after opening.

Some historical accounts have referred to Ford as a "president maker." That's doubtful, but he did help keep Colorado from attaining statehood until its proposed constitution allowed blacks to vote. In this effort, Ford sold or leased his Denver properties and went to Washington to lobby for his cause.

When he returned, after Colorado blacks had the franchise, he opened a restaurant at Blake and G streets.

In 1872, he built the 4-story Inter-Ocean Hotel at 16th and Blake streets, and helped found the Dime Savings Bank. He organized the Colored Republican Club and joined the Colorado Republican Central Committee.

Ford built the Inter-Ocean Hotel for $53,000 and sold it 2 years later for $75,000. At the request of a Cheyenne citizens committee, he built a hotel in the Wyoming capital but lost it during a financial panic.

He then opened a small restaurant, Ford's Chop House, in Breckenridge. Later, he acquired a larger restaurant there, the Saddle Rock.

By 1881, he was back in Denver with a new restaurant, the Oyster Ocean. Later, he bought a house at 1569 High St., and his wife was listed in Denver's Social Year Book for 1898, the first and only black on the list.

While Ford was fighting statehood for Colorado unless it came in as a free state, he told other blacks: "You must vote, but vote with knowledge."

He helped establish the first adult education classes in Denver in 1866 to teach reading and writing.

Ford died after a stroke in December 1902 and was buried in Riverside Cemetery beside his wife, who had died 3 years earlier.

Honors have followed Ford's death. The Barney Ford Memorial Association was organized in 1975 under the leadership of Kathryne McKinney. In 1981, the legislature placed a commemorative stained glass window in the capitol.

A chair carved with his name was dedicated in the Central City Opera House, and the building at 1514 Blake St. was listed on the National Register of Historic Places and declared a Denver landmark.

A housing project at East 20th Avenue and Clarkson Street opened in 1968 as Barney Ford Heights. And Ford Elementary School in Montbello, in the Denver Public Schools system, is named for him.

November 18, 1984

Children and grownups headed up Bulldog Mountain for the yule log hunt at Palmer Lake. It's an old custom, revitalized in the Colorado community for the enjoyment of one and all.

Christmas tradition logs half a century

IN 2 weeks, Palmer Lake will observe the 50th annniversary of one of the loveliest Christmas traditions in the country.

In 1934, this little town that sits around a lake on the Continental Divide adopted the English custom of hunting and burning a yule log. It started with an idea hatched by the Rev. Eva-lena Macy, then pastor of the Little Log Church at Palmer Lake, and Lucretia Vaile, a librarian.

Over the 50 years, thousands have traveled to Palmer Lake for the hunt, which is followed by drinking punch and burning the log in the Town Hall's huge fireplace.

The 1984 hunt will start at 1 p.m. Dec. 16 with the sounding of a trumpet in front of the Town Hall.

The guest of honor will be Charlie Orr, 97, longtime Palmer Lake resident whose home was the setting of the first few yule log ceremonies.

Following tradition, the yule log has been cut and hidden on Sundance Mountain northwest of town. The identity of the person who hid the log remains a secret until the log is found.

When the trumpet sounds, hundreds of log hunters, many wearing red or green capes, will start out escorted by trail leaders. Those who stay behind will be treated to Christmas carols and other entertainment in the Town Hall.

Searchers will walk nearly a mile — often through snow — until a second blast from the trumpet tells them they are within 200 feet of the log.

Then it's every man for himself, and whoever finds the log gets to ride on it back to town, pulled by the others.

In front of the Town Hall the log will be sawed in two, with the finder on one end of a two-person saw. Half the log will be burned in the Town Hall fireplace, and half will be saved to become the starter for next year's fire.

To begin a yule log tradition, a starter splinter must be obtained from a yule log in another town. Palmer Lake's splinter was sent from a yule log ceremony in Lake Placid, N.Y., in 1933. Since then, the Colorado town has sent splinters of its yule logs to other towns around the country.

As the log burns, some of Palmer Lake's 6-year-olds will carry the ancient silver wassail cup and ladle to the stage, singing an old English song: "Here we come a-wassailing, among the leaves so green." Everyone will repeat the ancient toast: "Wassail — health to you," and the crowd will move to a silver punch bowl for a drink.

The first drink will go to the one who found the log, the second to the one who hid it. Roger Voelker will concoct this year's punch from a recipe that includes hot cider, baked apples, ground oranges and lemons and spices.

Several days ahead of the main event, the yule log committee meets for a covered-dish supper in the Town Hall, then stays to decorate the hall and make souvenirs.

After the meal, men and boys will cut tiny souvenir lapel logs; women and girls will tie crimson ribbons on them. Everyone who attends the ceremony will get a souvenir log.

Palmer Lake residents expect the 1984 yule log ceremony to be one of the best ever, in honor of the 50th anniversary.

December 2, 1984

Finding Shangri-La

A reader in Springfield, Ill., has written asking about Shangri-La, the Denver mansion built by theater magnate Harry Huffman.

Marie Harper writes: "On a recent trip to Denver I finally found and visited Cranmer Park, which was Mountain View Park when I first visited Denver. On my first visit I was particularly fascinated with the Shangri-La, which, as I recall, was a handsome home elevated and surrounded by a stone wall, on a corner. I'd like to know if it still exists. It is evidently obscured by trees and the lovely homes around the park.

"The land for the park, I understand, was donated by the Cranmer family. A smaller sun dial replaces the original one.

"I'd appreciate any information on the park and Shangri-La."

She said she is glad to see D&F Tower still standing and hopes the Brown Palace Hotel "will be spared the wrecking ball."

Dear Miss Harper:

Time and distance sometimes alter things in our memories. I have the impression you think Shangri-La was placed to overlook Cranmer Park, which is at East Second Avenue and Cherry Street. The house called Shangri-La stands at 13 Leetsdale Drive, on a hill with several homes below it. (They are about 4 blocks apart.)

At the time you last saw it, this subdivision probably was just a grassy hill. The expanse of greenery beyond it is Burns Park, which was donated to the city by real-estate agent Franklin Burns when Harry Huffman bought acreage for the house.

Huffman was a registered pharmacist with his own drugstore at West Colfax Avenue and Lipan Street around the turn of the century.

Rocky Mountain News

Shangri-La stands on a hill in southeast Denver just off Leetsdale Drive. It was built in 1937 by Harry Huffman and designed from plans for the monastery, Shangri-La, in the movie *Lost Horizon*.

In 1906, he opened a nickelodeon slide show adjoining the pharmacy, inspired by the idea that showgoers would stop for a soda after the show. Clerks hired for the store had to be able to sing during the slide show.

The nickelodeon proved to be more of a success than the pharmacy, and Huffman began to expand in show business until he headed the Fox-Intermountain chain in Denver. In 1926, he built a fine theater — the Aladdin on East Colfax Avenue — designed in the style of a Moorish palace. In 1929 Huffman awed movie-goers by showing the first talking motion picture in the city at the Aladdin. The picture was *The Jazz Singer*, starring Al Jolson.

In the 1930s, Huffman with his wife, the former Christine Keehn, bought 6½ acres on a hill overlooking Leetsdale Drive, where he planned to build a Spanish-style home with a red-tile roof. The land once was part of Leetsdale Farm, a subdivision started in 1889 by Denver realty agent John Leet.

Huffman changed his ideas about the house when he saw the movie, *Lost Horizon* with its monastery, Shangri-La.

He got plans for the building from Columbia Pictures and had them modified by Denver architect Raymond H. Ervin. The house's center faces Mount Evans, the north wing looks toward Longs Peak and the south wing faces Pikes Peak.

The house was built in 1937. Its most unusual feature is the art deco entryway, which soars two stories above the stairway and is decorated with a chandelier of large dangling glass balls.

The Huffman home became a focal point for large receptions and dinners honoring figures of the entertainment world. Mrs. Huffman decorated the entryway lavishly during each holiday season.

Huffman died in 1969 at 85. Two years later the house was sold to a 21-year-old bachelor, David Rumbough, son of actress Dina Merrill and grandson of Marjorie Merriwether Post of the breakfast-food fortune.

Rumbough, a University of Denver student, drowned Sept. 9, 1973, when the shaft of his high-powered motor boat gave way at 60 miles an hour, and he was thrown overboard into Gardiners Bay at East Hampton, N.Y.

Now, longtime Denverite A. Barry Hirschfeld owns Shangri-La. It's hard to see unless you know what you're looking for, but it may be spotted from East Alameda Avenue or South Colorado Boulevard.

December 30, 1984

Rocky Mountain News

Mr. and Mrs. Harry Huffman entertained at many lavish parties at Shangri-La.

Chapter 5

Molly Brown found Field quite unsinkable

MRS. J.J. Brown, Denver's famous "unsinkable Molly Brown," learned the poems of Eugene Field in her youth and enjoyed them throughout her life. In an interview in the late 1920s, she said:

"The first money I ever made was when the miners rolled silver dollars on the stage when I recited Field's poems at Leadville. When I, with Judge (Ben) Lindsey, sponsored the first Juvenile Court benefits, I always recited his poems.

"I recited Field's poems in New York, when 2,000 assembled at the Waldorf-Astoria to greet me when I came up from the Titanic disaster. I have read his poems to soldiers and miners, and he has always gone over big."

Field, on his own, achieved considerable fame in Denver, both as poet and prankster. He was managing editor of the *Denver Tribune* from 1881 to 1883 and wrote a column, which started under the name *Nonpareil,* but was changed to *Odd Gossip.* He left Denver when he was 33 to write his famous *Sharps and Flats* column for the *Chicago Morning News.* He died about 12 years later.

In Denver, Field wasn't above fabricating a news story. Among these works was a supposed interview with 12 wives of Brigham Young. He also had a bottomless chair in his office, with the defect covered by newspapers, and he delighted in offering this to visitors.

Brown, as a fan of Field's, was a natural to save the cottage in which Field had lived at 315 W. Colfax Ave., just across from the Denver Mint.

Field lived in the house during 1881 and 1882 with his wife, Julia; daughter, Mary, 6; a son, Melvin, 4; and an infant, Eugene Jr. Julia Field left for St. Louis late in 1882 for the birth of another child.

Brown was approached to save the house by the late Elizabeth Kuskulis, president of the Colorado branch of American Penwomen, and the group's vice president, Caroline Dier.

"We met in the rotunda of the Brown Palace Hotel," Kuskulis said later. "Mrs. Brown was all interest and enthusiasm. . . . While she was quick and generous in assuming all expenses entailed, she left to us all the research and planning necessary for the restoration, although she was intensely interested and insisted on making it a trio whenever any selections of materials or work were to be made."

Brown paid rent on the dilapidated little cottage for 2 years, from 1928 to 1930, and maintained it as the Eugene Field Memorial.

In a later interview, she said the house had been preserved as it was, including "the little chair where Eugene Field's son, the inspiration for *Little Boy Blue,* left his toys the night he died of the croup." *Little Boy Blue,* his most famous poem, was written in a bedroom in the home in less than 2 hours.

Brown finally bought the little cottage for $350, turned it over to the city, then left on a trip to Europe.

The land remained under other ownership, and in 1930, the owner demanded that the cottage be removed. Malcolm Wyer, then librarian of the Denver Public Library, persuaded the city to give the house to the library and move it to Washington Park.

Brown was in Paris in 1930 when she learned that Field's cottage was to be turned into a branch of the library. She was not pleased.

"You see," she said to friends, "we are such utilitarians at home that, in spite of all our space, we must utilize one of our greatest poet's homes as a library. . . . They will paint it up, put frescoes of nursery scenes on the walls, and poems on the ceilings. . . . "

The house was moved to a corner of Washington Park at 715 S. Franklin St., where it was used as the Eugene Field Branch Library. When a library was built at 810 S. University Blvd. in

1970 and named the Eugene Field Library, the city gave the cottage to the Park People for their headquarters.

The Field cottage has been declared a Denver landmark and is listed by the Colorado Landmark Preservation Commission. Sue Cannon, president of the Park People, says the house has been restored and furnished as a meeting place. Heating and wiring have been modernized and a garden added to the grounds.

The statue of Wynken, Blynken and Nod, based on Field's poem, *Dutch Lullaby*, stands not far away.

February 3, 1985

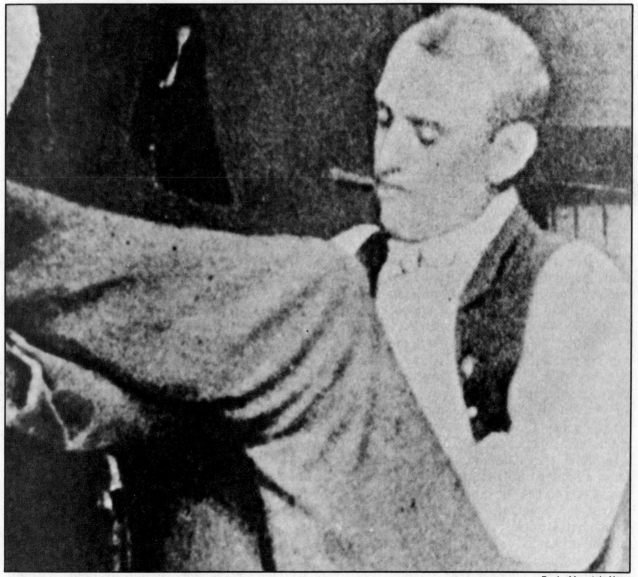

Rocky Mountain News

Eugene Field, who achieved fame in Denver as a poet and prankster, relaxed at his newsroom desk. He once lived in a cottage on West Colfax Avenue, which has been moved to Washington Park.

Denver street names put past in present

BURNETT Meyer of Denver has opened a treasure chest of interesting material with a question on the naming of Denver streets.

"I have been wondering when the present system of numbered streets and avenues was instituted in Denver," he writes. "The oldest maps I have seen do not have any numbered streets. . . .

"It would be interesting to know why 1st Street and 1st Avenue were located where they were. I cannot find 1st Street on current maps, but I assume there was one before the Valley Highway (Interstate 25) was built. It must have been in a location which was quite a distance from the center of town. Even stranger is the location of 1st Avenue, which must have been several miles out in the country."

Dear Mr. Meyer:

You'll be glad to know that "wasoola" is an Arapaho Indian word for "short and fat." This is a tidbit I uncovered while looking for an answer.

Court Place first was called Wasoola Street, but no one seems to know why. Some say it didn't mean "short and fat," but was the name of William McGaa's Indian wife. Other historians maintain that "Wewatta" was the name of McGaa's wife, and we still have a street named for her. McGaa and John Smith, both early mountain men, furnished city fathers with many of the Indian names given to streets.

In his *History of Denver*, published in 1901, Jerome Smiley wrote that in 1860 many street names were changed in the towns of Auraria, Denver and Highlands. The three towns were consolidated by an act of the Jefferson Legislature in December 1859, and Denver became a legal fact during the first Colorado Territorial Legislature in November 1861.

The names bestowed by the Aurarians and Highlanders disappeared, and by 1900 a majority of Denver's street names had been changed.

Denver's clerk and recorder Felicia Muftic gave us help on this question, along with city engineer Tex Pool and design engineer Frank King. A map in the City-County Building shows downtown streets before they had numbers — when they were known by alphabetical letters, A, B, C, D, E, etc.

Pool said that in 1859, Auraria, across Cherry Creek from Denver, was changed to West Denver. An ordinance passed in 1873 abolished the alphabetical series and instated the present numerical system, applying to 16th Street and its parallels. Jackson Street became 1st Street, a street that disappeared under the Valley Highway.

These streets did not run on a true line east and west, but when the avenues were put in later, they were aligned with points of the compass, Pool said.

"A" Street was changed to 10th Street in 1875, "B" became Speer Boulevard, "C" was 12th Street, and so on until "F" became 15th Street.

The story was different for other street names. S.S. Curtis, a director of the Denver Town Co., is quoted in Smiley's *History of Denver:*

"The intention of the directors of the Denver Town Co. in naming the streets was to give those running in a northeasterly and southwesterly direction alternately names of members of the town company and Indian names. . . . "

"Champa, I think, is Arapaho for some common animal — deer, antelope, horse, steer, buffalo or dog. . . . " Another theory is that Champa may be a corruption of the Indian word, "yampai," pronounced yampa, for bear.

Other streets were named for pioneer sheriff E.W. Wynkoop; oldtime merchant Charles H. Blake; McGaa for mountain man William McGaa; Larimer for Gen. William Larimer, a leader in the Denver Town Co. along with Charles A. Lawrence (Lawrence Street) and S.S. Curtis (Curtis Street).

McGaa Street later was changed to Holladay Street to honor local stage operator Ben Holladay. After that, it became Market Street.

Stout Street was named for E.P. Stout, first president of the Denver Town Co., and Welton was named after N.W. Welton, who arrived in 1858 and was one of the first shareholders in the Denver Town Co. Glenarm Place was named by McGaa after Glen Arm, an estate he admired in Scotland.

Tremont was first called Clancy Street after William Clancy of the Denver Town Co. Clancy moved to Butte, Mont., and the city council changed the name to Tremont. Many believed it was intended to be "Fremont" after John C. Fremont, an early western explorer known as "the pathfinder."

Court Place originally was called Parkinson Street, after Capt. T.J. Parkinson, who arrived in October 1858 and was identified with both Auraria and Denver. It next became Wasoola and was changed to Court Place when the courthouse was built. (The courthouse has since been torn down, and the downtown May D&F store occupies the site.)

Streets were named, and then changed as subdivisions appeared, Pool said. The avenues were not all named at once. Colfax Avenue, for instance, was named with the Henry C. Brown addition in 1868. The present 16th Avenue, running east of Broadway, was first called Sheridan Street, then became 16th Street under an 1873 ordinance. Finally, it became 16th Avenue.

March 3, 1985

The readers said . . .

ELIZABETH Hall of Denver wrote:
"My grandfather, A.J. Williams, settled in Denver in November 1858. He was a partner of Charles Blake. My grandmother told me there was a Williams Street below Blake Street, and that when the railroad tracks came through Denver, Williams Street was obliterated. However, the farthest street in Capitol Hill was then named Williams Street. It was quite far out in the country then.

"Does this agree with your research on the streets of Denver?"

Dear Mrs. Hall:

Your information mainly is correct. There was a short street named Williams in lower downtown Denver. After a few years, the name of Williams Street was changed to Chestnut, and maps still show a Chestnut Street in the vicinity of the tracks. In order, going southeast, the streets were Bassett, Chestnut, Delgany, Wewatta, Wynkoop, Wazee, Blake, Market, Larimer, and so on, as we know them now.

When Williams Street became Chestnut Street, another Williams Street was placed "uptown," where it remains today, between Gilpin and High streets.

May 19, 1985

Potato Clark — popular and profane

A letter asking for a little history on "Potato" Clark comes from Mrs. Ford Fox of Denver. She writes:

"In 1942, we purchased the old 'Potato' Clark home at 1398 S. Santa Fe Drive, with six lots, from the Mary Elizabeth Bates Foundation. We paid the unbelievable price of $3,500 for it, $35 down and $35 a month. It had stood vacant for more than a year when we bought it.

"We fixed it up, but didn't stay in it long because we felt it was dangerous for our daughters to be crossing the railroad tracks to get to school.

"There were kennels attached to the back of the house. The Dumb Friends League Kennels were in the block just north of us. I always have been curious about Dr. Bates' role in founding the Dumb Friends League. Can you tell me about it? Also, I'd like to hear Potato Clark's story."

Dear Mrs. Fox:

Let's begin with Clark. Rufus "Potato" Clark was profane and hard-drinking and had lived a lifetime of adventure by the time he came West.

Clark was born in Coventry, Ky., Dec. 4, 1822, into a family that traced its descent from the Clark who was a mate on the Mayflower.

Rufus left the family farm when he was 16 to ship out on whaling vessels operating around the Cape of Good Hope and in the Indian Ocean.

He was shipwrecked on the Navigators Islands, now known as Samoa, in 1852 on a voyage to Australia. After his rescue he found work in Australian gold mines. That wasn't to his liking, so he quit and walked 400 miles to Melbourne.

Two years later, Clark, at 32, had worked his way back to Connecticut. He had no money, but he moved to Taylor County, Iowa, where he farmed, built a sawmill and married Lucinda Watts.

With the discovery of gold in Colorado, Clark and his bride headed West by ox train in April

Rufus "Potato" Clark got his name by auctioning potatoes to help 1871 Chicago Fire victims.

1859. Three months later they took up 160 acres of land along the South Platte River, 7 miles south of Denver.

Clark grew a variety of vegetables, but concentrated on potatoes, selling them at inflated prices. He is said to have made $30,000 from one crop.

Despite that success, he was regarded as a drunkard. However, he was known as a man of his word and was well-liked. He invested in land around Denver and at one time was paying taxes on 4,500 pieces of property.

Clark's wife died in 1861. He was elected to the territorial legislature in 1864 and he became a member of the Arapahoe County School Board in 1867.

When news of the Chicago Fire flashed across the country in October 1871, he drove into town with a wagonload of potatoes that he auctioned to aid fire victims. One sack brought $270, and the auction raised $7,200 that was sent to Chicago.

Clark joined the United Brethren Church in 1873 and helped found the Salvation Army in Denver. He also quit drinking and gambling and spent hours in prayer. After his conversion, he said:

"Everything I touched seemed to turn to money."

He deeded 80 acres of land in southeast Denver to former Gov. John Evans in 1886 as the site for the University of Denver, which was downtown at the time, and added $500 in cash to help build it. In return, he was named a trustee of the university.

That was only the start of Clark's benefactions. In 1886, he and his fourth wife, the former Ella Perryman, built a three-story stone building for the Rufus Clark and Wife Theological Training School 60 miles from Freetown on the West Coast of Africa in what is now Sierra Leone. The school was to educate missionaries.

In the early 1890s, Clark sold half of his homestead land but retained the house. The rest of the land became Overland Park.

Clark died in the house Oct. 14, 1910, at the age of 87, one of Denver's most honored citizens. He left no children, but Lois Guyer of Boulder and Dr. John Perryman of Englewood are a great-niece and great-nephew through his marriage to Ella Perryman.

March 3, 1985

Our dumb friends can thank Dr. Bates

COLORADO history is peppered with re-markable women. One on the Denver scene until recently was Dr. Mary Elizabeth Bates.

Bates, born in Manitowoc, Wis., in 1861, did unorthodox things in a ladylike way. Among other things, she was the first woman intern to train at Cook County Hospital in Chicago, and none followed her for 5 years.

When she arrived in Denver in 1890, she became one of the first women to wear a divided skirt for bicycling. She helped establish the Denver Dumb Friends' League and the Colorado Humane Society, and lobbied through many of the state's present humane laws.

When she was 16, Mary Elizabeth Bates attended commencement exercises of the Women's Medical College of Chicago, later part of Northwestern University, and there was inspired to become a doctor. She graduated from Women's Medical College before she was 21, and her diploma had to be post-dated to make it legal.

As an intern in Cook County Hospital, she performed 14 amputations before her 21st birthday.

Describing her 18 months as an intern, she later said it was "6 months of hell, 6 months of purgatory and 6 months of heaven after they found out I intended to stick."

Bates spent the year after her graduation doing post-graduate work in Vienna. She also learned fencing there, and preferred swashbuckling with a broadsword to making dainty jabs with a foil.

She returned to work several years in Chicago as a professor of anatomy, lecturing at the Women's College.

She moved to Denver in 1890 for her health, got a license to practice medicine and established an office in the Kittredge Building downtown.

The woman doctor was something of a novelty on the Denver scene. She was tall and thin and wore her auburn hair in a knot on the back of her neck, with the sides cut short and frizzed. She had a salty sense of humor and a ready tongue to flay anyone who got out of line. If anyone made a smutty remark in her presence, she assumed her famous "baby stare," and the joke fell flat.

Bates' involvement in civic and social matters began almost as soon as she arrived in Denver. At the time, agitation was strong for women's suffrage, and the doctor became a leader in the movement. The bill passed in 1893.

Bates' first venture was a campaign for street drinking fountains. She visited the president of the Board of Public Works and suggested their installation. He said the Denver City Charter prevented installing them.

Bates came back a few days later, carrying a copy of the city charter. She put her finger on a passage that allowed "such other improvements which in the discretion of the Board of Public Works would be desirable."

Not long after, 26 drinking fountains were installed downtown, 13 on the West Side. The fountains, at Bates' suggestion, included bowls for dogs' water.

Bates became involved in humane legislation when Edwin K. Whitehead, secretary of the Colorado Humane Society, called on her to help push through laws on the age of consent, white slavery, indecent liberties with children, horse-docking and the feeding of starving deer, elk and antelope when snow covered their grazing fields.

It took hard work and several legislative sessions, but Bates finally lobbied through all the bills.

In 1910, Mrs. John H. Gower of Denver was trying to organize a Dumb Friends League patterned and named after a smiliar organization in London. She asked Bates for help, and the doctor responded with zeal.

The motto of the organization was: "Every

Rocky Mountain News

Dr. Mary Elizabeth Bates was a pioneer physician with a particular love for animals.

creature, brute as well as human, has the right to food, drink and shelter, to work, rest and play, to comfort and happiness, to be free from unnecessary pain."

When the league started, Bates said she begged paint, whitewash and linoleum from businessmen and cleaned up a drafty shed for the animals' first building. Kittens were housed in the caretaker's home.

Later, when the league expanded enough to build a shelter, Bates located the old Rufus "Potato" Clark property at 1295 S. Santa Fe Drive and bought 11 lots. She headed the fund drive and directed the erection of buildings.

The property came up for sale on the steps of the courthouse when the builder put a lien on the buildings. Bates bought the buildings for $5 more than the lien and deeded them to the Dumb Friends League. For many years she was secretary of the league and paid the organization's deficit out of her own pocket.

In 1942, Bates was named secretary to the board of directors of the Colorado Humane Society and served until she retired in 1946. But in 1947, at the age of 86, she still was campaigning for funds to expand the Dumb Friends League.

She died in 1954, aged 93.

March 31, 1985

Bat Masterson worked both sides of the law

A letter from a woman who believes she is Bat Masterson's daughter asks for information on this famous figure of the Old West, who operated on both sides of the law.

Fact is well-mixed with fiction in the legend of William Barclay Masterson, but no one disputes that he was one of the great characters of the early days. Some of his colorful adventures took place in Colorado.

When Masterson was 27, it was said that he'd killed 26 men, stretched to "one for every year of his life." His nickname was patterned after Baptiste Brown, a famous hunter and dead shot of frontier days.

When Masterson died in New York in 1921, aged 67, the *New York Tribune* said in his obituary: "One who knew him in the West said, 'Masterson improved the world considerably by the people he removed from it.'"

In a strange twist of fortune, the former frontier marshal, gunman, buffalo hunter and Indian fighter, wound up in New York as a sports writer on the *Tribune.* Said the newspaper:

"He died at his desk, gripping his pen with the tenacity with which he formerly clung to the hilt of his six-shooter. . . ."

Masterson, wearing full dress, had been known to carry the gun to a ball, and he played many a poker game with the gun in his pocket. In later years, he carried the six-shooter in a front trousers pocket or in winter in an overcoat pocket, in preference to a holster.

He was born in Fairfield, Ill., in 1855, and the family moved to Wichita, Kan., when he was 14. By the time he was 16, he was a buffalo hunter for the Union Pacific Railroad.

From then on, his career moved fast. He was severely wounded when he joined Captain Baldwin's scouts against the Indians in the Battle of Red River. He recovered and returned to buffalo hunting. By the time he was 19, he was a crack shot with rifle and pistol.

Before he was 21, he got a call from Wyatt Earp, marshal of Dodge City, Kan., to help him keep order in that rough-and-tumble town. Masterson and his brother, Ed, devised a scheme to cool off Dodge's quarrelsome drunks. They dumped them in a 15-foot well with not enough water to drown them but too deep for them to crawl out.

By the time he was 22, Bat was elected sheriff of Dodge City, and Ed was town marshal. Ed was killed when he tried to disarm two drunks in front of the Lady Gay Saloon. Bat killed both when he learned of the tragedy.

Masterson moved on for a short time to Leadville, where he indulged in mining and gambling, then went to Tombstone, Ariz., and back to Dodge.

Next, he was appointed city marshal in Trinidad, Colo., in 1882, and the word spread that "the new marshal never misses." He also operated the gambling concession in a saloon in Trinidad.

He was deputy sheriff for a time in Creede. An article in the *Colorado Sun* on Feb. 25, 1892, said of Masterson:

"No man ever got the drop on him, nor did he seek a quarrel. Masterson is a man of 38, of muscular build and pleasant face. He is quiet in demeanor and sober in habit. There is no blow or bluff or bullyism about him. He attends strictly to business.

"He has been known to take a slap in the face from some drunken fool who didn't know his record and not resent the insult; but woe betide the fellow who offered him an affront in cold blood.

"It is probably owing to Masterson's presence here . . . that we have had no bad breaks yet. He is here in the interest of peace, having a commission from certain Denver parties to maintain order in their gambling places."

Masterson spent the greatest part of his Colorado time in Denver, where he worked as a faro dealer in Ed Chase's Arcade, then acquired his own gambling house and burlesque theater, the Palace on Blake Street.

Performers were given a set of rules laid out by Masterson:

"Performers writing to this house for an engagement will state the quality and quantity of their wardrobes, and the amount of salary they will work for, not what they want, for we make all the allowances for a performer's gall. We care nothing about how they 'split 'em up the back at Grand Rapids,' or how they 'knocked 'em silly on the Coast...'

"The proprietor doesn't care whether the performers worked one or 30 seasons with Tony Pastor; all he expects of you is to please the hobos of Blake Street."

On Nov. 21, 1891, Masterson married Emma Walters, a singer. She was in New York with him when he died.

While he was in Denver, Masterson refereed prize fights and managed boxers. As a boxing promoter, he hung around newspapers and decided he wanted to be a sports writer.

Eventually, when he began drinking heavily, he was ordered out of Denver, and took a train to New York. While he hadn't made it as a sports writer in Denver, he got a reporting job in New York. In 1905 he became U.S. marshal in New York, but continued covering sports.

Two years later Masterson resigned as marshal because he couldn't manage both jobs and preferred sports writing. He became sports editor of the *New York Morning Telegraph* and for 14 years had a column, *Masterson's Views on Timely Topics.*

He was writing a prize-fight report when he slumped over dead at his desk.

April 14, 1985

The Scottish castle of Daniels Park

A mansion in the style of a 1450 Scottish castle arouses the curiosity of Phyllis Os-trander of Denver.

"What history can you find concerning the

Rocky Mountain News

The manor house of the Cherokee Ranch near Sedalia was built in 1926 for a Denver real estate magnate. It now is owned by Tweet Kimball and she raises Santa Gertrudis cattle on the property.

castle down by Daniels Park?" she writes. "I understand it originally was built for some queen."

Dear Mrs. Ostrander: No, the castle wasn't built for a queen. It was built in 1926 on a rocky crest of a mountain near Sedalia, south of Denver, as the manor house for a 2,500-acre estate owned by Mr. and Mrs. Charles Alfred Johnson.

Johnson had made a fortune in Denver real estate. He and his wife dreamed of building a castle in Colorado, and the castle on the crest, called Charlford, was the culmination of their dream.

Charlford was named for their two sons, Charles A. Johnson Jr. and Gifford Phillips, Mrs. Johnson's son by a previous marriage, who was an heir to the Phillips Milk of Magnesia company's fortune.

The castle was designed by M.B. Hoyt and Merrill Hoyt, and was built of native stone quarried on the property. Exterior and interior stone is in hues of pink, maroon and garnet, and it gives the castle particularly attractive coloring. Three gargoyles decorate three faces of a tower on the northwest corner.

Charlford has 24 rooms, eight baths, eight fireplaces and a six-car garage. The main room, a great hall with two fireplaces, is 40-by-25-feet.

A swimming pool, tennis courts and a small guest house were added later.

A private road winds to the castle, through scrub oak and pine trees, and the building is visible from several points along U.S. 85.

The Johnsons filled the castle with beautiful furnishings they collected at art galleries in Europe and America. They used the house as a permanent residence until World War II, and entertained lavishly in it. They usually closed the castle after New Year's Day and spent the winter traveling, re-opening Charlford in the spring.

In 1955, Mr. and Mrs. Merritt Ruddock of Moab, Utah, bought the castle and its acreage after the death of C.A. Johnson. Mrs. Ruddock, now Mrs. Tweet Kimball, changed the name of the property to Cherokee Ranch and runs it as a working ranch, raising Santa Gertrudis cattle.

Most of the furnishings collected by the Johnsons were sold at auction before the property was sold.

Kimball has furnished the castle appropriately in antiques, and she entertains extensively in it. One of her parties was a private dinner for Princess Anne of Great Britain in June 1982.

May 19, 1985

'Miss Denver' sank at Lakeside

Rocky Mountain News

Fountains in City Park lake spout water into the twilight sky. It's been an attraction since 1908.

T HE motor launch that plied the waters of City Park lake long ago and the fountain in the middle of the lake have inspired a question from Kathy Jackson of Arvada. She writes:

"I remember as a child going to City Park to watch the fountain and ride in a boat around the lake. What happened to them? I can see that the fountain is still there, but never working. And what became of the boat?"

Dear Ms. Jackson:

Information on *Miss Denver,* as the launch was cllaed, is scarce. We do know she was a favorite attraction chugging around City Park's large lake for years. The boat was 56 feet long and motor-powered. She came Denver by rail from chicago in 1929, and was an instant hit.

Pat Gallavan, deputy manager of Denver parks, said the boat hasn't been operated in the lake since the early 1960s.

In 1972, it was sitting out dry at City Park, and Donald R. Swanson of Denver bought it for $1 from Araserv Inc., the park concessionaire.

Swanson renovated the boat in his back yard. After he had invested several thousand dollars in the renovation, he renamed her the Miss Colorado and launched her at Lakeside Amusement Park. That year 17,800 people bought rides on her at 35¢ each.

Outside pressures the next year, including an investigation into the boat's safety, kept Swanson from operating *Miss Colorado.* For several years she sat idle and gradually sank at Lakeside.

Swanson gave the boat to Channel 6 for its fund-raising auction in 1976. But the highest bidder didn't come up with the money. Station supervisor Donald Johnson wanted Swanson to take back the boat. But Swanson didn't want it. And Lakeside wanted nothing but to get the lame vessel off its premises.

"I don't know what finally became of it," said Gallavan. "The last I saw, 6 or 7 years ago, it was in a junkyard south of the Colfax Viaduct."

As for the City Park Fountain in the middle of the large lake, it is alive and well and last week played for the public the first time this year. (It had a rehearsal ahead of the performance.)

Martha Guevara, Denver manager of parks and recreation, says the fountain will be operated all summer for one hour each evening, starting at dusk.

The fountain has been a major civic attraction since 1908, and still is the only municipal musical dancing water fountain in the United States.

When it was installed in the middle of City Park lake 77 years ago, it cost $25,577. In the fountain's early years it cost $30 a night to operate it. Now the cost is more than $100.

James Bible, retired parks superintendent, tells us the fountain was a pet project of Mayor Robert W. Speer. The installation was done by Fred W. Darlington, an electrical engineer.

A pumping plant for the fountain stands on the north shore of the lake, and two electrical pumps force water drawn from the lake into pipes supplying the fountain, with pumping pressure of 80 to 90 pounds.

The pipes lead to 2,100 nozzles that create the fountain displays. Each group of nozzles can produce several effects, but one of the favorites starts with "beehives," then can be adjusted to make "sheaves of wheat" and finally "vases."

On normal settings, the fountain sends up about 1,200 gallons of water per minute. When all the valves are opened to maximum, and that's seldom, the fountain uses 4,000 gallons of water a minute.

A man in the righthand tower of the park pavilion operates the switches that control the fountain formations. Switch No. 2 creates the 90-foot jet which has been named Old Faithful. In the fountain's earlier days, four men were needed to operate it nightly. One manned the pumps, one operated switches in the tower to choose the types of water jets and the colors, and two worked in a 30-by-60 foot pit under the fountain in the middle of the lake.

The men in the pit faced a certain amount of danger if the tower operator got the pressure too high.

The fountain always has been associated with concerts by the Denver Municipal Band.

On nights when the band is playing in other parks, the City Park fountain is accompanied by recorded music broadcast over loudspeakers.

June 2, 1985

Classy Ed Chase ran the best saloons

DONNA J. Chase of Lakewood writes: "In your (April 14, 1985) article on Bat Masterson, I noticed the reference to Ed Chase's Arcade, where Masterson worked.

Western History Department, Denver Public Library

Ed Chase operated many saloons and gambling parlors, later became a philanthropist.

"I am Ed Chase's great-great-granddaughter and would very much like to hear anything about him that you can tell me."

Dear Ms. Chase:

Ed Chase, along with various partners, ran some of the most interesting saloons and gambling places in Denver, and newspapers often published stories about him.

Being tall, blue-eyed, with premature white hair, and always immaculately tailored, he cut a dashing figure. He also was well-respected. Mary Lathrop, a famous woman lawyer in Denver's early years, was Chase's attorney. She once recalled that he never used profanity.

"No man ever was more steadfast or loyal in his friendships," she said. "Whenever any of his employees got into trouble, he went the limit for them, looked after their families, and, if a killing was involved, spared no expense in their defense.

"Any old-timer could always get $10 from him, merely for asking. I know, for I disbursed his funds. Whenever an indigent old-timer passed away, it was Ed Chase who provided the funeral — flowers, carriages, music, all — even the burial plot."

Chase was born in 1838 in Saratoga, N.Y., where his parents, Richard and Maria Chase, ran a fashionable hotel. In this atmosphere, he acquired some of the skills that helped him when he went into business in Denver. He also met some famous guests at the New York hotel, including Daniel Webster and Henry Clay.

Chase came west in 1858, stopping first in Montana. It was too cold there, however, and he moved to Colorado.

"I was something of a wing shot then," he recalled later, "and I spent most of my time coming over the Plains shooting buffalo."

After a few months in Golden, he was asked to start a recreation business in Denver because he was the only one in town who knew about billiards and pool — games he had learned in his parents' hotel. The first pool table in Denver came across the Plains by oxcart for Chase's recreation room.

Chase and Francis P. Heatley became owners of the Progressive Club, which proved to be a popular and profitable saloon and gambling parlor in Denver.

Saloons and gaming rooms attracted a certain amount of trouble. Chase's place didn't escape. One night, a man named Kelly, who had lost at gambling, pretended to yawn and then drew on Chase. The proprietor recalled later:

"When I looked up, there was a big hole in front of my eyes, and Kelly, who was an Indian fighter, would have sent a bullet down that hole into my brain in a second if I had moved. He backed out of the place, swinging his revolver to cover the crowd while everybody in the place ducked. The next minute he was on his horse and gone."

No one went after the gunslinger, Chase said.

From then on, Chase positioned himself on a high stool in the gambling area with a shotgun across his lap. He never used the gun, but its presence may have staved off more trouble.

In 1873, Heatley and Chase built the Palace Theater on Blake Street, an establishment for drinking, gambling and entertainment, sort of a forerunner of the Las Vegas scene. The Palace became the best gambling spot in town.

Chorus girls sang and danced between serving drinks to gamblers and members of the audience. The program also included black-faced comedians in minstrel routines. In addition, a large orchestra accompanied the performers and played for dancing.

Chase ran this place for many years, and according to reports, it was "conducted with decorum."

Although he was a busy entrepreneur, Chase also found time for romance and married several times. One wife sued for divorce when he was running the Progressive Club, contending that he maintained a love nest at the club.

At the Palace, the entertainers included the Barbour Sisters, and in 1880, Chase married Frances Virginia Barbour, his third wife. He bought her a home at 2859 Lawrence St.

Later, he bought a house at 1492 Race St., which years later was torn down to build the Aladdin Theater, which also has been torn down.

After the Palace, Chase ran the Interocean Club with other partners, Robert Austin and Barney Boyce.

Chase apparently did not like to work without a partner. With another partner, Vaso L. Chucovich, in 1909, he acquired the Brinker Institute in the 1700 block of Tremont Place and changed its name to the Navarre. The Navarre across from the Brown Palace Hotel, had been built in 1880 as a girls collegiate institute operated by a professor, Joseph Brinker.

It was said that a different kind of girl was featured when the building became the Navarre.

With still another partner, Ed Gaylord, Chase invested heavily in Denver real estate over a period of years. They went out of this business in 1907 but their property investments had made Chase rich.

June 16, 1985

Roots of stately elm reach to Shakespeare

JOHN L. Russell, who was superintendent of Denver parks during World War I and after, made a hobby of getting cuttings from famous trees and growing them in Denver parks.

One of the trees for which we may thank Russell is the Shakespeare Elm in City Park. This handsome tree was only a slip when Russell saw a newspaper ad offering cuttings from an elm growing at Shakespeare's birthplace and burial spot in Stratford-on-Avon, England.

Russell sent for a cutting of the Shakespeare Elm, and the slip was planted in City Park on April 23, 1916, the 300th anniversary of Shakespeare's death. Ten years later, Russell installed a bronze plaque near the foot of the tree, giving its history.

The Shakespeare Elm, 69 years old at this writing, stands about 100 yards north of East 17th Avenue and 75 yards west of Colorado Boulevard.

About the time Russell sent for the Shakespeare Elm, he also acquired a slip of the Washington Elm, a tree at Cambridge, Mass., marking the spot where George Washington took command of the Continental Army on July 3, 1775.

The Washington Elm was planted in Washington Park and flourished there. In recent years, however, it became a victim of Dutch Elm disease, according to Ray Howe, city forester, and was removed.

"We replaced the elm with an oak tree, but we left the plaque there," Howe said. The plaque states that the Washington Elm was presented to the city by John L. Russell and was dedicated May 3, 1917, by the Denver, Colorado and Peace Pipe chapters of the Daughters of the American Revolution.

June 23, 1985

Rocky Mountain News

The Shakespeare Elm is in the southeast corner of City Park.

Nikola Tesla — a hair-raising genius

AT the turn of the century, an electrical genius of the caliber of Thomas A. Edison lived and worked in a laboratory at the foot of Pikes Peak. He was Nikola Tesla, a Yugoslavian born in 1858.

Tesla, who had many eccentricities along with his genius, was an electrical engineer in Europe.

When Tesla arrived in the U.S. in 1884, he was convinced of the possibility of a worldwide wireless electrical system. He worked briefly with Edison in Orange, N.J., but the two could not get along.

Legend says that in 1915, Tesla and Edison were considered jointly for the Nobel prize in physics, but Tesla turned it down because he didn't want to share it. In fact, there's no evidence that Edison ever was considered for the award; his work was not in theoretical physics.

It is said that Tesla would have given the world free electricity as a result of his experiments in Colorado Springs in 1899, but big-business interests, concerned with the fortunes to be made from the sale of power, suppressed his work.

All that was needed to use Earth's energy for electric appliances, Tesla said, was a 200-foot antenna, a condenser, a ground connection and a coil, the same as is used in a radio receiving unit.

Tesla based his works on alternating current, which was said to be more efficient than Edison's direct current. To prove that his alternating current was safer than direct current, Tesla once lighted lamps held in his hands through several thousand volts of high-frequency electricity passing through his body. If the frequency were high enough, he said, alternating currents of high voltage electricity would be harmless.

Tesla first experimented at his Houston Street Laboratory in New York. There he had a powerful oscillator that produced 4 million volts of current and lights and sounds that frightened his neighbors. His first important discovery was the alternating current polyphase motor, which still is used in electrical systems.

Tesla decided to head for Colorado's wide open spaces where he felt he could conduct experiments that might be too dangerous in urban areas.

He arrived in Colorado Springs on May 17, 1899, at the age of 43. He was tall and thin with dark curly hair and intense gray eyes. He told reporters he planned to send a message through the air from Pikes Peak to Paris. This was 2 years before Marconi's trans-Atlantic transmission.

Tesla had chosen the Colorado Springs area, he said, because of its many electrical storms accompanied by vivid lightning displays. The area also had plenty of open country.

His stay in Colorado proved to be both interesting and eventful. In one experiment, he knocked out the electrical system of Colorado Springs. In another, some people believed that the gigantic electrical impulses emanating from his laboratory had brought replies from extra-terrestrials.

Tesla came to Colorado Springs fairly well-prepared for the work. John Jacob Astor had lent him $30,000 and M. Crawford, a dry-goods merchant, had contributed $10,000. Leonard E. Curtis, a local attorney, arranged for Tesla's laboratory to get free service from the Colorado Springs Electrical Co.

Tesla built his laboratory on the plains outside Colorado Springs, east of the Colorado School for the Deaf and Blind. The building was 100 feet long by 25 feet wide, and was topped by an 80-foot tower shaped like an oil derrick. A pole 200 feet long was attached to the tower and the top held a copper ball 3 feet in diameter. The ball was wired to an electrical apparatus in the lab below.

The laboratory also contained what Tesla called a "magnifying transmitter." A huge coil buried under the floor was 51 feet in diameter, and wrapped with copper. A secondary coil of the huge transformer was at one end of the lab.

It was a dangerous place for strangers, and Tesla surrounded the property with a high fence and a large sign, "Keep Out — Great Danger!" The only person admitted to the lab beside Tesla was his assistant, Kolman Czito. Tesla lived at the Alta Vista Hotel, where he choose room 207, a number divisible by 3, and thus humored one of the many superstitions which ruled his life.

He daily commuted to his laboratory, driving a rented horse and buggy, with one leg over the side, ready to jump, since he greatly feared horses. He also had a phobia about elevators, and often walked many flights of stairs rather than take one. He was afraid, too, of all kinds of germs.

In Colorado Springs, Tesla said he intended to see if the Earth contained an electrical charge, and if so, to alter its magnitude with experiments. He wanted to send out electric power without wire by making the Earth a giant oscillator.

He later said his experiments had convinced him it was "possible to transmit power in unlimited amounts to any terrestrial distance and almost without loss." In his book, *The Life of Tesla,* John J. O'Neill said that the coils in Tesla's laboratory were tuned to vibrate in resonance with the Earth's surge of energy and built up potentials of more than 100 million volts.

"No scientist since ever has succeeded in building up currents with one-tenth of that potential," said O'Neill. To accomplish this, Tesla used only about 300 horsepower of energy.

Many strange phenomena were noted while Tesla conducted his experiments in Colorado. His magnifying transmitter was so powerful that light bulbs within 100 feet of the laboratory glowed even if they weren't turned on.

"At times the very grass seemed to crackle with electricity, and sparks an inch long could be drawn from the water hydrant at a distance of 300 feet from the laboratory," wrote O'Neill. People walking in the vicinity were startled as sparks flew around their feet.

One summer night in Colorado in 1899, while

Western History Department, Denver Public Library

Nikola Tesla made a name for himself, indeed, while he carried on experiments in Colorado.

experimenting with electric power, Tesla received a series of signals on his instruments which he believed came from another planet, probably Mars or Venus. He didn't mention this occurrence until the following January, perhaps fearful of being scoffed at.

The extraterrestrial messages, he said, were only a simple counting code, such as 1, 2, 3. But he maintained that his signals were of sufficient power to affect a receiving instrument on another planet with 10 times the necessary force. Today it is believed that the strange signals did not come from space.

On the night that Tesla had determined to turn up his machinery to its greatest power, he donned full evening dress — and rubber boots. His assistant, Czito, was to remain in the barn and throw the switch feeding the generated power into the condensers.

It later was reported that when the switch was thrown, the barn was bathed in a violet light, and the copper ball crackled and sent out jagged arms of lightning 130 feet long. Thunder created by the experiment was heard in Cripple Creek, 15 miles away.

Suddenly everything stopped. Tesla thought the Colorado Springs power company had cut him off. He grabbed the telephone and begged the company to restore power. The answer was curt:

"We can't restore your power. You've ruined our generators and plunged the whole town into darkness."

Thus ended Tesla's free power in Colorado Springs. Astor also refused to continue his financial support, although Tesla presented him with ideas for electric clocks, a world broadcasting system and pictures that could be sent to a receiving set, what we now call television.

Tesla left Colorado Springs on Jan. 13, 1900, and returned to Long Island, N.Y. He was heavily in debt in Colorado Springs, and several years later his laboratory and tower there were torn down to pay wages and satisfy creditors.

Back on Long Island, Tesla hoped to establish a world broadcasting system. But funding was difficult. He did, however, develop the theory of a rotating electrical field, and his transmissions of power with conduit led to the invention of the fluorescent tube, among other things. He also predicted the laser beam and the guided missile defense system.

Scientists referred to his death in 1943 at age 85 as "the loss of one of the great intellects of the world, who paved the way for many of the technical developments of modern times."

Colorado Springs remembered Tesla and his experiments with a memorial marker placed on the former site of his laboratory.

July 21, 1985

Ninety-seven people were killed in this 1904 railroad disaster near Eden. The train, nicknamed the World's Fair Flyer, was loaded with people going from Denver to the World's Fair in St. Louis.

The night the Flyer plunged into doom

THE head-on collision of two Burlington Northern freight trains near Westminster on Aug. 2, 1985, occurred just five days shy of the date 81 years before when the Missouri Pacific's World's Fair Flyer was wrecked at Eden, Colo. *The Denver Republican* the next day reported it as "the greatest railroad disaster Colorado has suffered, and one of the greatest in the history of the country."

The tragedy killed 88 people. Another eight were missing and believed dead on the night of Aug. 7, 1904, when the Flyer plunged off Bridge 110-B on the main line of the Denver & Rio Grande Railroad, near Eden.

Tony Fisher of Pueblo died a month later of injuries from the accident, bringing the apparent death toll to 97. Most died by drowning, according to the coroner's report.

The locomotive and three cars plunged into the arroyo, and the locomotive floated about half a mile downstream before it lodged against the bank.

In his book, *Tragedy at Eden,* Dow Helmers gives an interesting and accurate account of the event.

The St. Louis World's Fair was in progress

that summer, and the Denver, Kansas City and St. Louis Express, a crack Missouri Pacific train, was running daily between Denver and St. Louis with a temporary name change to *World's Fair Flyer.*

Between Pueblo and Denver, the trains used D&RG tracks, crews and engines. Rio Grande locomotive No. 1009 was assigned to haul the Flyer to Pueblo on Aug. 7. At Pueblo, the train would get a Missouri Pacific crew and engine.

The crew out of Denver included: Henry Hinman, the engineer; David C. Mayfield, fireman; James Smith, conductor; Thomas Reese, baggageman; E.T. Betts, Pullman conductor; and A.A. Robinson, trainman.

The train glided out of Denver at 5 p.m. Aug. 7, reaching Colorado Springs on time, at 6:55 p.m. A slight rain was falling, and the engineer was advised of heavy rain the rest of the way to Pueblo and was cautioned to run carefully.

The train was full, and the dining car was operating at capacity because most passengers liked to eat between Denver and Pueblo.

Before the train reached Hogan's Gulch, not quite 9 miles from the Pueblo depot and close to the tiny town of Eden, a cloudburst broke over the gulch and washed out a wooden bridge on a county road. Wreckage of the bridge washed downstream and hit D&RG Railroad Bridge No. 110-B, a single-track bridge that crossed the gulch.

The collision weakened the bridge, which began to shake as the engine started over it, although the train had been slowed to around 20 mph instead of its usual 50 to 60. Hinman threw on the power and got part of the train to the other side of the gulch, but suddenly there was a terrific jolt. The bridge supports buckled, the engine slid back and dropped into the arroyo, dragging three cars with it.

When the train's air line was broken, it caused brakes on the rest of the train to engage automatically, and the three remaining cars were stopped before they jumped into the chasm. The diner was one of the cars that was stopped.

It was a little past 8 p.m. and, because of the storm, very dark. But when rescuers arrived, they could see one Pullman car hanging over the edge of the drop.

News of the wreck was flashed from Eden. The railroad provided free transportation to the scene for members of victims' families. Volunteers searched for bodies, as did men hired by the railroad at $2 a day plus $25 per body found. The search was organized by then Pueblo Mayor B.B. Brown.

Four undertakers were hired to handle the 88 bodies, and embalmers were brought in from Colorado Springs, Pueblo and Denver.

One of the strangest stories to come out of the wreck was that of William M. Henry, a middle-aged man who appeared at the scene in torn and muddy clothing and told a grim story of surviving the wreck. Henry was hospitalized, and further questioning revealed that he was suffering from hallucinations and had not been in the wreck.

An investigation was held to determine the cause of the accident, and on Aug. 20, a jury stated:

"The jury finds that the appalling loss of life and property at Bridge 110-B on Aug. 7, 1904, was due to the negligence of the D&RG Railroad." The jury blamed the wreck on the cheap, inferior class of the bridge and said there should have been a better system of reports and more night operators as well as track walkers and flagmen who might have seen and averted the impending trouble.

Because no felonious action was shown, no charges were brought against the railroad.

The railroad announced that it would contest claims by mourners. Colorado law at the time limited claims for accidental death to $5,000, but the railroad managed to pay most families only $1,000 for loss of a family member.

The D&RG estimated its own damage costs, including the engine, at about $25,000.

The engine later was pulled out of the creek, cleaned and repaired, to serve another 32 years.

The broken bridge was repaired quickly, and trains continued regularly on their rush to St. Louis and the World's Fair.

August 11, 1985

Chutes Park grew into a stewpot of fun

CHUTES Park, once one of Denver's glamor spots, is the subject of a question from Eliot Wager of Denver. He asks for a story of the park's origin and some of the events that took place there.

Dear Mr. Wager:

A newspaper account at the time the park opened characterized it as "an ollapodrida of exubrant fun." To save our readers from scurrying for their dictionaries, an "ollapodrida" is a "medley or mixture" and sometimes is even applied to a stew.

In 1892, a group of Denver businessmen, including Robert W. Speer, one of Denver's more famous mayors, organized Arlington Park at about East 4th Avenue and Corona Street. It became a favorite spot during the Gay '90s.

Theatrical spectacles were one of the park's greatest attractions. Perhaps the most famous of these was *The Last Days of Pompeii,* presented on July 4, 1892, to mark the park's grand opening. The production ran through Aug. 13.

Three hundred actors were assembled to dramatize the famous novel, *The Last Days of Pompeii.* A backdrop of Mount Vesuvius 54 feet high provided the setting. The production was billed as *Pain's Historical Pyrotechnic Spectacle* and was staged by Henry J. Pain of London. The grand finale, the eruption of the volcano Vesuvius, accompanied by an elaborate fireworks display, was beyond everyone's expectations.

After each performance, a concert in the Grove was offered by the Arlington Military Band.

Fifteen years later, the park had a change of owners — and name. Messrs. Harris and Baumann took over, and had the "chutes" constructed. This was a graded waterfall with a lake at its foot. Passengers rode small boats down the slide to the lake and called it "shooting the chutes." The boats were on chains by which they were pulled them back to the top.

Western History Department, Denver Public Library

1899 drawing showed elks diving at Chutes Park at East 4th Avenue and Corona Street.

Chutes Park opened on May 27, 1898, amid much fanfare at a time when troops were being mustered for the Spanish-American War. On opening night, W.H. Brown, a one-legged cyclist, was one of the featured entertainers as he coasted down the chutes on his wheel. Another attraction, much heralded, was the Boston Ladies Military Band of 25 women, led by Professor Ernest Fleck.

The park midway included a shooting gallery, mystery maze, baseball practice and strength testing machines and "illusions."

A small "scenic railway" wound through the park, and a newly constructed bicycle track was said to be one of the best in the country. The first wheel meet on June 4 offered $750 in prizes.

Over several years some stunning productions were presented at Chutes Park, using the lake as a prop. A theater in the shape of a boat was built to reach to the water's edge, and musicals and opera were offered there by Harrison and Baumann. *A Midsummer Night's Dream* and several Gilbert and Sullivan operettas were produced.

Each year a different spectacle was offered in the tradition of *The Last Days of Pompeii*, including *The Battle of Manila* and *The Battle of San Juan Hill*.

There were other attractions, too. Denver bicycle race meets were held at the park, and amidst much ballyhoo in May 1899, Sadie Boynton came to town to shoot the chutes on her bicycle, "then dove gracefully over the handlebars into the lake."

Boynton's act was followed by Professor W.H. Barnes and his "diving elks." On cue, the animals marched up a steep platform, and at a signal, one-at-a-time plunged off the platform into a tank of water 60 feet below.

The Denver Republican reported on May 28, 1899:

"The elks seemed to enjoy the performance as much as did the people in the grandstand."

In August 1898, when the show of Gertrude Charlotte Planka, the "lady of the lions," failed to attract the crowds expected, the producers hyped it with a marriage "in the lions' den."

On Aug. 8, 1898, Jenny Allen and her fiance, Charles Rogers, had their wedding ceremony performed in the lions' cage at Chutes Park.

The Denver Times reported the next day that while Madame Planka stood by with chair and whip, and a pistol on her hip, the trembling young couple entered the cage for the ceremony. Three female lions sat on stools to watch, but a male lion, Brutus, was banned from the proceedings because he was untrustworthy.

Madame Planka discouraged Justice of the Peace Hunt from entering, so he performed the ceremony from outside the bars.

A crowd of 5,000 watched, and "everyone was very nervous." The tension was increased because the ceremony was performed in the late afternoon, near the lions' dinnertime, and the beasts several times interrupted the wedding party with loud roars.

The stunt was so successful that the next year, another couple, Mary George and Felix John Hettwer, accepted $500 to be married in the lions' cage. It was even more elaborate than the first affair.

With all the expected trimmings, Mary and her bridesmaid, Tracy Platzer, walked down a path decorated in flowers to meet John and the best man, who was Mary's brother, Joseph George.

The wedding couple stepped inside the cage while their attendants and the justice of the peace, Justice Towers, stood outside. The lions sat on stools, and Madame Planka stood by with a whip and a gun. A handful of riflemen was stationed outside.

As the betrothed couple stood trembling, Towers intoned:

"And now join your right hands
"And hear me pronounce
"The sentence for life, 'ere beasts
"On you pounce.
"By virtue of law shall this contract abide.
"As man and wife go, and down the chutes glide."

On July 7, 1900, at the height of the season, a fire caused the park to close. Six months later, on Jan. 21, 1901, fire again raged through the park, but this time the amusement spot was destroyed.

After reconstruction, the park reverted to its name of Arlington Park.

Fire again destroyed the park in 1903. It went into receivership, and a high board fence was erected around it. Not long after, East 3rd Avenue was graded through the former park grounds, and the land was parceled into building sites.

Aug. 18, 1985

National Guard Armory in Golden is said to be the nation's largest cobblestone structure.

Centennial House, also made of stone, was a stage stop between Golden and Central City.

Old stone walls are standing still

EFFIE St. John of Arvada writes: "I would like to know something about the Centennial House about 10 or 12 miles up Golden Gate Canyon — a large rock house that was used for a stagecoach stop. Can you help me?"

Dear Ms. St. John:

None of my sources mention anything about a Centennial House near Golden. I did learn of the old National Guard armory in Golden, which is said to be the largest cobblestone building in the United States. It's doubtful this is the structure you have in mind, but it's an interesting building, all the same.

Georgina Brown gives a good story of the building in her book, *The Shining Mountains.*

The armory, at 13th and Arapahoe streets in Golden, was built for Company A Engineers Corps of the Colorado National Guard.

Company A was composed of students at the Colorado School of Mines. A National Guard training course granted credits toward graduation from the School of Mines. Brig. Gen. John

Chase, who mainly was responsible for organizing the group, believed that these college men would be good officer material.

James H. Gow of Golden was appointed architect and subcontractor for the building. He must have anticipated building such a structure because in 1910, he started collecting large cobblestones, which he hauled in a horse-drawn wagon.

The building he designed resembles a castle, with a tower 65 feet high, approximately 4 stories. Window slits on each floor and rounded corners enhance its resemblance to a fortress.

The excavation was begun in December 1912, and the cornerstone was laid on June 14, 1913. The estimated cost of the building was $43,666.

The armory took 3,300 wagonloads of cobblestones, which are held together with mortar mixed from 5,500 sacks of cement. Gow insisted to critics that the building would be as strong as if it were built of bricks. Most of the walls are 3 feet thick.

The completed armory included a kitchen and

mess hall, library, dormitories, baths and a large drill hall. The Golden post office was on the ground floor.

The post office was ready for Christmas business in 1913, but the rest of the building wasn't completed for nearly 3 years.

Through the years, the armory has had a variety of uses. Jefferson County Civil Defense got quarters on the second floor in February 1951 and held drills and training sessions there.

Twenty years later, when the building was in danger of being torn down, Ronald Weiszmann, of the Golden law firm Devitt and Weiszmann, bought it.

"We remodeled it in a period from 1972 to 1974," Weiszmann said. "Now, we're remodeling it again, opening the upstairs ceiling to expose beams and roof joists." Many of the interior rock walls that had been covered with paint have been sand-blasted to show the bare stones, he said.

We're still looking for the Centennial House, and maybe some of our readers will help us find it.

August 25, 1985

The readers said . . .

ROSE Koch Lyon of Greeley answered our plea. She said the house is 10 miles north of Golden, on the Golden Gate Canyon road.

"The house was part of our family for many years," she wrote. "My folks bought it from the original owners, Daniel Booten and his wife Americus, who built it in 1876. A stone above the front door carries the date.

"It's true that the house was halfway between Golden and Central City. There originally were 12 rooms, with walls 3 feet thick, of stone. My father combined some of the rooms to make seven, and put a bath in later. During the remodeling he took out wheelbarrow after wheelbarrow of rock.

"My mother's family, the Theodore Kochs, lived next door to the Bootens, and when Mother was married nearby in Robinson School in 1903,

a wagonload of lilacs from the Bootens' front yard provided the decorations.

"The Bootens, who were Quakers, used the house as a stage stop between Golden and Central City. They kept milk cows and provided fresh milk for the guests. The ladies had a living room upstairs, and the men stayed downstairs.

"After my father's death, my brother, George Koch, who was sheriff of Jefferson County for some time, lived in the house. Raymond Koch, a cousin, took the house later and eventually sold it to a Denver dentist for a summer home."

October 6, 1985

Melvin B. Swena of Siloam Springs, Ark., also had the answer. He wrote:

"I was born in Denver in 1905. My father moved our family up Golden Gate Canyon Road just 1 mile beyond the Centennial Ranch. The next ranch west of us was the Michigan, sometimes called the Junction Ranch, because it is where Jefferson County and Gilpin County meet.

"At that time Golden Gate Canyon was the only wagon road from Denver and Golden, so it was the main stage route to the rich gold-mining area of Central City and Black Hawk. There were numerous stage stops along the way, the Centennial House being one and Michigan Ranch another. In fact, every ranch was equipped to take care of travelers, something like the stores along the highways of today try to accommodate tourists in every way they can. Tourist dollars have always been an attractive source of income.

"The Centennial House was built by Mr. Booten for this purpose. He was attracted by the rich gold strikes in the area, but he never cared to risk going down into those miserable mine shafts, perhaps contracting miners' disease or miners' consumption like so many men did, so he chose running a stage stop, or as some called them, a roadhouse."

Swena added that he believes some members of the Booten family still live in Maybell (in Moffat County). Three of Booten's children, he said, Dan, Rose and Alma, never married but lived in the Centennial House until just before their deaths in the 1920s.

November 10, 1985

Auditorium curtain ended up in the dump

THE handsome oil painting that adorned Denver's City Auditorium stage curtain some years ago is the subject of a question from Stan Oliver at the University of Southern Colorado Library in Pueblo.

Oliver enclosed a *Rocky Mountain News* clipping from March 15, 1945. The clipping said Colorado Daughters of the American Revolution were "annoyed" that the curtain, which the DAR gave to the city in 1909, was hanging unused, far above the stage, gathering dust instead of admiration. At that time, the women were promised that the curtain would be used for some forthcoming concerts.

"I would like an update on this DAR curtain," Oliver writes. "Is it still there or did fire laws on curtains cause it to go?"

Dear Mr. Oliver:

First, there are few details about the curtain.

A newspaper article on Sept. 18, 1909, said that the "handsome drapery and magnificent curtain" were to adorn the proscenium arch of the auditorium whenever it was used as a theater.

The curtain was ceremonially presented to the city by Mrs. James Benton Grant, former regent of the Colorado Chapter of the DAR, and was received by Mayor Robert W. Speer.

At the presentation, according to the *Denver Republican*, "Patriotism ran riot. ... The presentation was made an occasion of social brilliance and the boxes held many of Denver's most prominent people." As part of the ceremony the audience sang the first two verses of *America*.

Four hundred yards of red silk velour decorated with 1,000 pounds of gold fringe, tassels and embroidery were used. The draperies and painted curtain were valued at $10,000.

The painting, by Albert Herter, was created in the Herter Studio in New York, and finishing touches were applied in the Vanderbilt Library, because of the great size of the work — 60 by 33 feet.

The DAR had ordered "an allegorical painting descriptive of revolutionary times." The Herter curtain showed Washington, Hamilton and Lafayette standing under the Stars and Stripes borne by angels with flame-colored wings. The nation's liberty, peace and prosperity were represented by robed female figures following the three men.

Herter explained the work:

"Progress is symbolized by a youth bearing in the glow of dawn the torches of enlightenment high above the mountains and valleys of the new country, while below from the valley of mists, war and conflagration, the spirit of blind Justice seems to float distinct but indefinable — forerunner of the Revolution."

Three Indians in the shadow of a knoll were described as "slinking into oblivion ... fleeing before the light of progress and the dawn of a new era in America."

A mammoth American eagle flanked by bison heads formed the center base of the painting, with connecting garlands of painted fruit.

The answer to "What became of the curtain?" was supplied by Bobbie Niles, business manager for the Denver Convention Complex. She said that when the Auditorium Theater was remodeled in 1955, the curtain and drapes were hauled to the dump.

"After 50 years of use, the curtain was just a rag," she said. "It had deteriorated to the point where very little was left of it. And there was no way to clean the velvet drapes. No cleaner was big enough to handle them."

The replacement drapes which went up in 1955, she said, lasted until recently. A new curtain of red with gold trim was used for the first time in July 1985, with the presentation of *42nd Street*.

September 1, 1985

Denverite cultivated flowers-by-wire

THE inspiration and perspiration of a Denver man many years ago are credited with bringing life to flowers-by-wire, the service that sends floral gifts around the world.

It was 75 years ago this year when the late John A. Valentine, who was owner and general manager of Denver's Park Floral Co., persuaded 14 other florists to join him in organizing the Florists' Telegraph Delivery Association. Bill Gunesch, present owner of Park Floral, has a collection of scrapbooks that tell most of the story.

Valentine became a florist accidentally. He was born in Keosauqua, Iowa, in 1859, and graduated from the State Law School in Iowa City in 1880.

After working for both the Chicago, Burlington & Quincy Railroad and the Northern Pacific, he moved to Denver for his wife's health. He practiced law, and it was through his friendship with another lawyer, Allen B. Seaman, that he became involved in the flower business. He told the story at a florists' convention more than 60 years ago. The story was repeated in *The Florists Review*.

"In 1894, Seaman put some money into the erection of some greenhouses to help a florist friend of his," Valentine recalled. "In January of 1895, Seaman discussed with me the possibility of abandoning the investment as it seemed unprofitable. But he and I believed that if more money were invested and larger greenhouses were built, the business could be made profitable. I agreed to give some attention to the bookkeeping and handling of accounts.

"Later on it became apparent that the only way to save the investment was for me to take hold of the active management. I knew absolutely nothing about the business, and, in fact, there were a great many of the common flowers that I did not even know by name. I realized I was up against a tough proposition."

John A. Valentine of Denver organized the Florists' Telegraph Delivery Association in 1910.

Valentine immediately subscribed to the two florists' publications then in existence and read widely about the flower business. He also traveled extensively, visiting florists in different parts of the country.

He said later that his attendance at meetings of the Society of American Florists was "the best expended dollars that I have spent in the florists' business."

Valentine's dedication paid off. Several times

he read papers on flower growing at the society's national conventions, and in 1908, he was elected president of the society. That year he read a technical paper before the American Carnation Society meeting in Boston, and 5 years later was elected president of the society.

Park Floral Co., Gunesch said, started with a lease from the city on what now is East High School's grounds, from York Street to Josephine Street and from East Colfax Avenue to East 17th Avenue. In 1923, the company bought out Beers Brothers Greenhouses and moved to 1090 W. Hampden Ave. The slogan was "Mile High Quality at Sea Level Prices."

When Seaman died in 1904, Valentine took over management of the estate's interest in the flower firm and reorganized it on a cooperative plan. Several employees were allowed to acquire small blocks of stock.

Concerned that flowers couldn't be sent across the country and arrive fresh, Valentine conceived the idea of the Florists' Telegraph Delivery Association which came into flower in January 1910, at a meeting in Rochester, N.Y. From then on, inter-city floral gifts could be delivered fresh, from local supplies.

Valentine became the first president of FTDA, a cooperative owned by member florists, and served several terms. In recent years the name was changed to Florists' Transworld Delivery Association.

When Valentine was 58, he died in an auto accident in Jarre Canyon, near Sedalia. He was on a fishing trip to Deckers with his wife and two friends, Mr. and Mrs. Frank D. Woodson.

It was believed that defective steering caused Valentine to lose control of the car, which overturned and crushed him. The others escaped with minor injuries.

E.P. Neiman and B.E. Gillis owned Park Floral after Valentine, and Gunesch bought the company from them.

Today the association Valentine helped found has more than 21,000 members and annual sales of $500 million. Many FTD florists now use computers to send and receive their flowers-by-wire orders.

September 8, 1985

Denver's 'flying cross'

A question about Denver's "flying cross" comes from Bill Nicholsen of Denver, who writes:

"Do I remember this, or am I dreaming? Two questions, please.

"During the early 1930s, every Christmas Eve, did Denver have a flying cross? This plane would take off with a lighted cross under the fuselage and criss-cross our city. During these years, was one of the pilots Marcus Schellenberg?"

Dear Mr. Nicholsen:
Many people who were living in Denver from 1930 and later remember that cross.

It was started by the late Ray Wilson, pioneer Denver aviator, and founder of Monarch Airlines, which merged with three others to form Frontier Airlines.

Wilson's widow, Alverta Wilson, and Everett Aden, former chief pilot for Frontier Airlines, provided information about the cross.

The first lighted red cross flew over Denver in 1929, attached to the bottom of a Curtiss Robin monoplane piloted by Wilson, said Alverta Wilson. At the time, Ray Wilson was an instructor as the Curtiss-Humphrey Flying School, and he operated out of an airfield at East 26th Avenue and Oneida Street. It was the only field in the region then lighted for night flying.

The plane had a takeoff speed of 50 mph and a cruising speed of 95 to 100 mph.

"Ray was a Christian, and he just thought it would be nice to have a flying cross for Denver on Christmas Eve," recalled Alverta Wilson.

The project was sponsored by *The Denver Post,* and the ingeniously wired framework of wood, wire and neon that formed the cross was fastened under the plane by Electrical Products Consolidated.

"Denver was a small town then, and the suburbs were even more so," Ray Wilson said in an interview a few years ago. "I'd circle over Denver, then make a sashay over Arvada, Englewood and Aurora. From the air at night there

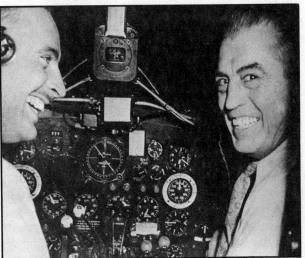

Everett L. Aden

Everett L. Aden, left, and Ray Wilson flew the Christmas "Flying Cross" over Denver.

were big black gaps between the towns."

Through most of the 1930s, Wilson flew the flying cross over Denver, never missing a Christmas Eve trip. Most of the time the weather was good, but at times he took off in ice or snow, and one year ice built up on the wing struts so thick that he "had to land fast."

The flying cross was received with great enthusiasm, particularly during the Depression. Often during the 1930s, as Wilson circled over residential areas, he would be greeted by the flicker of flashlights and spotlights pointed toward him.

Occasionally, some of Denver's business people would telephone Wilson, asking him to fly over their homes, Alverta Wilson said.

Although things went very well most of the time, there were a few touchy moments. One time, magnesium flares were attached to the edges of the wings to attract more attention.

"That was almost a disaster," Ray Wilson said. "The light blinded me, and the heat and burning particles from the flares almost burned off the horizontal stabilizer. The fabric covering on those ships was highly volatile."

Another time, the neon company decided to make a star instead of the cross, but the bulky framework created too much wind resistance and slowed the plane.

During World War II, the cross was discontinued when Wilson went to Chickasha, Okla., to operate a flying school where he trained more than 10,000 pilots under a contract with the Army Air Forces.

When he returned to Denver, Wilson reinstated the flying cross in 1946, but he stopped flying it himself after that year.

The job of flying the cross was taken over by Capt. Everett Aden, who at that time was chief pilot for Monarch Airlines. He flew the cross every Christmas Eve until it was discontinued in 1959.

"I really enjoyed it," Aden said. "As far as I know, it was the only flying cross in the country. And every year that I flew it, the weather was great. It really was amazing."

During the last years of the flying cross, Aden said, a DC-3 was used, and people continued to wave flashlights at it during its 90-minute flight over the city and suburbs.

"I liked those lights from the public," he said. "You didn't feel so alone up there."

Aden added a special turn over Buckley Field, at the request of Buckley residents. The air base had not been on the original schedule.

In an editorial in 1961 explaining why the cross had been discontinued, *The Denver Post* said that among other things, the newspaper had conducted a survey of about 1,300 families, asking whether any member of the family had seen the cross on Christmas Eve. Only 300 responded that they had.

The paper also had received criticism for displaying a cross for Christmas. A cross, said the critics, is for Good Friday or Easter.

"So, for those who remember and who found a little inspiration in the annual display, there must be understanding," said the editorial. "It was a beautiful idea in its time, but its time had run out."

As for Nicholsen's second question, Aden remembers Marcus Schellenberg as a pilot but doesn't think he ever flew the cross.

September 15, 1985

Colorado owns a chunk of Glenn Miller

GLENN Miller, who died in a 1944 plane crash in the English Channel, was once the highest-paid band leader in the world.

In 1944, it was estimated that one of every three nickels dropped into the nation's jukeboxes played a Glenn Miller record. In a *Downbeat* magazine poll, Miller collected more votes for swing and sweet music combined than any other orchestra leader. Benny Goodman got more for swing.

Miller always has had a special place in the hearts of Coloradans, not so much for his band's renditions of *Old Black Magic, Tuxedo Junction, Chattanooga Choo Choo* and the Miller theme song, *Moonlight Serenade,* as for the fact that he went to high school in Fort Morgan, then attended the University of Colorado at Boulder. In fact, he worked his way through CU playing a trombone in the college band.

The university was so proud of him that a campus ballroom built in 1953 was named the Glenn Miller Ballroom. Many of these details are in the movie, *The Glenn Miller Story,* which first appeared in 1953. (Miller was born in 1904 in Clarinda, Iowa.)

Miller, who became famous both for his trombone playing and for his distinctive arrangements, earned his first instrument by doing odd jobs when he was 14. He played in bands in Fort Morgan and after graduation joined the Boyd Senter Band, which traveled in western states.

By 1923, however, he had decided college was important, and he enrolled at CU.

In Boulder he joined the Holly Moyer Orchestra, a dance band that played 3 nights a week at Citizens' Hall, where college students hung out. He was serious about a career as a musician, and declined to play football for fear of having his teeth knocked out, disastrous for a trombonist.

He was tall and thin and was not a warm personality. Before long he had earned the nickname "Gloomy Gus" because of his serious air and strict personal discipline. He also was so shy that, when he organized his own band, it was difficult for him to get up in front to lead it, but he loved the music so much that he made himself stand there.

He stayed at Boulder for a year, then left school because he wanted to get started on his musical career. For several years he worked for different bands, both on the West Coast and in New York, as trombonist and arranger.

In 1928, he married his college sweetheart, Helen Burger, in New York.

About that time Ray Noble asked Miller to help him put together an orchestra and do the arranging for it. Most of the nation knew this orchestra on Ray Noble's *Coca-Cola Hour.*

Still itching to be on his own, Miller organized a combination of "strings and swing" that recorded for Columbia Records in 1935. Miller's big band was formed in 1937, but a year later he disbanded it and started over. By 1939, the band was a national hit, playing in the famed Meadowbrook Roadhouse and the Glen Island Casino. His band's recording of *Tuxedo Junction* in 1939 was the first million-disc seller in nearly 10 years.

Then came radio's *Chesterfield Show,* which starred the Miller Band.

In 1942, Miller turned the band over to Harry James and enlisted in the Army Air Force. He was appointed conductor of the Army Air Force Band and given the rank of major.

The Air Force band was playing in Paris in December 1944. Miller was flying ahead of his group to another engagement in France when his plane disappeared over the English Channel. No trace was ever found.

The movie stars James Stewart as Miller and June Allyson as his wife. Henry Morgan had the role of Miller's buddy, "Chummy" MacGregor.

Much of the filming was done on location in the Denver area in 1953. About 3,000 airmen from Lowry Air Force Base performed as extras in a scene showing a USO performance in England in December 1944. Although it was an extremely hot July in Denver, and the temperature inside the hangar was around 100 degrees, the airmen wore heavy wool winter uniforms.

Another day's shooting took place on the CU campus in Boulder. In later years, Miller had remembered his college days by playing songs of the university on his radio program and by making an occasional appearance at the college with his famous orchestra.

About 5,000 Denverites were extras for scenes filmed at Elitch Gardens Trocadero Ballroom, which was torn down in 1975. Stewart's wife, the former Gloria McLean, was in the crowd.

Miller's 82-year-old mother, Mattie Lou Miller, who lived in Greeley, came to watch the ballroom scenes being filmed and met Stewart.

"He's a fine actor," she commented, "but he doesn't look a thing like my boy."

Civic Center was the locale of another scene, showing Miller stopping to make a phone call from a booth in 1926. Antique-car collector Arthur Rippey provided the vehicles for the scene.

September 22, 1985

Rocky Mountain News

Glenn Miller, famous for his big band and his skill on a trombone, went to high school in Fort Morgan and attended the University of Colorado which named its famous ballroom after him.

'Phantom Canyon' tantalizes the curious

VIRGINIA Pemberton of Montrose writes: "I am a native Coloradan, but after much research I cannot find why the area south of Cripple Creek toward Penrose has been called 'Phantom Canyon.' There must be a legend that the history books haven't told. Can you please

A Florence and Cripple Creek train rumbled on the narrow gauge track through Phantom Canyon in the 1890s. The area originally was known as Eight Mile Canyon, the scene of many accidents.

help me?"

Dear Mrs. Pemberton:

I can't find the answer, either.

When the last of the big mining strikes was made at Cripple Creek in 1890, railroads were needed to haul ore out to the mills and bring in supplies.

The narrow-gauge Florence and Cripple Creek Railroad was built in 1894, snaking its way through Eight Mile Canyon, which later became known as Phantom Canyon. This rail line connected with the main line of the Denver & Rio Grande Western at Florence.

Nothing I have read indicated why the name was changed to Phantom Canyon. It was suggested that an early-day photographer, L.C. Mc-Clure, who made many pictures in the canyon, changed its name, but no reason was given.

Mabel Hall, who wrote *The Story of Phantom Canyon,* said several movie companies, including one owned by Tom Mix, used the area for locations, and she speculated that the name might have been changed by some of the movie makers simply for romantic interest.

There were a number of accidents in the canyon, and possibly these brought the change of name. Or perhaps cliff dwellings in the canyon near Manitou Springs inspired the name.

By 1914, it was suggested that the rail line be changed into an auto road. This was done in 1918, and it still is a favorite scenic drive.

What is the real story behind the name of Phantom Canyon?

September 23, 1985

The readers said . . .

MARY Joy Martin, author, artist and composer from Montrose, had a bit of information.

"Colorado's phantoms have been my passion for many years," she wrote, "so it was impossible for me to resist temptation when your column presented several stories of Phantom Canyon. During the 8 years I researched historical ghost sightings in Colorado (for my book, *Twilight Dwellers*, Pruett, 1985) I never came upon any historical tales of ghosts in Phantom Canyon.

"The ghost story from *Old West Magazine* sent by N.C. Gross was borrowed from an original written by Fitz Mac in 1892. In the original, the convict's spirit was seen in the narrows of the Arkansas River Canyon, not Phantom Canyon. Fitz Mac gave the man a name and a prison number, but no such person ever was incarcerated at the state penitentiary, according to its records.

"There were some historical ghosts sightings over the eastern ridge of Phantom Canyon in a place called Cemetery Park. But these spooks seemed content to stay in their haunt, even though there was a trail from the park to the Holbert cabin on East Eightmile Creek.

"I never discovered how the canyon got its name, although I strongly suspected Hollywood's finger in it. The name was changed only by degrees, not all at once. On all my old maps up to the 1930s, the name is Eightmile Canyon. A 1951 map still calls it Eightmile, and a 1954 map calls it Phantom.

"Pinning down the actual reason and person behind the name change is like pinning a ghost to a telegraph pole."

More information on Phantom Canyon came from Ray Brady of Wheat Ridge.

"A number of years ago, in the mid-1930s, I believe, radio station KOA used to have a series of programs on the West," said Brady. "The stories were told by Old Waggin' Tongue, a character portrayed by Roscoe Stockton.

"One of these stories was about Phantom Canyon. In it, a man presumably followed a ghost horse and dog to the edge of the canyon. Later, the man dug around below the spot where they went over, and found the skeleton of a man and a horse.

"Presumably, that's how Phantom Canyon got its name."

December 15, 1985

Welcome Arch glowed in its brief life

A reader writes: "With Denver's Union Station figuring so prominently in the news these days (as possible site for a convention center, later defeated by Denver voters), I have been wondering what happened to the sign at the arched entry? It said 'Mizpah,' which I think was Arabic. Maybe it's still there, on the inner side."

Denver's Welcome Arch, as it was known, was erected in front of Union Station in 1906, in time to greet the national convention of the Benevolent and Protective Order of Elks. It became the most widely remembered landmark in Denver.

Mayor Robert W. Speer presided at the dedication ceremony on July 4, 1906, while a crowd of 10,000 surrounded the structure.

At the time, the word "Welcome" appeared on both sides of the arch. In 1908, the wording as you faced the station was changed to "Mizpah," while "Welcome" remained on the other side to greet arriving travelers. The word Mispah is Hebraic and was taken from Genesis 31:49. It is translated to mean "The Lord watch between me and thee when we are absent, one from another."

An East High School student, Mary Woodsen, designed the arch in a contest for children. Architects followed her design.

The arch was built by the Denver Iron and Wire Works and was 65 feet high by 86 feet wide. It was made of steel coated with bronze and weighed 70 tons. The crown of the arch was decorated with Denver's seal.

About 2,000 four-candlepower lights were used on the arch, making it a glorious nighttime sight. Total cost of the structure was variously reported at $22,000 to $32,000.

In his dedication speech, Speer said:

"(The arch) is to stand here for ages as an expression of the love, good wishes and kind feeling of our citizens to the strangers who enter our gates."

The mayor was partially mistaken. The Welcome Arch stood for only 25 years.

By 1931, Denver traffic was beginning to find the arch troublesome, and Mayor George D. Begole said lighting the structure cost a staggering $9,000 per year. On Dec. 6, 1931, dismantling began.

But during its brief life, the arch welcomed many celebrities to Denver. Its famous visitors included four presidents — Warren G. Harding, Woodrow Wilson, Theodore Roosevelt and William H. Taft. Queen Marie of Romania and the crown prince, Nicholas, passed under the arch. So did Ethel Barrymore, Paul Whiteman, Sarah Bernhardt, Caruso and John Philip Sousa.

There were many others in other fields — Cardinal Patrick Hayes, Coach Knute Rockne, evangelist Aimee Semple McPherson, inventor Thomas A. Edison, politicians William Jennings Bryan and Al Smith among them.

Many who remember miss the Welcome Arch as one of the great mementos of Denver in bygone days.

October 13, 1985

Rocky Mountain News

Both sides of the arch said "Welcome" in the early days. This side was changed to "Mizpah."

The statue *Broncho Buster*, in Civic Center east of the Denver City-County Building, was dedicated in 1920. The artist was Alexander Phimister Proctor, and the work was a gift of J.K. Mullen.

Horse thief bucks in Civic Center

PRACTICALLY everyone who has strolled through Civic Center has admired the bronze sculpture of a cowboy and a horse called *Broncho Buster*.

The model of this sculpture, which is so appropriate for Denver, supposedly was a horse thief.

The artist was Alexander Phimister Proctor, who was born in 1872 in Ontario and came to Denver when he was 12.

Proctor studied art in Denver, then studied at the Art Students League in New York City. He later earned a scholarship to study in Paris for 2 years.

Cowboys, Indians and animals became his favorite subjects, and when a City Beautiful project was begun by Mayor Robert W. Speer, Proctor was selected to create a sculpture for Civic Center. The work was a gift of J.K. Mullen, millionaire flour miller, who paid $18,500 for it.

Stories vary on Proctor's model for the cowboy. One version is that the artist was attending the Pendleton Roundup in Pendleton, Ore., where he was struck by the "typical cowboy" features and mannerisms of Bill "Slim" Reddings, a rodeo performer.

Before Proctor was ready to start work, Reddings was arrested for "borrowing" a horse, and was jailed in Pendleton. Proctor persuaded Sheriff Till Taylor to let the cowboy out long enough to pose for the sculpture.

One version of the story is that Reddings returned to jail to be tried after the statue was complete. Another version is that Proctor persuaded local authorities to withdraw the charges and let the cowboy go.

Sheriff Taylor later was shot and killed by some escaping prisoners. When Proctor heard of it, he expressed a desire to make a sculpture of the lawman, and pennies from schoolchildren and larger contributions from adults in Pendleton paid for it. The statue of Till Taylor stands in the city park in Pendleton.

Proctor was a meticulous craftsman, and it is said that he worked a full year getting the horse for *Broncho Buster* modeled to his satisfaction. With human figures, he first made a nude, then clothed the figure.

Broncho Buster was dedicated in December 1920. A smaller version was made to be awarded as a trophy for champions in the Pendleton Roundup. A small copy, perhaps one of the Pendleton trophies, is displayed on a pedestal in the Western History Department of the Denver Public Library.

Two years after *Broncho Buster* was installed in Civic Center, it was joined by another Proctor sculpture, this time a figure of an Indian on horseback, brandishing a lance and called *On the War Trail*.

This work was a gift to the city from Stephen Knight, a Denver manufacturer and member of the Board of Education. Knight was inspired to make the donation after hearing a speech by Speer, urging listeners to "Give while you live."

The model for the Indian statue was Eddie Big Beaver of Browning, Mont., a Blackfoot Indian. Both Indian and cowboy sculptures are 1½ times life size.

Proctor went on to make more statues in many parts of the country. He died at the age of 89.

November 10, 1985

Ghosts of glamor live at Ken-Caryl Ranch

MIKE Caruso of Aurora has a question about Ken-Caryl Ranch.

"I recently attended a wedding at the Manor House at Ken-Caryl Ranch and I was fascinated by the house and its history," he writes.

"Can you tell me more about the original ranch — its size, the family who owned it, and especially about the house. I saw some old pictures in it of a stone house, and I wondered if the present house is a different house or was the stone house remodeled?"

Another question about Ken-Caryl comes from Christy Martin of Littleton, who writes:

"I learned recently that a man named Perley was buried near the Bradford House on the ranch. Are any living relatives of Perley in Denver?"

The story begins with Maj. Robert B. Bradford, a partner in the firm of Russell, Majors and Wadell, freighters who hauled merchandise into old Denver.

Bradford came to Denver to establish a store to be stocked by the freighter. He also had ambitions to build a toll road into the mountains and a hotel along the way.

In 1860, he established the town of Bradford in the foothills on some of the land that now is Ken-Caryl Ranch. He built a log cabin and a larger building of stone cut from a limestone ridge nearby. This became known as the Bradford Hotel, the first stage stop out of Denver on the way to Fairplay.

The stone building once had a third story, but after it was struck by lightning a third time, Bradford removed it.

The "shortcut" that Bradford advertised as being "shorter than any other" to South Park, went up a steep hill behind the stone house, and became known as "the terrible Bradford Hill." It was impossible for some travelers to get over it, and the gold seekers took other routes. This was the principal reason the town did not pros-

per.

James Adam Perley purchased the hotel in 1895. After his death Charles Boettcher acquired it on a public trust deed for $3,709.70. Boettcher sold the property to Colorado Portland Cement in 1910.

John C. Shaffer of Chicago and Indianapolis acquired the property in 1913 for $9,844.40.

Shaffer was the property's most interesting owner. He was a financier, philanthropist, arts patron and a founder of the Chicago Opera Company. He owned streetcar companies in several cities and was a grain speculator.

He also was a newspaper publisher, which is what brought him to Denver. He owned the *Star* newspapers of Indianapolis, Muncie and Terre Haute, Ind., and the *Chicago Post*. In 1913, he purchased the *Rocky Mountain News* and the *Denver Times* from Sen. Thomas M. Patterson. He then bought the *Republican* from Crawford Hill, and merged it with the *Times*, causing considerable unemployment in Denver's newspaper industry.

Shaffer's principal home and art collection were in Evansville, Ind., but he bought 12,000 acres west of Littleton (the ranch property) and in 1914, built a $100,000 colonial-style home called Manor House.

The house stands on the highest section of the land. It originally contained 20 rooms, six baths and a living room 80 feet long with fireplaces at each end.

Shaffer named the property Ken-Caryl after his two sons, Kent and Carroll.

In 1926, he bought the Perley place (Bradford's property) then bought land known as the South Ranch from Frank Mann.

Some interesting details of life on the ranch under Shaffer's ownership are told in *Ken-Caryl Ranch — a Look Through History*, by Jo McCormick.

The Shaffers entertained lavishly. Their

The Manor House at Ken-Caryl Ranch was constructed in 1914 at a cost of $100,000. It was built by John C. Shaffer, and he named his property Ken-Caryl after his two sons, Kent and Carroll.

guests included Presidents Theodore Roosevelt and William Howard Taft, as well as stars of the Chicago Opera Company, advice-to-the-lovelorn columnist Dorothy Dix and the president of Northwestern University, Walter Dill Scott.

Shaffer's wife Virgie was the daughter of a fundamentalist Baptist preacher and sometimes objected to the lavish living. It was said that she wore cotton knit underwear beneath her fine party gowns so the elegant fabrics wouldn't touch her skin.

Shaffer decided to raise cattle on the ranch and chose Hereford stock — the best available.

Scripps Howard bought Shaffer's Denver newspaper interests in 1926. In the 1930s Shaffer lost the ranch property, which was acquired by William Allen for $100,000. His wife sold it to a hair stylist for $250,000 while her husband was out of the country, and made Allen very angry.

Cap McDannald, Texas oil baron and cattleman, bought the property in 1949 for $350,000. The Johns-Mansville Corp. (now known as the Manville Corp.,) bought it from McDannalds' estate in 1972 for $7.75 million. In June 1974, the company announced plans for a $450 million residential, commercial and recreational development.

Three builders were constructing on it by 1977.

December 8, 1985

Index